CREATIVE TEACHING OF MUSIC
IN THE
ELEMENTARY SCHOOL

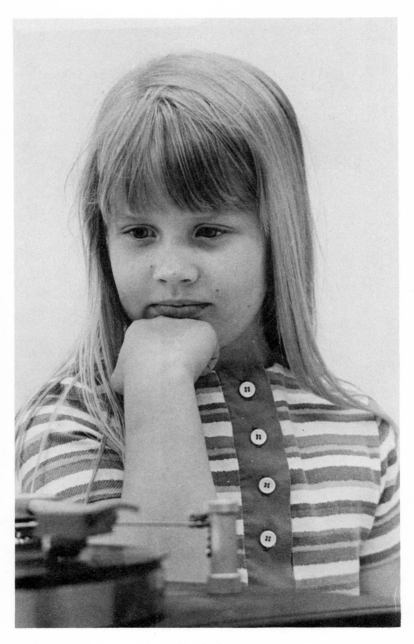

Frontispiece

Creative Teaching
of
Music
in the
Elementary School

DOROTHY HICKOK
JAMES A. SMITH
*State University of New York
at Oswego*

Allyn and Bacon, Inc.
Boston

TO OUR STUDENTS, PAST AND PRESENT

CONTENTS

CHAPTER IV: Music for Its Own Sake 121

PART TWO: THE NURTURE OF CREATIVITY THROUGH THE TEACHING AND USE OF MUSIC

CHAPTER V: Music Through the Creative Arts—In Music and Movement 163

CHAPTER VI: Music and Dramatics, Literature and Art 185

FOREWORD

In the Foreword of the first edition of the Creative Teaching Series, E. Paul Torrance expressed a concern that many exciting, meaningful, and potentially important ideas have died because no one has translated them into practical methods and that this could be the fate of the creative movement.

Fortunately, this concern has not been realized. In the past ten years educational literature has been flooded with reports of research studies, theories, and experimental programs that focus on the creative development of each child as a goal in modern education.

Including the developing of creativity in each child as an educational objective is a staggering challenge for all school personnel. It calls for the invention of new materials and tools, the development of new time schedules and new patterns of organization, a new approach to child study, the invention of new testing methods and new instructional materials, the devising of unique evaluation processes, and the creation of new textbooks and teaching procedures. And most of all the task calls for a commitment and dedication on the part of many people to take risks, to make choices and decisions, to push their own creative potential to new limits.

This has been done! In the past ten years the creative spark has caught fire. Thousands of people in all walks of life have found in the creative movement, self-realization and the challenge of making life meaningful for others. The educational scene in America has become peppered with experimental projects in the development of creative thinking.

No movement in education has swept the world as the creative movement has. The need for creative people across the globe today is tremendous. Developing the creative potential of each child has become an educational objective even unto the far corners of the world. The authors of the Creative Teaching Series hope these volumes will contribute in some bold measure to the changes necessary in teaching methods in the elementary school to realize this objective.

DOROTHY HICKOK
JAMES A. SMITH

PREFACE

To title a book *Creative Teaching of Music* . . . appears in itself to be a contradiction. Can music which is a creative product be taught uncreatively? Indeed it can, and sometimes it is. Lack of knowledge of the real nature of creativity and how it can be developed left music educators and classroom teachers of the past to their own resources in attempting to awaken the spark of musical creativity within children.

We know that most all children have the gift of creating. We know that music is a universal behavior in mankind. To develop these two qualities in the child—his musical ability and his creative ability—has been the goal of the public school since music was incorporated as part of the curriculum.

The compartmentalization of music has taken it from the realm of life and placed it into the realm of "subject." To be effective and to truly develop musical ability and creativity, music should be an integral part of every day for children. They should dance and play to music, hear the music of the countries they study, know the arithmetic and science of music, and be exposed to all kinds of music continually to learn the qualities of each kind and to develop their own appreciation and taste.

Circumstances in the past have assigned music to a role much more subordinate than most educators believe it should rightfully play. Problems of teacher shortages, lack of equipment, population explosions, and a shift to a strong emphasis on the sciences have often derailed music programs from their original goals. Music, a creative form of expression, has become a victim of cognitive classification. Instead of teaching music in a manner which will release the heart and soul of the child, it has often been taught as the memorization of a body of skills and the rote learning of a series of words, symbols, and facts. The creative aspects, the very soul of music, have been neglected.

There is a movement in America today to humanize the curriculum: to return to the concern for human relations and the finer things of life. Accountability has also become a popular theme. But accountability, to many parents, does not mean solely that schools account for the programs of their students in reading, language arts, and social studies. The authors believe that within a few years a majority of parents will be asking, "Why has my child's creativity been stifled?" and "How is it my child does not sing more or play a musical instrument?"

This book is written on the premise that soon the responsibility for teaching music to children will be shared by the classroom teachers *and* the music teacher, and that these teachers, working as a team or as part of a team with other teachers, will provide music experiences to *all* children which are meaningful and directed toward developing musical ability and creativity.

The authors feel that the music teacher (and the art teacher) must have a legitimate place in every team teaching situation. We feel that music should be taught both as an end in itself and as a means to an end through the use of social studies, language arts, art, physical education, and mathematics.

Chapter I and part of Chapter II incorporate a summary of those principles of creative teaching that the authors feel are basic to creative presentations and an understanding of creative development. The remainder of the volume concentrates on developing the creative powers of children and proposes ways by which teachers may develop both their creative and musical ability.

Throughout the book we have referred to teachers as "she" except when specific male teachers are mentioned. Some of our readers will object to this, but we took the liberty of doing it because most of the teachers we observed or most of the ones with whom we worked were women. For each of the many illustrations in this book, the image of a particular woman teacher comes to mind. It seemed, therefore, more comfortable to refer to each as "she."

The authors wish to express their appreciation to all the people to whom they are indebted for materials in this book. Among them are many children and their parents who granted permission to use pictures and creative materials, our teacher colleagues who tried many of the ideas in this book with their children, our college students (especially student teachers) who dared to be creative and allowed us to watch them at work, and teachers and parents who "lent" us their children and/or their classrooms so we could experiment with our own ideas.

Special acknowledgement must be made to Miss Nancy Wood and Miss Ruth Birmingham of the Onondaga Road School in

Camillus, New York for their material on the pollution unit; to Mrs. Holly Weller, Miss Kathy King, and Mrs. Mary Dixon of the Palmer Elementary School in Baldwinsville, New York, for the material on the Arts Festival; to Mrs. Dorothy Clark of the Oswego Campus School for pictures of her classroom activities; to Mrs. Mary Ann Sterling for some exciting days in her preschool classroom; to the students in Miss Hickok's Saturday morning classes; and to Dr. Charles Rhinehart of the Campus School at Oswego for his kind assistance and enthusiasm.

DOROTHY HICKOK
JAMES A. SMITH

PART 1

The Nature of Creativity and Music

CHAPTER I

The Nature of
Creative Teaching

*Good teachers are guided by the conviction that the poten-
tiality for creative experience belongs to all children. They
know that, although the abilities among children vary widely,
understanding, encouragement, and help lead children to develop the abilities they have.*

—MANUEL BARKAN[1]

INTRODUCTION

The material in this chapter is a summary of Book I, *Setting
Conditions for Creative Teaching in the Elementary School.* We
advise you read that volume as a companion to this book. This
summary chapter will help pull from Book I all those principles
uniquely related to the teaching of the creative art of music.

CREATIVE PROBLEM SOLVING WITH MUSIC

Learning the Scale and Pitch Intervals

"*I think we ought to have a song for Robin Hood to sing
as he and his merry men come on to the stage,*" *said Jimmy.*
"*Right,*" *said Bill.*

1. Manuel Barkan, *Through Art to Creativity* (Boston: Allyn and
Bacon, 1960), p. 1.

The children of a middle school group had written a play and were now planning the production of it. Mr. Farrell, their teacher, was sitting in on the planning conference. He was particularly pleased this day because he was working with a group of boys who had refused to sing at the beginning of the school term. Singing, to them, was "sissy." But Mr. Farrell had begun his program with camp songs and had gone on to fun songs and then to other forms of music, and now here he was, listening to one of his early rebels suggesting that music be added to their current production.

"Mr. Farrell," Tom turned to him. "Could we have time this morning to work on a song?"

"How about our report period at 11:30?" asked Mr. Farrell. "I think we can work it in there."

So at 11:30 Mr. Farrell asked the children to meet in a circle to make up a poem for a marching song. To determine the tempo of the lyrics and the music Mr. Farrell asked the boys to march like Robin Hood's band around the room and invited the other children to join in. Soon they were clapping the beat of the marching. As soon as they were again seated in a circle Mr. Farrell asked anyone who had an idea to write it on the chalkboard. Rhythm was clapped for the ideas and soon the following poem took shape.

The March of Robin Hood's Men

We are the band of Robin Hood
Marching, marching!
Each day we do our deeds of good
Marching, marching!
We take from the rich and give to the poor
We go from forest to field and to moor
We help all we can to save and to store.
Marching, marching!

Mr Farrell then asked some of the boys to bring in a set of tuned bells (which the class had used many times previously), and the boys on the production committee explained the problem of creating a song to the group.

Mr. Farrell asked anyone who had an idea to try it out on the bells. He explained that, as the children experimented and each became satisfied with his tune, it would be recorded so they could later remember what each sounded like. He encouraged children to work for entire tunes or phrases. Mr. Farrell had placed pieces of colored tape on each bell. As each child came up with an idea that he thought was a good one, he was asked to make a notation on the chalkboard.

The notations were simply made: pieces of chalk, the same

colors as those on the bells, were on the chalk tray and a child who played a tune went to the chalkboard and repeated the color scheme from the bells on the chalkboard. Past experiences of the children were utilized to give the phrases proper accent and beat. The poem looked like this on the chalkboard.

> *Red-Red-Red-Red-Red-Red-Red-Blue*
> *Blue-Red   Blue-Red*
> *Orange-Orange-Orange-Orange-Orange-Orange-*
> *Orange-Violet*
> *Violet-Orange   Violet-Orange*
> *Orange-Orange-Orange-Orange-Orange*
> *Yellow-Yellow-Yellow-Yellow-Yellow*
> *Yellow-Yellow-Yellow-Yellow-Yellow*
> *Green-Green-Green-Green-Green*
> *Green-Green-Green-Green-Green*
> *Blue-Blue-Blue-Blue*
> *Red-Blue   Blue-Red*
> *Blue-Red   Blue-Red*

Mr. Farrell utilized every situation in which the children were highly motivated to develop new concepts and skills in music. His class had previously learned the names of the notes; consequently, in this experience he saw the opportunity to extend the teaching of musical knowledge to build musical literacy in his children. He also hoped to teach creatively enough to sustain the enthusiasm and productivity of the group.

Before the class met the next day he constructed a melody chart. He felt this chart would serve two purposes: (1) It would help the children in taking a step toward notating their song, showing pitch intervals, and (2) it would lead to a creative scene in the play. Placing the melody graph before the children, he encouraged them to transpose the color symbols of the song into note names on the scale. The melody graph appears below (Fig. 1–1). The children knew note values, so notes were used.

The children could easily sing their melody using the note names. Mr. Farrell suggested that it might be fun to show the audience of their play how easy it is to compose songs by using the note names and showing how this particular song was composed. The figure below (Fig. 1–2) shows the idea that came out of the discussion at this time. Eight boys each took a note name and stuck his head through the hole in the scale. The entire play was produced as though a large book opened to a new chapter for each act. When the book opened a scene was posed to represent the new story to be dramatized. Immediately after the scene

A Melody Graph. The March Of Robin Hood's Men.

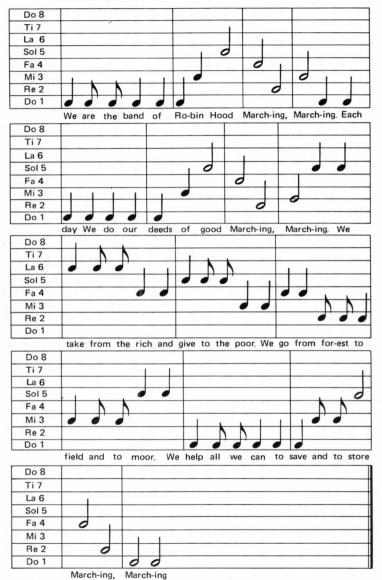

FIGURE 1–1

where the marching song was sung the book opened and the boys stuck their heads through the note holes and sang the marching song by singing the notes, each boy his own note. The effect was delightful and original.

Mr. Farrell did not lose sight of the fact that once the children had made the melody chart he could easily help them to notate the music to a scale by adding key signature, time measure, and tempo terms. Here the children worked directly on music paper. After the task was accomplished, each child received a dittoed copy of the song for himself.

In this illustration Mr. Farrell demonstrated the principles and special strategies of creative teaching, both to develop divergent thinking, as in the creation of the song and the poem, and to develop convergent thinking, as in the forms of notation applied immediately to a scene in the play and to the dittoed papers for all to have a copy of the song (Fig. 1–2).

THE NATURE OF CREATIVE TEACHING

Creativity cannot be taught; we can only set conditions for it to happen. Because it is a quality deeply imbedded in the human personality, it can be developed by reinforcement when it does appear, but the main function of the creative teacher is to maintain certain physical, psychological, socioemotional, and intellectual conditions within the classroom so it will be free to rise to the surface and she can get at it and develop it. The conditions set for developing creativity, then, become very important in the regular classroom.

Research in the past decade in this area has been extensive, and it has helped us to understand creativity, what it is, and how it can be developed.

What Is Creativity?

Creativity, in this volume, is defined as the ability to delve into past experience and to come up with something new. This product need not be new to the world, necessarily, but it must be new to the individual. The most creative acts in the world are those which result in something new to the world. A backlog of experiences, especially sensory experiences, is essential for the development of creativity.

The March Of Robin Hood's Men

We are the band of Ro-bin Hood March-ing, March-ing. Each

day We do our deeds of good March-ing, March-ing. We

take from the rich and give to the poor. We go from for-est to

field and to moor. We help all we can to save and to store

March-ing, March-ing.

FIGURE 1–2 The "March of Robin Hood's Men" (the children's song).

BASIC PRINCIPLES OF CREATIVITY

The research in the area of creativity has guided the authors in evolving a set of principles that are fully developed in Book I of this series.[2] A review of this list of principles follows to form a foundation for the current volume.

1. *All children are born creative: Creativity is not a special talent doled out to a chosen few.* It is present in every individual, though it varies in degree and is somewhat related to intelligence. Its development depends largely on the environment into which it is placed.
2. *There is reasonable relationship between creativity and intelligence.* Highly creative people are always highly intelligent, but highly intelligent people are not always creative. Although creativity is a form of giftedness inherent to some degree in each individual, intelligence determines the level of quality in the creative product. Even slow learning children can be creative.
3. *Creativity is a form of giftedness that is not measured by current intelligence tests.* J. P. Guilford[3] explains this by indicating that our creative powers are developed through the exercise of our divergent thinking abilities and that this particular component of the intellect has been grossly neglected in our teaching in the elementary school up to this time. Almost all learning has been conceived as the development of the convergent thinking processes, which are those that the child uses to come up with a correct answer. In divergent thinking, many answers are possible and the uniqueness of answer may be the important factor in solving a problem. All intelligence tests up to this time measure only convergent thinking processes. Consequently, creative powers are not usually predictable by these tests.
4. *All areas of the curriculum may be used to develop creativity.* The development of creativity is not limited to the program in the creative arts. Creativity can be developed through all areas of the curriculum (as this series of books shows again and again in the many examples of creative teaching that are presented). Creativity is not something to be added to the heavy schedule of teachers, or something that can be taught at a given time once or twice during the week. It is a quality, a characteristic, and a *way of learning.* Some research has shown that as a way of learning, it excels other

---

2. James A. Smith, *Setting Conditions for Creativity in the Elementary School* (Boston: Allyn and Bacon, 1965).
3. J. P. Guilford, "Three Faces of Intellect," *American Psychologist* XIV (1959), pp. 469–479.

FIGURE 1–3   Creativity in music is a process and a product.

ways of learning, accomplishing more and better learning in a given time period than more traditional methods of learning. Creative learning calls for creative teaching and creative teaching is a method of teaching that differs from other methods.

5. *Creativity is a process and a product.* Although research is not conclusive in this area, most researchers will accept the following steps as those which humans go through in the creative process. Mary Lee Marksberry has identified these steps in her book, *Foundation of Creativity*,[4] as being a part of the creative act: (1) First is a period of preparation when the creator identifies with the problem at hand; (2) next is a period of incubation when the creator lives with, and is even tormented with the problem; (3) this is followed by a period of insight when all parts of the problem seem to become clear; (4) then comes the period of illumination or inspiration when the ideas or answers seem to come (this may also be labeled the "moment of discovery"); and (5) a period of verification, elaboration, perfecting, and evaluation occurs when the product is tested for its worth and tension is relieved.

6. *All creative processes cannot be developed at one time or in one lesson.* The total personality of the creative person is

4. Mary Lee Marksberry, *Foundation of Creativity* (New York: Harper & Row, 1963).

made up of many things: characteristics, skills, and qualities, each of which may be developed when teaching is directed towards it. Just as all skills in reading cannot be developed in one lesson at one time, each of the component skills of creativity may be a target for instruction, thus contributing to the development of those qualities, skills, and characteristics that make the creative individual. The development of creativity requires a long period of time. It is developmental and is affected by the kind of environment into which it is placed (Fig. 1–4).

7. *Creativity cannot be taught.* Although some of the component parts of the creative character can be taught such as visual acuity, evaluation skills, comprehension skills, and others, total creativity cannot be taught as such. We can only set conditions for it to happen and insure its reappearance through reinforcement.

8. *Knowledge, skills, and facts are required of each individual in order for him to be creative.* Inasmuch as creativity is seeing new relationships, the more a person learns, thinks, or perceives, the more material he has at his command to put into new patterns. All the knowledges and the skills he knows can be of help to him. A child who knows a great deal about music, composers, notation, music symbols and who has learned the technique of writing or recording notes in one manner or another, is better equipped to create and perhaps more likely to create than the child who has no knowledge of music and no concept of recording sound. The illustration of Mr. Farrell's children used at the beginning of this chapter was chosen because it demonstrates so well this point: the use of learned skills and knowledges in promoting creativity.

9. *The theories of creative development lead us to believe that the unconscious plays a role.* Children must be free to tap all life's experiences in order to become truly creative. Unnecessary rules and actions may force much of children's experience into the subconscious where it cannot be used, where it is not available to the child because of his fear of losing social status if he taps this resource for the purpose of creating.

If a child has difficulty in drawing, for instance, it means he has not had a highly personal reaction of his own with the object he is trying to draw. It is better to help him recall or enter again into his past experience with the object, or to give him a new experience with the object than it is to give him stereotyped patterns to copy.

10. *Excessive conformity and rigidity are true enemies of creativity.* Conformity is necessary to maintain a society, but excessive conformity is the greatest killer of creative development.

FIGURE 1–4   *Creativity in music is encouraged by setting an environment in which it may flourish.*

11.   *Creative teaching and creative learning can be more effective than other types of teaching and learning.*
12.   *Children who have lost much of their creativity by poor teaching may be helped to regain it by special methods of teaching.* This, of course, means the employment of the

methods of creative teaching in the classroom. These methods of creative teaching are derived from a set of basic principles of creative teaching culled from the research on creativity.

BASIC PRINCIPLES OF CREATIVE TEACHING

Following is a condensed version of the basic principles of creative teaching as they were developed in *Setting Conditions for Creative Teaching in the Elementary School.*[5]

1. *In creative teaching, something new, different or unique results.* In the creative teaching of the creative arts, every piece of sculpture, every painting, every poem or song from each individual would (and should) be different from all the others. Because each child's experiences differ in perception and form from all other experiences, each interpretation of his or her experience will be different or unique. No two people can create the same thing.

Miss Arnes selected a record to play to her class. She asked the children to choose one media to interpret the music from several she had placed on a table. Sadie chose the colored chalk; Marcia selected finger paint; Jimmy used tempera paint. As the children listened to the record, they used their chosen media. Every product was unique and different from every other product. (Figs. 1–5 and 1–6 are examples of this.)

2. *In creative teaching, divergent thinking processes are stressed.* Divergent thinking processes as stated above are not concerned with an absolute or correct answer. In divergent thinking knowledge, facts, concepts, understandings, and skills learned through convergent thinking processes are put to new uses—and new answers rather than absolute or correct answers are the result. Divergent thinking processes develop such qualities as flexibility of thinking, originality, fluency of ideas, spontaneity, uniqueness, and are the basis of creative thinking. It has been pointed out above that creativity is a kind of giftedness and the current IQ tests do not measure divergent thinking processes so they do not identify creatively gifted children.

The training of the divergent thinking processes in the elementary schools up to this time has been grossly neglected in spite of its importance because little was known of the nature of creativity and how it develops. Research in this area has added substantial understanding of our knowledge of thinking processes, and ne-

5. James A. Smith, *Setting Conditions for Creativity in the Elementary School* (Boston: Allyn and Bacon, 1965).

FIGURE 1–5   Mr. Glenn's eleven to twelve year olds chose a word, which suggested a mood, then painted a picture, and composed a short song to show the mood. This is John's interpretation of "lonesome."

FIGURE 1–6   And John's song.

glect of training in this area of the intellect is no longer justifiable.

In teaching music, the teacher is provided with innumerable opportunities to develop the divergent functions of the mind. Learning the identification of certain music symbols such as a G clef is an example of a memorization of facts, and illustrates convergent thinking processes (see Fig. 1–7). The actual composition of a tune is an example of a divergent process in action. All compositions are different, unique, individual.

3. *In creative teaching, motivational tensions are a prerequisite to the creative process; the process serves as a tension relieving agent.* Motivation is an essential to all learning but this is particularly true in creative development. A "passion for learning" must plague the creator—the drive to use the *right* word, the *right* color, and the *right* note. Although many children will paint, and compose spontaneously, in *teaching* for creative development one condition that must be planned with great care is the introduction to the lesson, which sets the mood and fires the imagination of the children.

Motivation can be "natural" or contrived. Natural motivation is that which centers the interest of all the children on a particular activity without much preparation by the teacher. Actually, "natural" motivation is, to a large degree, the ability of the teacher to take advantage of a current interest or teachable moment. For example, *the music itself may serve as a motivation.* Contrived

FIGURE 1–7   An open-ended assignment, "Make a G clef character to use on our Community People song sheets," resulted in these figures. Songs were later composed using these characters in the notation.

motivation is that which is stimulated by careful planning by the teacher as part of a lesson plan. Both "natural" and "contrived" motivation can result in some highly creative teaching.

4. *In creative teaching, open-ended situations are utilized.* Open-endedness in teaching means that children are presented with situations in which they are allowed to put their knowledge, understandings, facts, and skills to work. The one great difference between lessons which develop convergent and divergent thinking processes is that in the former, the lesson ends when the knowledge is learned, while in the latter a situation is provided in which the newly acquired knowledge is put to work to solve a problem. The acquisition of knowledge *begins* the divergent thought processes.

> *Miss Parker took her first-grade class to the zoo. After the children returned to the classroom, they discussed the animals they had seen. Pictures were mounted and labeled. The movements of the animals were dramatized.*
>
> *One day, Miss Parker saw an opportunity to develop some abstract concepts in a creative way. She asked the children to make up a musical story about an animal who went to the zoo. She structured the story to the degree that she suggested*

the story animal be a rabbit because it was the only animal that did not make a sound.

Janet suggested that the rabbit might go to the zoo in search of a sound he could make. Everyone liked Janet's suggestion so Miss Parker developed the story from this point on.

The elephant was the first animal that Mr. Rabbit met.

"We have used the piano a great deal for singing and dancing," Miss Parker said. "Now listen carefully while I play each key. You tell me which keys make the high notes and which ones make the low notes."

The children identified the high sounds and the low sounds and then Miss Parker asked, "Now tell me, what do you remember about the elephant? Was he big or little? Light or heavy?"

Of course, the children answered in a chorus, "Big! Heavy!"

"Johnny, show me with your hands how big the elephant is, and then show me how he walks."

Johnny put the heel of his hand on the floor and pressed until his fingers touched the floor also. Then he proceeded to walk his hands across the floor.

"Good," encouraged Miss Parker. "Now children, think where Johnny would put his hands on the keys to show that the elephant walks slow and heavy."

The children pointed to the proper end of the keyboard. "Heavy sounds can be made with the low notes then, can't they?" asked Miss Parker. "Johnny, come to the piano and walk your hands on the low notes just as you did on the floor and we'll see if it sounds like an elephant."

The children were delighted with the result. "Well, what animal will Mr. Rabbit meet next? Can you think of one where we might use the high notes?"

The deer was suggested. Paula made her fingers play the high notes in a dainty, dignified manner. The children added the kangaroo next, who bounced over the keyboard from the low notes to the medium notes and back again. Soon many animals were represented by music. Then the children suggested the rabbit should have a musical theme, too, so Mary made her fingers hop the whole length of the keyboard and back again.

The story was ready to put together. One child told how Mr. Rabbit set out on a trip to the zoo to find a sound he could make. First he came to Mr. Elephant (at this point, Johnny played the elephant music), but he decided he didn't like the elephant sound so he went on until he met Miss Deer. (Paula then played deer music.) And so the story continued.

An amusing twist to the story came when Jimmy suggested the ending. "The zoo is so noisy, let's have all the animals make their noises at the same time, then Mr. Rabbit will go home 'cause he's glad it's so quiet there!"

No sooner said than done, and the creative musical story was complete, concepts were taught meaningfully and the divergent powers of the children had been teased.

Using the trip to the zoo as an open-ended experience, Miss Parker was able to teach a great deal of music—especially about pitch, tempo, and rhythm—and to develop the creativity of the children as well.

5. *In creative teaching, there comes a time when the teacher withdraws and the children face the unknown themselves.* At this moment the teacher and the children, in a sense, change roles. The teacher, in building highly motivated tensions, is the planner, the leader, the guide, and the producer. However, at one point in the lesson, she withdraws from this role and the children, spurred on by these tensions, become the planners, the guides, and the producers. Each leads himself to the fulfillment of the creative act. It is essential that each individual solves the problem in his own way, arriving at his own solution or product.

The preceding illustrations demonstrate this principle. Miss Arnes played a minor role in her classroom when the children began to listen and paint. Miss Parker played a minor role in constructing the story about the rabbit once she had developed certain keyboard skills which permitted the children to progress on their own steam with their story.

6. *In creative teaching, exact outcomes are unpredictable.* Because the *products* are unique, individual, or new, the teacher cannot know to a full degree exactly what they will be. This is another specific quality of the creative teaching process. It differs, for example, from an arithmetic lesson, in which the *process* being used by the children and teacher may be very creative but where teachers know at the onset of the lesson that children (with possible exceptions of a few slow ones) will know the correct answers, or the *product.*

Although Miss Arnes knew there would be painting as a result of her lesson, she could not tell what those paintings would be like. Miss Parker was not absolutely certain how the story about the rabbit would go or what the results would be. Outcomes in creative teaching are never completely assured.

7. *In creative teaching, conditions must be set which make possible preconscious thinking.* Children are encouraged constantly to draw from all their experiences and from their memory. Ideas are rarely considered as silly or impossible—each is considered

and eventually evaluated. Conformity to preconceived rules is omitted. If a child decides he would like to try finger painting with his knuckles or the palm of his hand, he is encouraged to do so even if someone previously had told him to use only his fingers. The rigid, conforming rules under which children often labor for status or approval are relaxed.

Helping children to form associations with past experiences encourages them to delve deep into their subconscious and to assemble past experiences into new patterns. Mr. Gaines wanted his children to create sounds for a sound orchestra. He encouraged the children to brainstorm ideas such as: How can we create percussion sounds with materials we have available so we can use them in an orchestra? Following are some of the children's ideas. Notice that, as most brainstorming goes, the more commonplace ideas appear first on the list and the more creative ideas emerge toward the bottom of the list.

Percussion Sounds We Could Make

Clap blocks of wood together
Strike wooden spoons together
Clap pan tops together
Strike pans with a stick
Clap sticks together
Stamp on the floor
Beat cardboard boxes with a stick
Ring bells
Put water in glasses and tap them with a metal spoon
Make a marimba
Hang flower pots of various sizes and hit with a metal bar
Hang pipes of different lengths and hit with a metal bar
Fasten roofpaper washers to paper plates and make like tambourines
Hang up different sized bottles and tap with metal bars
Change tones of bottles by adding water to the bottles and tap with bar
Shake a cluster of measuring spoons
Beat the sides of our filing cabinet
Shake a large piece of tin
Make drums from large juice cans, waste cans, etc.
Play a metronome
Clap the soles of our shoes together

8. *Creative teaching means that students are encouraged to develop and generate their own ideas.* Research in identifying the creative personality indicates that creative children often are treated along punitive lines by their teachers and are considered to have "silly" or "senseless" ideas. Yet many of the world's great-

est discoveries and inventions have come from such "silly" ideas. Unusual, different, original ideas are the threshold of creative discovery and should be encouraged.

Mrs. Pomeroy had a knack for turning catastrophe into fun. During the rage for calypso music she one day faced a problem in showing a film. She used the occasion to develop a calypso song with the children. This illustration demonstrates the concept of natural motivation.

What Happened to the Movie?

Verse: *One day we had a movie*
The film was put in wrong.
When she started the projector
We all laughed loud and long.

Chorus: *The funny movie!*
The funny movie!
What happened to it?
What happened to it?

9. *In creative teaching, differences, uniqueness, individuality, and originality are stressed and rewarded.* This is the necessary reinforcement which causes creativity to appear again and again so we can get at it and work with it.

Mrs. Colimay often encouraged the children to write *about* music. On certain days, she took a musical instrument to class for the children to observe and use. After the experience many children wrote creative stories and poems built around these classes. Some of the topics suggested were:

The Story of the Tuba
The Sound the Tuba Reminds Me Of
The Tuba and the Piccolo
Fatty the Flute
The Sound of Music

The following stories show some of the children's responses to this sort of stimuli.

Alfred the Tuba

Once upon a time, there was a tuba who was very lonely. He wanted to play in a band. His friends all teased him.

One day a band came into town and Alfred said, "This may be my chance," so he went over and they said they would try him out. They tried and tried and tried. But no noise would come out. The manager said he would have to be cleaned out.

So Alfred went to the "Annette Music School." They tried to clean him out but they just couldn't. Alfred was so sad he began to cry. He cried and cried and cried, and he cleaned himself out! The first thing he did was to go to the band and the manager said, "You're in!" And from that day on, Alfred was never lonely again.

DIANE, *Grade Three*

Finicky the Flute

I am a flute. My name is Finicky. I am here to tell you what happens to me when Carol plays me.

First of all, I must tell you that I belong to the woodwind family. My nice sweet tone is produced by a current of air blown into my mouthpiece. My great grandmother was once played by blowing into the top of the mouthpiece like a clarinet. The Greeks and Hebrews played this way. I am now a long tube. I have a little hole into which you blow. I have many keys which you push down to make different sounds. My brother is just a piccolo. He is much shorter than I am because he didn't eat his wheaties. He also has a higher sound than I have. We are both in the orchestra and the band.

LINDA, *Grade Five*

Polly the Piano

Polly was in a panic. She was a very unhappy piano. When you touched her key, it would hit the string and go "bong." She was out of tune and no one would fix her. The reason why she was out of tune was because she was unhappy, but no one knew that.

One day, a little girl and her mother came into the warehouse where Polly was. It was a warehouse for pianos. They said to the manager, "We would like to see a pretty piano." They looked at many pianos, but they weren't able to find a piano like they were looking for.

Then, all at once, the little girl said, "Mommy, look! Here is a very pretty piano."

The manager said, "Yes, she is very cute, but some of her piano keys aren't in tune. . . ."

"Oh, we can fix her," said the little girl. "Please, can we get her?"

Finally her mother said it would be all right. So they bought Polly. Now Polly was happy, and they found out that she could play well, but they never found out why Polly wouldn't play in tune in the warehouse.

LOIS, *Grade Five*

10. *In creative teaching, the process is as important as the product.* The process of creative production occurs more often when it is practiced or repeated. In some instances creativity is fostered more readily by the process than the product, as would be the case in the creative teaching of arithmetic.

Mr. Arnold's first graders experimented with many instruments including the triangle. They discovered that it can make many different sounds if it is held in various ways. Here are some of the sounds they made which the triangle reminded them of:

Soft Sounds

little baby's feet
prayer song
collar bell
tinkle bell
Tinker Bell
baking a gingerbread man
tiny little bell
ding bell

Sounds When Held in Hand

hammer on a rock
bottle on a rock
two plates crashing together
two sticks hitting
water dripping
gold
rain
school alarm

Loud Sounds

bells
chimes
supper bell in olden days
train bell
jingle bell
school bell
storm
church bell
ice cream bell
store bell
rooster
fire engine bell
chuckwagon bell
bicycle bell
two bottles hitting
horn
cow bell
wake-up bell
police bell
telephone
siren

11. *In creative teaching, certain conditions must be set to permit creativity to appear.* The unique conditions necessary to develop creative production in music will be developed later in this book. There are some general conditions necessary to all creative production, however. Most obvious among these are the *physical conditions.* The classroom must be a learning laboratory with material readily available, and the room must be arranged in such a manner that the task at hand can be readily accomplished. (See p. 42.)

Certain *psychological* conditions are also necessary. Good rapport must exist between the teacher and children, and among the children themselves; they must be comfortable with and accepting of each other. An air of expectancy must pervade; children must feel they are expected to create, but the atmosphere must be permissive to the degree that children feel comfortable at experimenting, manipulating, exploring, and, in so doing, make mistakes (see no. 12 below).

Certain *intellectual* conditions must also prevail. Children must be motivated to think, the imagination must be teased, problems must be posed in such a way that *all* children are thinking most of the time. A great deal of material, and many facts and skills must be available to the child. Many of these facts and skills will be taught by convergent thinking processes but will be taught to be put to divergent uses. The more knowledge, skills, facts, and ideas a child has in his experience, the more there is available for his use when he taps these experiences in order to create.

Sound *social* and *emotional* conditions must prevail in a comfortable relationship among the children. Children who are emotionally upset may often find outlets for their pent-up emotions in creative products if the proper social climate exists—one of acceptance and understanding. Under such circumstances, creative energy may be channeled into creative, constructive acts rather than acts of aggression or violence.

12. *Creative teaching is success- rather than failure-oriented.* Disapproval, sarcasm, disfavor, and other forms of verbal punishment may be interpreted by any single child as failure. There is a difference between "failure" and "failure experience." Failure experiences help children understand the true conditions of life and play a part in building character. Often, failure experiences provide the impetus for creative production. Repeated failure, on the other hand, can only result in psychological damage to personalities and a lowering or eventual destruction of self-concept. Children will fail many times in their experimentation with problem solving, but failure promotes growth if it is resolved.

Criticism and disapproval can make a child feel he is a failure; it is dangerous unless a creative relationship has been established between the teacher and the student. Once this rapport is established, criticism and disapproval, used with a constructive goal rather than as punishment, may be useful.

Even at the onset of the creative act, excessive evaluation may be construed by children as disapproval and may check the creative flow: The work of many researchers would propose that evaluation and criticism of ideas be postponed until all ideas are out. This is often called the principle of "deferred judgment."

The creative child must be willing to make mistakes, but he needs to develop skills for finding out when he makes a mistake and how to correct it. This is one task of the teacher in setting the conditions for creative development. A set of criteria may be worked out with the child for evaluating ideas so that he under-stands that any criticism, disapproval, or rejection of his ideas is made because the idea is not appropriate or best for the solution to the problem at hand, not because he himself is unworthy.

13. *In creative teaching, provision is made both to learn many knowledges and skills and to apply these knowledges and skills to new problem-solving situations.* Learning to read music is a skill that can be learned by convergent thought processes, and one way the skill is best retained is when children use it to record and read the music they create.

Mrs. Peters helped her children learn about the composers of beautiful music. They read stories of these people and gave re-ports or dramatizations of their lives. Many children went to see moving pictures made on the lives of these composers and re-ported to the class. The children became so interested in the com-posers that they drew pictures and wrote poems about them.

Poems About Franz Joseph Haydn

Papa Haydn
When a boy
Used to have a little toy
He called a violin.
It went everywhere with him.
A very busy man was he
Didn't even stop to have his tea.
He wrote music oh so grand,
Even when he was an old man.

Franz J. Haydn was so very good,
He wrote music as no one could.
He loved to sing and dance so well,
He went to play a spell.
He loved to play his violin,
Singing and dancing went well with him.
He finally went to play in a symphony,
And this is what made him really happy.

14. *In creative teaching, self-initiated learning is encouraged.* The release of tensions accompanied by the esthetic satisfactions that come with the creation of a new product or with the working through of a problem make the creative process cyclic. This re-lease and satisfaction become a part of the high motivation required for successive creative acts. Children become truly cre-ative when they constantly occupy themselves with self-imposed problems and produce poems, paintings, dances, songs, and other creative products without the continual motivation of the teacher. (See Fig. 1–8.)

FIGURE 1–8 Putting learned skills to work—the making of an operetta.

Creative teaching tends to motivate more students in the learning processes and to make their learnings relevant to them to the degree that they initiate their own activities and reinforce or discover their own learnings.

15. *In creative teaching, skills of constructive criticism and evaluation skills are developed.* Many convergent thought processes are essential to the full development of creative thinking. Evaluation skill is one—and the application of this particular skill aids the creative act if it is practiced at its conclusion. A set of criteria worked out with the child to measure the effectiveness and the usefulness of his creative products will help him to be constructively critical and able to evaluate effectively.

Research in the area of creativity indicates that evaluation of creative products may check the flow of creativity if the evaluation comes too soon in the process. Consequently, evaluation of children's products is most effective when the product is completed. (See p. 23.)

Developing skills of evaluation also helps a child build his own perceptions of good music and taste in music. This does not mean that the teacher imposes her tastes on him. It does mean that she helps him to sense and discover those elements within a composition that give it its character and strength. Often this is accomplished through asking such questions as: How did you feel during the opening part of the composition? Why? At the closing? What did you think of during this part? Why? (She plays it.) What instruments do you recognize that the composer used to create his composition? What words would you use to describe the music at this place? (She plays it.)

16. *In creative teaching, ideas are manipulated and explored.*

Research shows that the more children are allowed to manipulate, explore, experiment, discover, and resolve their own failures, the more creative they become.

Mr. Forrester encouraged his children to write limericks built around musical sounds and musical instruments.

Limericks

There was a monkey who was a pet,
He was very good on the clarinet.
He played for his master
Until a disaster
Ruined his lovely clarinet!

There was a fish called a carp,
Who was exceedingly good on a harp.
He played for his mother,
And also for his brother
And all of them thought he was sharp.

PATTY, *Grade Five*

17. *Creative teaching employs democratic processes.* Because creativity is individualistic and because a basic principle to democratic ideology is that each individual is important, the development of democratic procedures in the classroom develops creativity in the children. Few people ever became great or famous or renowned by copying what others had already accomplished. In order to become self-realized as a democratic citizen, each person must remain an individual, contributing his own unique ideas to the total culture and helping it to move forward. These goals are synonymous with those of creative development, and true democratic living in the classroom calls for the development of the individual powers of each person—in short, all the creative power he can muster.

18. *In creative teaching, methods are used which are unqiue to the development of creativity.* Among these special methods are those suggested by Sidney Parnes[6] in his courses on creative problem solving at the University of Buffalo:

a. *Deferred judgment.* No evaluation of ideas is offered until after all ideas are out and all creative products reviewed. (Mentioned under no. 15 above.)

b. *Creative ideation.* In order to stretch creative thinking we apply the following criteria to creative products: adaptiveness,

6. Sidney Parnes, *Instructor's Manual for Semester Courses in Creative Problem Solving*, rev. ed. (Buffalo: The Creative Foundation, 1963), pp. 32–66.

new uses, modification, magnification, minification, substitution, rearrangement, reversing, and combining. Examples of this follow.

(1) *Adaptation.* A sample of adaptation, a low form of creativity, follows.

Often children in Mrs. Pomeroy's classes loved tunes (especially folk tones) so much that they hummed them much of the time. Mrs. Pomeroy heard them making up new words to go with these old tunes so she encouraged the children to develop this idea. Here are some samples of the work she received:

New Verses to "Old Michael Finnegan"

(*Each begins with "There was an old man named Mike Finnegan" and ends with "Poor Old Michael Finnegan.")*

He played tennis with his chinnegan.
He knocked the ball from here to Minnegan.

He grew up to a man again.
He grew down to a boy again.

He had a car and smashed it in again.
He bought a new one and turned it in again.

He ate an apple with a spoonegan
Then grew apples out his earsegan!

Golden Gold

(*Tune: "Sweet Betsy from Pike")*

O California here I come
With a washbowl on my thumb,
We crossed the plains, the mountains and hills
And all we ate was vitamin pills!

O I came in search of golden gold
All my pockets would ever hold,
All we did was wash rocks and soil,
O why do we have to do all this toil?

I found a few nuggets worth thousands of dollars
We got all that money in just a few hours,
It was lucky we had all those vitamin pills
Or the Indians would have put us in kilns!

MRS. COON'S *Fifth Grade*

(2) *New Uses:* An example of new uses is cited under no. 10 above.

(3) An example of *modification* is shown in Figure 1–9.

(4) *Magnification* means that we ask how we can make an object bigger, taller, louder, larger, or greater and thus make a new creation of it. In music this may mean that a song is made longer, parts are repeated, certain instruments are played louder, some parts are emphasized over others, and so on.

(5) *Minification* is the opposite of *magnification.* Everything in modern life seems to have gone mini. We have mini-cars, mini-skirts, mini-courses, mini-coats, mini-buses. Mrs. Olson had her children write mini-songs one day after they had discussed the word *mini* for some time. The object was to write a poem and set it to music with as few words and notes as possible. The children enjoyed this activity very much.

My Mini-Song

See my dog (Do sol do)
Scratch his fleas (Do sol do)
Scratch, scratch, scratch. (Do do do)

KEVIN

FIGURE 1–9   The principle of modification.

A Mini-Song

Right or wrong, here's (*Do Re Fa, Sol*)
A mini-song. (*Fa Me Re Do*)

MARLENE

(6) In the principle of *substitution* the question is asked: What can I use instead of one object to produce the same or better effect?

(7) *Combining* means that we use the principle of putting two or more ideas together to produce a new idea. Miss Arnes combined the idea of pitch differences which the children discovered with the child's idea of the heavy walk of an elephant: low pitches played in a heavy manner sounded like the elephant.

(8) *Rearrangement* means exactly what it implies: how can we change the structure, form or parts, within a product to make it more useful, more functional, or more esthetic?

(9) *Reversing* is a process whereby ideas, concepts, or objects are used in reverse to produce a new product. In one scene of Miss Parker's play (4 above) the rabbit hops to the top of the hill. The children played the scale from lower *do* to higher *do*, emphasizing one note for each hop. To bring him down hill, they reversed the process and produced a charming effect. No words were necessary to tell what Mr. Rabbit was doing.

c. *Brainstorming* is a special technique by which creative ideas can be put quickly before a group in a limited length of time. Brainstorming is most effective in a group of ten to fifteen, although it can be used effectively with larger groups under some circumstances. In brainstorming a problem has to be limited in scope: Too broad a problem generally leads to no specific solution.

In brainstorming the following procedures are observed: the moderator poses the problem very specifically and generally sets a time limit for the session. A recorder is appointed to list the ideas as they are spoken. All ideas, no matter how foolish they may sound, are recorded. No judgment is passed on any idea until the end of the session. The moderator may encourage the flow of ideas (creative ideation) by stopping the session and asking the recorder how many ideas have thus been recorded. He may say, "In the first ten minutes we have come up with fifty ideas. Let's see if we can double it in the next ten minutes." In order to keep similar ideas together on the recorder's list, the "hitch-hiking" technique is used. If one person gives an idea which sets off a related idea in another person's mind, he snaps

FIGURE 1–10   *Miss Cady's children created a new song each month to grace the monthly calendar.*

FIGURE 1–11   All were eventually put into a class book. This is the page for February.

his fingers and the moderator calls on him so his hitch-hiking idea will come after the one that prompted it.

After the session is closed, a committee meets and leisurely evaluates the ideas which resulted from the brainstorming session. Some are immediately discarded as impractical, too expensive, too time-consuming, etc. The rest are discussed further. (A sample of the results obtained in a brainstorming session may be seen under no. 7 above [p. 19]).

SUMMARY

There is a decided difference in the methodology of creative teaching and that of traditional teaching. In the area of the fine arts more than any other, homage has been paid to these differences over the past years. But even this area of the curriculum has not been free from its violations and neglect of the creative powers of children. Research in the past decade has provided us with a fuller understanding of the creative act, of creativity and the manner in which it develops.

The job the elementary school has always been to develop those component parts of the intellect which are necessary to life in a democratic society. We stand at the threshold of an age where creative powers are needed more than ever before. The basic principles of creativity and creative teaching as summarized in this chapter provide the framework for our action for the future. Now that we know so much more about creativity and how it is developed, we can join it to our knowledge of the fine arts—music in particular—and avoid the blunders made in the past.

Because people have been more receptive to innovation and individuality in the fine arts than in many other areas of the school curriculum, the area of the fine arts offers the greatest opportunity for the first giant step in revising much of the methodology currently employed by most schools. In the succeeding chapters, examples and ideas will translate the principles discussed in this chapter into action.

TO THE COLLEGE STUDENT AND THE TEACHING TEAM

1. Identify five great teachers from history. Read about them and decide which ones were creative in their approach to teaching. One group of students included in their list such

names as Socrates, Confucius, Jesus, John Dewey, Maria Montessori, Helen Keller, and Buddah. Would you include these on your list? Give a description about a great teacher under whom you have studied.

2. Do some research on the Montessori method of teaching and decide: What are the creative aspects of this method? The noncreative?

3. Send for some sample items on tests that measure creativity and examine the items. What aspects of giftedness do these tests explore that intelligence tests do not? Ask your college psychologist to give a demonstration of this test.

4. Using the material in this chapter, construct items that might be used with your college peers to measure their creativity.

5. Discuss ways you could measure the creative teaching abilities for a classroom teacher; a music teacher.

6. Can you think of other forms of giftedness that might not be measured by the intelligence tests? List them.

7. Check your own creativity by some of the following methods:
    a. Think of all the ways you could use a moving picture film in the classroom.
    b. Think of all the ways that audiovisual aids may be used to develop creativity.
    c. Think of all the ways that textbooks and workbooks can be used to develop creativity.

8. Can you identify the highly creative children with whom you work? How? Could you devise a check sheet of items which would help you, using the material in this chapter?

9. Can you identify creative teachers in your school? What will you look for in so doing?

10. Think of all the things you are doing which help in the development of creativity such as building visual and comprehension skills in a reading program, developing evaluation skills in social studies, etc. Make a list of the characteristics that develop creativity as they are described in this chapter and indicate which ones you are already working on through one or more of your instructional methods.

11. Which of the following sets of statements is likely to produce strong motivational tensions in children?

"Listen carefully while I explain each step of the dance. Once you know the pattern we will listen to the music." Or, "I have a very exciting dance record here. Listen and show me what it tells me to do."

"Now that we have read the story, let's make a play from it. I will have each of you read some parts and the best parts will be chosen for the play." Or, "Now that we have read the story, can you work in groups and tell it in new and different ways?

"When I nod my head all of you play your instruments to go with the beat of the music." Or, "Now that each of you has an instrument, let's let each person show us how he can play it."

12. In light of the discussion on creativity in this chapter, can we justify the grading of creative products in the elementary classroom with letter or number grades? Discuss this.

SELECTED BIBLIOGRAPHY

Anderson, H. E. (Ed.) *Creativity and Its Cultivation.* New York: Harper & Row, 1959.

Baker, Sam. *Your Key to Creative Thinking.* New York: Bantam Books, 1968.

Barron, Frank. *Creativity and Personal Freedom.* Princeton, N.J.: D. Van Nostrand, 1968.

Berman, Louise M. *Creativity in Education.* Madison, Wisc.: University of Wisconsin, School of Education, 1964.

Cobb, Stanwood. *The Importance of Creativity.* New York: Scarecrow Press, 1968.

Eisner, Elliot. *Think with Me About Creativity: Ten Essays on Creativity,* Dansville, N.Y.: F. A. Owen, 1964.

Fabun, Dan. *You and Creativity.* Beverly Hills, Calif.: Glencoe Press, 1968.

Gardner, John. *Self-Renewal: The Individual and the Innovative Society.* New York: Harper & Row, 1962.

Getzels, Jacob W., and Phillip W. Jackson. *Creativity and Intelligence.* New York: John Wiley, 1962.

Gowan, John, George Demas, and Paul Torrance. *Creativity: Its Educational Implications.* New York: John Wiley, 1967.

Gruber, Howard, Glen Terrall, and Michael Wertheimer. *Contemporary Approaches to Creative Thinking.* New York: Atherton Press, 1962.

Guilford, J. P. "Factors That Aid and Hinder Creativity," *Teachers College Record,* LXIII (February 1962), pp. 386–392.

————. *Intelligence, Creativity and Their Educational Implications.* San Diego, Calif.: R. R. Knapp, 1968.

Halprin, Lawrence. *Creative Processes in the Human Environment.* New York: George Braziller, 1969.

————. *The RSVP Cycles: Creative Processes in the Human Environment.* New York: George Braziller, 1969.

Hyman, H. *Some Experiments in Creativity.* New York: Random House, 1961.

Kagan, Jerome (Ed.) *Creativity and Learning.* Boston: Houghton Mifflin, 1967.

Karagulla, Shafiera. *Breakthrough to Creativity: Your Higher Sense Perception.* Los Angeles: DeVors, 1967.

Kneller, George. *The Art and Science of Creativity.* New York: Holt, Rinehart and Winston, 1965.

Kohl, Herbert. *The Open Classroom.* New York: Random House, 1970.

Kornbluth, Frances, and Bernard Baird. *Creativity and the Teacher.* Chicago: American Federation of Teachers, 1966.

Luck, James T. *Creative Music for the Classroom Teacher.* New York: Random House, 1971.

Marksberry, Mary Lee. *Foundation of Creativity.* New York: Harper & Row, 1963.

Mars, David. *Organizational Climate for Creativity.* Buffalo, N.Y.: The Creative Education Foundation, 1969.

Massialas, B. G., and Jack Zeven. *Creative Encounters in the Classroom: Teaching and Learning Through Discovery.* New York: John Wiley, 1967.

Michael, William. *Teaching for Creative Endeavor: Bold New Adventure.* Bloomington: Indiana University Press, 1968.

Miel, Alice. *Creativity in Teaching: Invitations and Instances.* Belmont, Calif.: Wadsworth, 1961.

Muenzinger, Karl F. *Contemporary Approaches to Creative Thinking.* New York: Atherton Press, 1967.

Osborn, Alex. *Applied Imagination.* New York: Charles Scribner's Sons, 1963.

Parnes, Sidney, and H. F. Harding. *A Source Book for Creative Teaching.* New York: Charles Scribner's Sons, 1962.

Patrick, Catherine. *What Is Creativity Thinking?* New York: Philosophical Library, 1955.

Reed, E. G. *Developing Creative Talent.* New York: Vantage Press, 1962.

Shumsky, Abraham. *Creative Teaching.* New York: Appleton-Century-Crofts, 1965.

Smith, James A. *Setting Conditions for Creative Teaching in the Elementary School.* Boston: Allyn and Bacon, 1966.

Taylor, Calvin W. *Creativity: Progress and Potential.* New York: McGraw-Hill, 1964.

————. *Widening Horizons in Creativity.* New York: John Wiley, 1964.

Torrance, E. Paul. *Encouraging Creativity in the Classroom.* Dubuque, Iowa: William C. Brown, 1970.

————. *Rewarding Creative Behavior.* Englewood Cliffs, N.J.: Prentice-Hall, 1965.

————. *Creativity: What Research Says to the Teacher.* Washington, D.C.: N.E.A., 1963.

————. *Guiding Creative Talent.* Englewood Cliffs, N.J.: Prentice-Hall, 1962.

Torrance, E. Paul, and R. E. Myers. *Creative Learning and Teaching.* New York: Dodd, Mead, 1971.

Williams, F. E. *Foundations of Creative Problem Solving.* Ann Arbor, Mich.: Edwards Bros., 1960.

CHAPTER II

The Nature and Setting of Music Instruction

Music is love in search of a word.
　　　　　　　—SIDNEY LANIER[1]

INTRODUCTION

In this chapter, the authors explore the nature of music and the objectives for including music in the elementary school program. The conditions which must be set in order to realize these objectives are also explored and some "verbal observations" are presented so that you may peep into the classrooms of a few teachers to see them providing the kinds of experiences that make music a means for creative development and a part of life.

Before you read this chapter, make a list of all the ways you recall that music influences your life in a week's time. Then, ask yourself how much the instruction in your school contributes to these influences. Considerable? Or was your taste and use of music acquired outside the influence of your school?

The music program in the elementary school should be designed for *all* children, not only for those who already appear to have a musical ability or a wide background of experience in music. While individual differences in ability must be met and individual skills developed, conditions in the classroom should be such that all children are provided with equal opportunity for creative development through musical expression. Setting condi-

1. Sidney Lanier in *The Symphony.*

FIGURE 2–1   Anticipating sounds indicates music memory.

tions for creative development through musical expression will include many considerations.

Music has always been one of man's best-known methods of communication. It has often been called the only existing international language. Through the use of music, man has been able to express his feelings and other men have understood what he was trying to say. The unique qualities of each culture have been imprinted in music and transmitted to the peoples of other cultures.

OBJECTIVES

There are three objectives to be kept in mind when teaching music in the elementary school:

1. To help children develop their own creative powers through music.

2. To provide opportunities for children to "discover" and to experiment with music in *all its forms* and to select for themselves that which best meets their growing needs.

3. To help children develop an awareness and a sensitivity to the esthetic aspects of music in our culture.

Music has not been used as much in our schools as a tool to develop creativity as it has been used for enjoyment. But music can provide ways of developing creativity comparable to art if it is utilized properly. A child who has experienced the joy of hearing his composition played or sung by his classmates is not only expressing himself creatively, but is also learning to build his own standards of appreciation and taste.

Music is sometimes taught by a music or classroom teacher who selects the songs and the skills that are to be taught, without much thought to the needs, interests, or readiness of the children. Children often build unpleasant associations with such music experiences, and they later form attitudes toward music that negate the objectives for including it in the school program. Music is best taught by using the equipment the child possesses and leading him forward, not by imposing the standards of the teacher on him.

Too often the goal for children in learning a song or playing an instrument is perfection. Children need, instead, to spend much of their time exploring, manipulating, and learning techniques so that they can better communicate musically. The thrill of discovering what *they* can do becomes a great motivating technique for children. Too much emphasis on other people's work and not enough experimenting on their own can discourage them. Music experiences, to be creative for each child, must be open-ended.

MUSICAL READINESS

Musical readiness is as important as reading readiness. Just as a child's reading powers rely to a degree on a background of speaking experiences, so do his musical powers rest on a background of musical experiences. A child who has had a great deal of experience with music at home has a built-in readiness for the program which the school has to offer. The child who comes from a deprived environment obviously needs a different type of readiness program for music. And, no matter how carefully school personnel may plan, there will be some children who are never ready for much music or for music experiences of great depth.

This readiness for music is not to be confused with a readiness for *reading* music. They are both important, but a readiness for music includes the following consideration: (1) does the child have the ability to listen; (2) has he developed a certain amount of audio acuity; (3) is his attention span developed to normal lengths for his particular age; (4) does he have the ability to understand and use simple symbols; (5) is he a member of a congenial group; (6) does he have the ability to reproduce heard sound and the ability to express rhythm; (7) can he recognize differences in pitch, contrasts in phrases, in the concepts of loud and soft; (8) can he hum a tune; and (9) does he respond differently to different music?

When children do not possess these simple skills on entering school, planned experiences need to be offered that will help them to mature in these skills. Many of them can, of course, be developed with short music exercises themselves.

Readiness for reading music is a specific kind of music readiness requiring a higher development of skills and a certain degree of intelligence. Some children are never ready for reading music, for one reason or another, and in these cases reading ability need not be developed.

In preparing to read music, the above skills for music readiness are especially necessary. When the child has a great deal of experience with music in school, he is ready for more difficult music with each successive step in his experience. He hears music a great deal, makes up his own songs, and learns to sing the songs of others. Then he is ready to recognize that " ♩ " can represent a musical tone. He later learns to record his own musical creations, and he learns to read the music of others. Notating his own music is one natural way for children to read the music of others. But when children are forced into reading music before they are ready, poor attitudes, accompanied by a dislike for the music situation, are usually the result. This negative feeling for music may persist throughout life.

Music Evaluation

The success of many school music programs is too often determined by the results obtained at a school concert during which a large number of students take part in singing, playing in a school band, or displaying instrumental accomplishments. Such a "show" does not necessarily imply a good music program, although it might indicate a good musical experience for several children. The true value of the teaching program can best be determined by the extent to which *each* individual in the school participates and enjoys music and the degree to which the music program develops each child's creative powers.

Following is a story to illustrate the above:

A visiting teacher entered a school building on a day near Christmas. From the auditorium came the sound of children's voices singing Christmas carols. The teacher paused, enjoying it. Drawn to the source, he pushed open the auditorium doors.

Before him, in the darkened assembly, only the stage was lighted. About sixty children of ten to twelve years of age stood singing on the stage before him, while in the orchestra pit, the music teacher directed them, and another teacher played the piano. This picture-card scene was soon shattered by an abrupt halt of the conductor's movements and an angry rapping of his baton on the music stand before him.

It was then that the visitor noticed the frightened look on the faces of the children, the tenseness of their bodies, and the wistful glances from their eyes toward the podium. The conductor proceeded to scold the children, calling them careless, and threatened to keep them all day until they sang the carol correctly. Some anxious children trembled; those who were more secure would have smiled if they had dared; all stood taut and tense while they waited for their verbal beating to end. After the irate teacher calmed himself, they were told they were to try it again—this time with no mistakes.

The teacher was striving for a finished product; what happened to the children in the process was of little consequence. One cannot help but wonder what pressures were

*being placed on him which made him treat the children in
such a manner. Just what this teacher hoped to achieve by
his exhibition is difficult to comprehend. Certainly none of
the objectives of education were being met.*

In another school a music teacher was preparing a Christmas
program in a different manner. The children were found to be
sitting around a tape recorder listening to a recording they had
just made of "Silent Night." There was much giggling and laugh-
ing as they heard themselves for the first time. When they finished hearing their performance, the director asked them if they
thought their mothers and fathers would enjoy hearing them sing.
They laughed and said perhaps they were not the greatest. Then
they began to talk about the song, what it meant, and how it
should be sung to create the mood of the words. They practiced
it once more with these ideas in mind. The contrast was obvious.
This time the result was a musical experience satisfying to the
children, as well as the director, illustrating that it is possible to
help children learn to sing musically and find joy in doing so.

As soon as we set perfection as our goal, our real purpose in
teaching music is lost. We should not be attempting to develop
adult musicians in our children; we should be guiding them to
have the richest musical experience possible at their age level.

The best evaluation of any musical program is not only how
well each child can sing or play, but does each child approach the
music experience with anticipation and joy; does he react emotionally and intellectually to music learning activities; and does
the music experience contribute to his creative development?

Setting the Conditions for the Creative Teaching of Music

Setting conditions for developing creativity through music will
include the following considerations.

1. *There will be many musical materials available in the
classroom.* If children are to experiment, explore, and develop
music technique, a classroom environment must be established
that will provide opportunity for this, through both the ample use
of materials and a well-planned classroom program that develops
a wealth of musical experience for children. (See p. 45.) A
music center should contain materials that challenge children to
explore on their own. A record player with a variety of favorite
records can be obtained or borrowed. Children enjoy sharing their
records from home. Simple musical instruments should be acces-

sible. These can be inexpensive but true to pitch such as a fluto-phone, a simple marimba, a recorder, a metalaphone, or a xylo-phone.

Handmade instruments should be ready for immediate use. Children can explore musical tones by use of homemade marimbas, pitched water glasses or pitched varied-size flower pots. Spikes suspended by strings produce clear, bell-like tones when struck. A horseshoe or a piece of pipe makes a beautiful substitute for a triangle. Castanets can be made with hollow nut shells. Tambourines can be created from the plastic tops of ice cream containers and inexpensive dime-store bells.

Some commercial rhythm instruments should also be available. There should be a pad of music paper handy. Many attractive music books should be accessible. If possible a radio should be added. Pictures of musical instruments and of musical activities should be on file. Ideally, a well-tuned piano should be part of each classroom.

Most of these materials are not expensive. If they are expensive, such as the record player, the school curriculum may have to be adjusted to meet the needs of several groups. A record player or piano may have to be placed on rollers to be easily shared among groups, but this need be little deterrent to the music program if the teacher utilizes the materials to the best advantage when she has them on hand. Children should be given a great deal of opportunity to explore the instruments by themselves, and to find out the many sounds and combinations of sounds they can make with them. This does not mean each classroom must be in a constant state of noisy confusion. It does mean that some time must be set aside or some organization is planned whereby all children may use the music materials without infringing on the rights or privacy of others.

2. *There must be a continual program of experiences which serve as stimuli for musical interpretation.* The individual child's musical experience is based on his own development, his particular needs and interests, or his particular feelings. The subject matter of music is constantly changing and differs at various age levels. (See page 50.) Also, this subject matter varies from generation to generation. The child entering the kindergarten today has, as a whole, much more contact with music through television, radio, phonographs, and the movies than a child of a generation ago. He has probably seen more band concerts, attended more musical festivals, and seen or heard music used in more ways than children of previous generations. The school curriculum must, therefore, be constantly changing.

We teach the nursery rhymes and jingles to children in kindergarten today at the expense of boring those who have already learned them at home through a "Sesame Street" type of program and are ready for more enriching experiences. One purpose of the school is to economically transmit the culture, and not to hold children back from learning in an area. Each teacher should know each child and his home and background experiences so he does not run the risk of overemphasizing the areas the child already knows at the expense of challenging him to move forward.

A three year old sat before a television set, watching a rendition of scenes from "Carmen." A famous opera star was singing the arias and dancing the scenes. For one full hour the three year old sat spellbound, watching the performance, and then said, "That was a good play. Pretty music, too!"

Two-year-old children who have had access to many books and whose parents often read and sing to them, quickly recognize words as symbols and will also begin to hum when, on turning a page, they see a staff with notes on it. At this very early age the child already has the concept of music and of music symbolism.

The subject matter utilized in the music for the young child is a representation of the world around him. Children like to sing about everything they see and hear. They are very responsive to noises and will practice making noises in certain rhythmical patterns in all sorts of ways, if given the opportunity. A little girl walks up and down the pavement, up and down the floor, up and down the stairs, up and down the hill, up and down, and she says, "Hear the pretty noises my shoes make, Mummy." Children sing sentences to little tunes, and hum little tunes as they work or play. These are our cues for determining the music curricula.

In art expression children paint their world; and in music they sing about their world. As the boundaries of this world expand, so do their interests; thus the subject matter for the music program is always expanding. As their interests and ideas develop, the techniques for teaching music expand also, and more and more children learn to use the tools of music. Music experiences in the classroom should be planned so the psychological and physiological needs of children are developed. A third grader may be very interested in folk music, and a fifth grader may be interested in Indian music, but an eighth grader or high school boy is apt to be more interested in current popular music. By experiencing all sorts of music at the time when the child is most receptive, he learns to evaluate, to understand and appreciate. A good music program relates to many areas of the curriculum and many facets of life. (See Part 2.)

Some musical "content" presents placement problems. Samples of these problems are: where to teach music symbols formally, where to teach the reading of music, and where to do "part" singing. These problems have sometimes been answered by setting them at a certain grade level and teaching them religiously at that grade level *regardless of the readiness of the children, or the interests and abilities concerned!*

The value of teaching sight reading to children has often been debated. To deprive children of any experience that promotes their growth or an understanding of their culture is questionable. Obviously, these skills should be taught, but to teach them in a fixed pattern at a fixed time is certainly not the way to help each child grow to maturity in his musical abilities or in his creative development. A better plan is to set conditions in the classroom so understandings emerge and are not imposed.

There are many instances in the child's life when he should sing for the sheer joy of it. Each teacher should develop a reservoir of songs children enjoy singing. She should also know of many recordings children can hear. Musical experiences, for the enjoyment and satisfaction they give, should be a part of the subject matter of any school's program.

3. *The emotional tone of the classroom must be such that it encourages musical experiences.* The children and the teachers described in the classrooms above are living in a creative, congenial, comfortable environment. The emotional tone of the creative environment is one in which children are not afraid to take risks, to experiment or to explore (see Fig. 2–2). To this end, plans are made so individual differences and interests are considered and respected. Children are encouraged to take part in class planning and evaluating. Those characteristics peculiar to the creative child are analyzed and respected. Competition is minimized in the emotionally healthy classroom and cooperation is stressed. Teaching is success-oriented. Children are helped to make decisions and to pass judgments for these traits are closely related to the development of creativity.

A conscientious effort is made to inform and instruct parents in understanding the music program and the musical interests of their children. Music offers a natural, normal way for emotional growth. Often, when they have mastered a few skills, children use music as a means of giving vent to strong emotion. Sometimes this becomes a means of ridding oneself of negative feelings in a positive way. Attitudes about music are formed at an early age during the child's first associations with music. It is very important that his first experiences be pleasant yet stimulating.

As a recipient of music-planned activities, the child plays many

FIGURE 2–2   Percussions: Children need the chance to experiment with all forms of music.

logical roles: He may be a listener, a participant, and an evaluator all in one lesson. (See pp. 78–86.) His emotional reactions to all forms of music must be respected. His feelings and tastes for music should come from within and should not be imposed from without. The stimulus comes from without but the reaction comes from within. No one can teach a child how to appreciate or love music; they can only interest him in music and respect his personal reactions. The teacher can help the child to understand and react more richly to music, but only the child and his culture can label the music good or bad, worthy or unworthy.

4. *Music must be experienced for its esthetic values. Esthetics,* according to Webster, is having to do with the beautiful as against the scientific. Garretson[2] says, "Beauty is a personal thing. What is beauty to one person may not be to another. Therein lies a reason for broadening a person's understanding of the nature of music." He goes on to add that schools should help their future citizens to become *consumers* of music. As a consumer of music, a child must develop his ability to weigh one piece of music against another: to develop a taste for music.

2. Robert L. Garretson, *Music in Childhood Education* (New York: Appleton-Century-Crofts, 1966), p. 2.

If the school program is to develop a consumer of music it will assume the responsibility for developing "taste" in a child. Many music educators have pointed out that this objective has been a popular one in the past and that the objective, as such, has never really been met. This may be due to the fact that agreement cannot readily be reached as to what taste is. The behaviorists would have us believe that objectives need to be spelled out in behavioral terms in order to be measured. This calls for a statement as to what the "behavior" of good taste is.

In like manner, a common goal found in music manuals of the past was "to develop a love and appreciation of music in children." Yet, too many youngsters have come to adulthood without a visible "love" or "appreciation" of music. This is probably due to the fact that a "love of music" or "appreciation of music" has never been defined in terms of behavior acceptable to all mankind—and they probably never can be. *Taste in music, love for music*, and an *appreciation of music* are all terms which are highly personal. They involve emotions and knowledge caught within the heart of each person. They can rarely be described in terms of common behavior. What one person loves in music may turn another off.

The inclusion of these objectives in the music programs of the past often meant that the classroom teacher or the music teacher saw themselves as mature people who had learned enough about music so that they were in a position to pass along their knowledge and learned tastes to the unsophisticated child. Consequently, "taste" or "appreciation" in music often meant the imposing of middle-class standards and values on children.

This book avoids the use of such generalized terms in their music objectives and substitutes this statement instead: "To help children develop an awareness and a sensitivity to the esthetic aspects of music in our culture" (see p. 39). This objective is broader. It is the *awareness* to music that we are trying to develop, and we believe that it is an unusual child, indeed, who can experience the situations described in this book and not be aware of them. We believe that conditions can be set which can make children *aware* and sensitive to *music*. We believe that such conditions allow for broad interpretation of music on the part of the child, they permit free and unashamed emotional reaction on the part of the child, and they encourage diverse and personal reactions on the part of the child.

Nonetheless, the objective calls for a definition of the word "esthetic," for it is not only an awareness and sensitivity to music but to the *esthetic* aspects of music that we are after. What do we mean by the esthetic aspects of music? Esthetics has to do with beauty. Are there aspects of esthetic growth that can be identified and primed by the classroom teacher? Yes, there are.

First of all, knowledge and understanding builds a love for beauty. But this knowledge is not knowledge as it was doled out to children by the music teacher or the classroom teacher in the past. It is knowledge sought after by the child or discovered by him or learned by him through his experiences. It is knowledge that is internalized and not pasted on from the outside. Consequently the predetermined curriculum planned and used over long years of time may not do a thing to support the child's intuitive tastes in music.

Second, the development of esthetic awareness means that the child must be exposed to all kinds of music so that he can make choices for himself and come to understand the differences in music expression by the many comparisons he is continually making. He should be in a position where he has many options from which he can make these choices. Under this procedure he is constantly training his ear to hear the differences in music forms rather than having someone *tell* him what they are.

Third, the music of the classroom must be the music of his life, so that he may constantly be sensitive to his school experiences when he is out of school and to his out-of-school experiences when he is in school. The programs of yesterday, which focused on preserving the musical art of the past, were misguided programs that implied that the only music that was worth learning was the music of the past—that constancy and tradition were the character of good music, whereas the true character of music is evolution and change. Music is ever-changing, many-sided, living, vital, and dynamic—but not in terms of the past. It is dynamic to us in terms of *now*.

What children know and appreciate about older music can be learned and appreciated best in terms of what they know about music today, by using the songs they bring to school, the music they hear on television and radio, the music from the football games, the parades, the marching bands, the state fairs, Broadway shows, and the dance floors. The first job of a teacher is to discover children's preferences in music as they exist at the moment and then to expand their experiences into the past.

There is something sad about a culture that finds so little of value in its own music and tends to worship the music of its ancestors. In many schools, even today, music education is taught historically, which means that modern music comes for short periods at the end of long lists. We contend that most music education today should begin with the children's music that reflects modern life and culture and that affords the children a link between home and school, present and past. An understanding of today's music (including music from the past which is still used) can build strong esthetic and usable awareness in children.

Recently a whole new program has been evolved around "synaesthetic education." Synaesthetic education has come to be because of the prejudices, biases, and academic expectancies often associated with the term "art education." In explaining this new education, evolved from art and applicable to music, Andrews[3] states:

> In synaesthetic education the greatest concern is to permit all that is present in the activity to the learner. He should be permitted to participate in the fullest and most vivid manner. The experience must be above all an individual-centered experience. The moment action is extrinsically directed in such a way that the directions eliminate the need for encounter between the person and the environment it ceases to be creative. It should, therefore, be born in mind that the effectiveness lies in empathizing, in the need for encounter and the wholehearted enlistment of the learner in developing rapport. Synaesthetic education is a matter of intimate participation: that is, the satisfying of the need to resolve conflict between man and his environment.

Andrews also says: "Synaesthetic education is not an adjustment *to*, but an engagement *with* all that exists."

FIGURE 2–3   To what are they listening? Are they all involved?

3. Michael Andrews (Ed.), *Synaesthetic Education* (Syracuse, N.Y.: Syracuse University School of Art and the Division of Summer Session, 1971), pp. 11, 14.

In developing esthetic sensitivity, references to value judg-ments will be avoided. Children are not asked what is "good" music or "poor" music. They will, instead, be asked such ques-tions as, "Does this music say something to you or make you feel any special way?" "Does someone else feel differently?" "What comes to your mind when you hear this music?" "Does someone else have a different picture?" "How does the composer make you feel the way you do?" "Can you tell what instruments he is us-ing?" "How else could he have done it?"

In approaching music listening in this manner, the teacher helps the children to probe below the surface of the music for those qualities and techniques that give him a critical eye for beauty. In esthetic listening certain knowledges can be developed which give each child the equipment he needs to become a critic of music. That is, he comes to understand, by listening to many kinds of music, those elements that make some music superior to other music in expressing meaning, in developing mood, or in communicating ideas. This is not to say that each child will agree with every other child on his evaluation of a piece of music. It will mean, however, that he will be able to present logical reasons for his choice or preference.

5. *The teaching of music will contribute to the development of the qualities of creativity.* The teacher will engage children in activities requiring divergent thinking. She will encourage discov-ery and originality. She will set conditions for teaching music that will bring about a flow of ideas and a joy on the part of the chil-dren in playing with and changing these ideas. She will develop the ability to redefine and elaborate these ideas. They will iden-tify closely with music as a means of creative expression.

In the following chapters, many examples are given to show how various teachers have put these principles into practice. These ideas also show how teachers used convergent thinking to develop skills which were put to use to create new products. Some examples show how teachers developed creative responses in chil-dren by giving them basic principles with which to operate. All these examples show the importance of the manipulation of ma-terials, tools, words, and ideas in obtaining the creative product. Some simply show how teachers have built a sensitivity to music as a creative communication medium.

THE MUSIC PROGRAM IN THE ELEMENTARY SCHOOL

A discussion of the musical experiences suitable for different grade levels leads to the problem of sequence. Should there be a set music curriculum to serve as a guide in the elementary school, one in which certain skills and knowledges should be mastered at indicated times, one in which certain songs are learned and specific accomplishments are expected at each grade level?

Such specific outlines, used extensively in the past, serve the purpose of exposing children to all aspects of music education by careful preplanning and help to avoid duplication from grade to grade, thus preventing boredom and waste of precious time.

However, such programs as a whole have been unsuccessful. Teachers, in their eagerness to "cover" the prescribed material, have often left the children behind by teaching too fast or by presenting material before the children were ready or able to take it. These teachers have failed to evaluate continually as to whether or not they have met their goals and as a consequence have often negated them. Children have disliked music, have been embarrassed by it, and have even rejected it. Since little musical ability can be developed if a child dislikes music, and since *no* appreciation and interest in music is developed under these circumstances, we do not favor a rigid, sequential music curriculum in the grades. This is not to say the music program should be incidental. Quite the contrary. To be effective, careful and detailed planning must take place between the classroom teacher, the music teacher, and the curriculum planners if the creativity of children is to be developed and if the objectives of the music program are to be met.

We recommend the type of program that grows out of the situation and begins with the child. An inner-city third grade requires a different music program from a wealthy suburb third grade which, in turn, requires a different third grade music program from a village nongraded primary school. The open classroom can support a different type of program from the departmentalized school. Planned graded curriculum outlines are ineffective in many schools today, but a program which starts with the child and the situation in which he finds himself is always effective if carefully planned.

In such programs duplication and time waste is avoided because the teacher keeps records of the work accomplished, which is then duplicated at the close of the year and passed along to the child's next teacher.

A nonstructured, preplanned, detailed program does not eliminate the concept of sequence. Obviously, some things must be learned before others because a second learning often depends on the first. It is just as obvious that maturity and development play a great part in learning and a child must be physically, socially, mentally, and emotionally ready to learn many things.

A CHILD'S INITAL . . . LISTENING EXPERIENCES

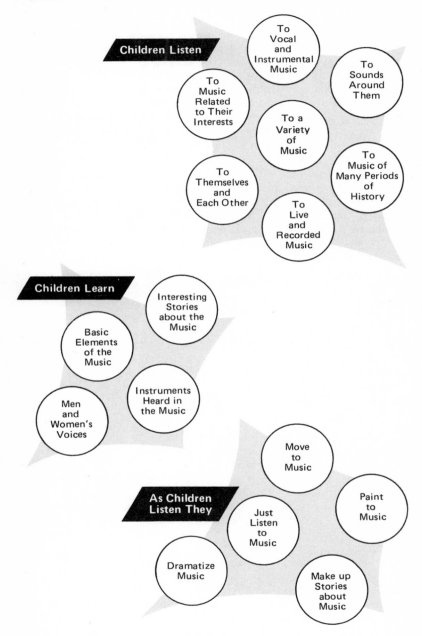

Children Listen

- To Vocal and Instrumental Music
- To Sounds Around Them
- To Music Related to Their Interests
- To a Variety of Music
- To Themselves and Each Other
- To Music of Many Periods of History
- To Live and Recorded Music

Children Learn

- Interesting Stories about the Music
- Basic Elements of the Music
- Instruments Heard in the Music
- Men and Women's Voices

As Children Listen They

- Move to Music
- Paint to Music
- Just Listen to Music
- Dramatize Music
- Make up Stories about Music

FIGURE 2–4 *The music program of the classroom is enriched when one child can accompany the singing of the others on any musical instrument.*

Many school systems are developing suggested outlines, putting in sequence those skills which rightfully belong there but not indicating a specific grade level in which any skill must be taught. Each teacher observes the children and then picks up his music experiences where he was left by the previous teacher. The sequence development in these instances is on a continuum or a thread, and the threads weave themselves in and out of the child's school years, making a tapestry of musical expression which gives the child skills in music when he needs them, and an interest in music at all times.

The following outline indicates the kinds of experiences which may be offered children by classroom teachers and music teachers, and lists some of the expected results from such experiences. These experiences should not be isolated but should be related to each other and to the child's psychological and physical growth in such a way that the child can enjoy the experience, become more interested in music, develop his skill in music and learn about music. The creative teacher will find many ways to include these experiences both in the music program and through related areas of study.

Through these initial experiences in listening many children:

1. Begin to select a repertoire of music that gives them satisfaction.
2. Extend their span of attention resulting in the ability to listen for a longer period of time.
3. Become aware of basic concepts in music.

They also learn about:

1. *Melody*   Based on an awareness of high and low pitches, the children recognize melodic patterns which are repeated, those moving by step and those having large intervals as well as the direction of the pitch of the melody: up, down, or of the same tempo. Some recognize major and minor tonalities.
2. *Tempo*   Move from the recognition of slow and fast tempo to the recognition of gradual changes in tempo.
3. *Rhythm*   Recognize even and uneven rhythmic patterns, discover the beat of the music and the accent grouping of twos or threes.
4. *Harmony*   Notice accompaniments, descants (either played or sung), more than one voice or instrument, and the need for chord changes when some one is accompanying the singing.
5. *Form*   Identify repeated and contrasting melodic patterns that lead to recognition of two- and three-part form.
6. *Dynamics*   Recognize range of dynamic levels from soft to loud as well as the more gradual changes.
7. *Timbre*   Identify many band, orchestra, and social (Tone Quality) instruments.

Through these experiences in listening which, in many ways, are an extension of the initial experiences, many students:

1. Expand their listening repertoire.
2. Discover a type of music that has a special interest for them.
3. Tend to listen more critically.
4. Become interested in playing an instrument or in singing.
5. Extend their knowledge and awareness of basic concepts in music.

They also learn about:

1. *Melody*   Discover the difference in sound between melodies based on major, minor, pentatonic, or modal scales as well as vocal or instrumental melodic lines.
2. *Tempo*   Notice flexibility of tempo such as retards (slowing down), accelerandos (speeding up), and the importance of a particular tempo to the interpretation of a composition.
3. *Rhythm*   Recognize more unusual accent groupings, syncopation, meter groupings, poly rhythms.
4. *Harmony*   Listen for tonality of a composition, changes of tonality (e.g., major to minor) within a composition, the use of scale patterns, including modal and pentatonic scales and chord sequences in song accompaniments.
5. *Form*   Explore larger forms such as rondo, theme and vari-

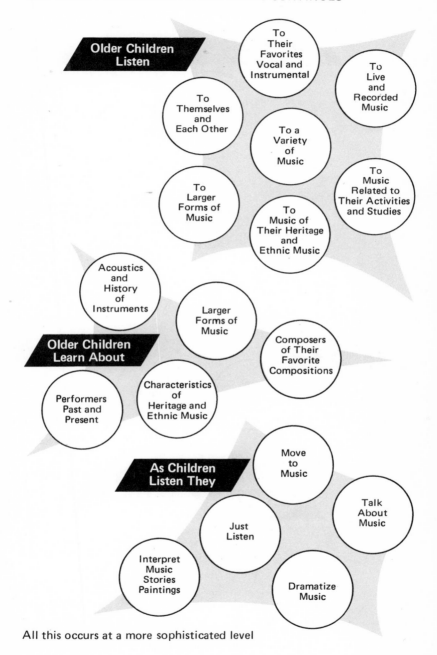

Older Children Listen

To Their Favorites Vocal and Instrumental

To Live and Recorded Music

To Themselves and Each Other

To a Variety of Music

To Larger Forms of Music

To Music Related to Their Activities and Studies

To Music of Their Heritage and Ethnic Music

Acoustics and History of Instruments

Larger Forms of Music

Older Children Learn About

Composers of Their Favorite Compositions

Performers Past and Present

Characteristics of Heritage and Ethnic Music

As Children Listen They

Move to Music

Talk About Music

Just Listen

Interpret Music Stories Paintings

Dramatize Music

All this occurs at a more sophisticated level

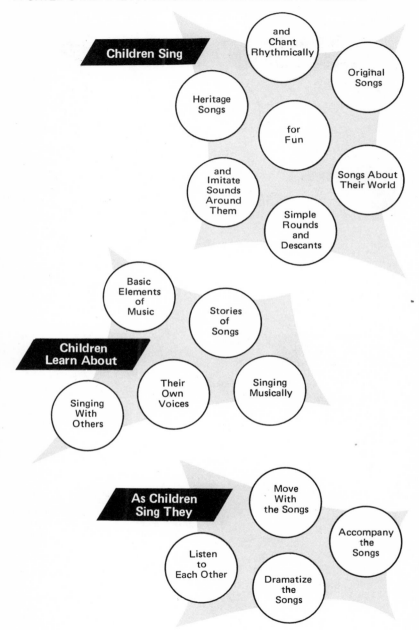

Children Sing

and Chant Rhythmically

Original Songs

Heritage Songs

for Fun

and Imitate Sounds Around Them

Songs About Their World

Simple Rounds and Descants

Children Learn About

Basic Elements of Music

Stories of Songs

Singing Musically

Their Own Voices

Singing With Others

As Children Sing They

Move With the Songs

Accompany the Songs

Listen to Each Other

Dramatize the Songs

FIGURE 2–5   *The music tells them what to do.*

ation, suites, symphonies, and art songs as contrasted with folk songs, operas, and oratorios.

6. *Dynamics*   Recognize importance of dynamic changes to the interpretation of a composition.
7. *Timbre*   Identify instruments in combination, give attention to quality of tone and range and classify voice types.

Many children, through these initial experiences in singing:

1. Discover the joy of singing.
2. Begin to select a repertoire of songs that give them satisfaction.
3. Discover a speaking voice and a singing voice.
4. Discover the voice moves up and down either by steps or leaps.
5. Learn to sing in a wider pitch range.
6. Learn to sing in unison with others and in parts; simple rounds, descants, and two-part music.
7. Discover the dynamic range of the voice.
8. Become aware of the characteristics of songs of many people.
9. Discover they can compose their own songs.
10. Gradually begin to investigate music notation and develop some skill in interpreting the printed page.
11. Learn to add interesting accompaniments (autoharps, percussion instruments, melody instruments).
12. Become aware and knowledgeable of some of the basic elements of music.

THE CHILD PROGRESSES . . . SINGING CONTINUES

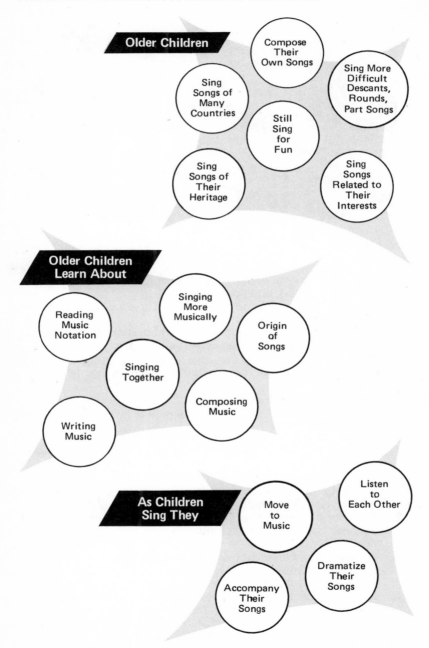

They also learn about:

1. *Melody*   Learn to sing more accurately and discover relationship of scale and chord patterns to the melodic line through the use of numbers or syllables.
2. *Tempo*   Discover the importance of tempo to the interpretation of a particular song.
3. *Rhythm*   Sing more accurately and feel the accent of the meter as well as the rhythmic pattern within the measure.
4. *Harmony*   Recognize the tonal patterns (major, minor, pentatonic) by ear and hear chord sequences I, IV, V.
5. *Form*   Become aware of phrases, length, repetition, and contrast.
6. *Dynamics*   Discover the relationship of the dynamic range to the interpretation of a song.

Things for the teacher to think about:
1. Respect individual differences by selecting a wide variety of music.
2. Repeat old favorites but continually include new compositions.
3. Call attention to the beauty of the music.
4. Choose the best of music in all categories.
5. Avoid placing a child in the position of having to make definite comments or any overt reaction to all the music.
6. Encourage listening to one another as children sing or play.
7. Adapt the length of the listening experience to the attention span of the child.
8. Enjoy listening with the children, remembering a teacher's most important contribution to a child's "musical life" may be creating an atmosphere that leads the child to discover the deep pleasure of listening.

Many children, through continued singing experiences (see p. 58):
1. Find even more pleasure in singing.
2. Explore a wide variety of songs.
3. Become more selective in their choice of songs.
4. Continue to enjoy old favorites in addition to learning new ones.
5. Enjoy singing with their friends and classmates in small groups.
6. Compose more of their own songs.
7. Discover new ways to use their voices.
8. Learn to add descants and interesting harmony parts to the melodic line by ear.
9. Find a satisfying way of expressing themselves through song.

10.   Learn to read music.
11.   Acquire further awareness and knowledge of some of the basic elements in music.

They also learn about:

1.   *Melody*   Develop the ability to sing more accurately (pitch, rhythm, tempo, etc.), realizing the importance of the melodic line and using appropriate tone quality and diction to bring out the expressiveness of the melody.
2.   *Tempo*   Become more critical of the importance of tempo in the interpretation of a song.
3.   *Rhythm*   Learn to sing simple and complex rhythms by note and by sight, and maintain interesting poly rhythms in part singing.
4.   *Harmony*   Extend their ability to hear and sing new tonal patterns both in the melodic line and in chord sequences. Add interesting harmony parts by ear and by sight.
5.   *Form*   Develop their ability to sing longer phrases by using better breath control and recognize the importance of attention to phrasing in interpretation.
6.   *Dynamics*   Become increasingly aware of the importance of dynamics in the interpretation of a song when sung in unison or parts and develop skill in singing with more subtle dynamic shading.
7.   *Timbre*   Develop individual voice qualities as growth and physical maturity occur.

Things for the teacher to think about:

1.   People of all ages seem to be sensitive about their voices so special care must be taken when working with children.
2.   Children are great imitators which means teachers should provide good examples of singing either by the use of their own voices or recordings.
3.   A variety of songs should be introduced so a child may be selective in building a repertoire.
4.   Individual talent varies in singing as in other areas. The child who lacks experience or confidence deserves attention as well as the child who sings easily. Neither should be ignored.
5.   Songs may be used to augment many areas of study.
6.   Songs may be used to bring unity to a classroom.
7.   A child may find great pleasure in composing his own song.
8.   Percussion instruments may be used to bring out special effects in the music.
9.   A child who can read music can be independent musically.
10.   Small ensemble and group singing offers great satisfaction both to the participants and those who hear them.

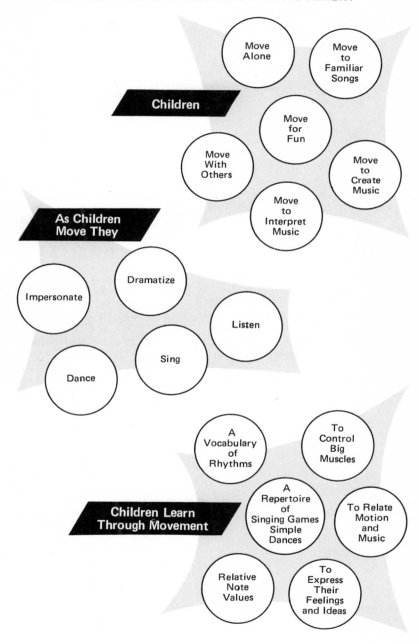

11.   It is important that children sing alone and with accompaniments. Social instruments are excellent at all age levels.
12.   There is a need for children to sing just for the joy of singing.

Many children, through these initial experiences with movement (see p. 61):

1.   Enjoy music more.
2.   Develop their rhythmic capacity.
3.   Become more perceptive listeners.
4.   Release their emotions.
5.   Develop control of their bodies.
6.   Become aware of the elements of music.

They also learn about:

1.   *Melody*   Recognize high and low pitches as well as sequence of melodic pattern through body interpretation.
2.   *Tempo*   Discover relationship of music and movement through moving with music and making music for movement at many tempos.
3.   *Rhythm*   Discover basic beat, accent, and rhythm patterns through movement.
4.   *Form*   Recognize phrase structure by moving with phrase patterns, changing motions to show repetition, contrast, and length of phrase.
5.   *Dynamics*   Recognize dynamic range through size and intensity of movement.

Through extended experiences with music, children:

1.   Move for fun.
2.   Move alone.
3.   Move more with others.
4.   Move to interpret music.
5.   Move to inspire music.
6.   Move to a wide variety of music.

Children learn:

1.   More about music.
2.   A larger repertoire of music.
3.   Characteristics of folk dances.
4.   Self-expression.
5.   A larger vocabulary of rhythms.
6.   To control movement more.

THE CHILD PROGRESSES ... EXPERIENCES WITH MOVEMENT

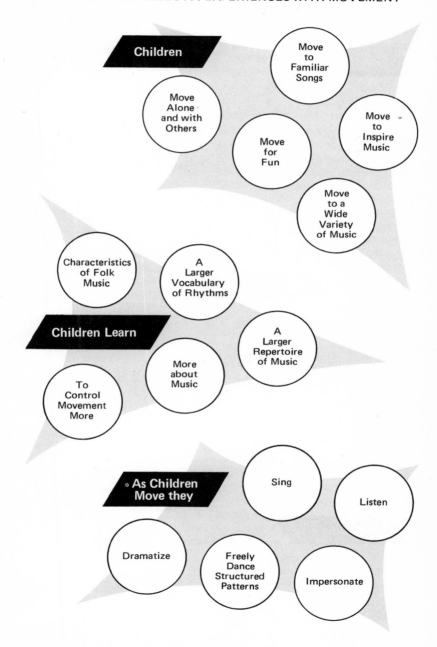

Children

Move to Familiar Songs

Move Alone and with Others

Move to Inspire Music

Move for Fun

Move to a Wide Variety of Music

Characteristics of Folk Music

A Larger Vocabulary of Rhythms

Children Learn

A Larger Repertoire of Music

To Control Movement More

More about Music

As Children Move they

Sing

Listen

Dramatize

Freely Dance Structured Patterns

Impersonate

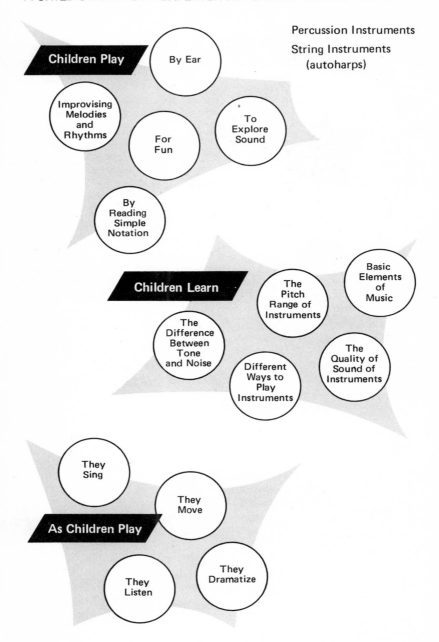

Children Play

By Ear

Percussion Instruments
String Instruments
(autoharps)

Improvising Melodies and Rhythms

For Fun

To Explore Sound

By Reading Simple Notation

Children Learn

The Pitch Range of Instruments

Basic Elements of Music

The Difference Between Tone and Noise

Different Ways to Play Instruments

The Quality of Sound of Instruments

They Sing

They Move

As Children Play

They Listen

They Dramatize

FIGURE 2–6   Experimentation with the piano keyboard can produce fascinating results!

As children move they:

1.   Sing.
2.   Dramatize.
3.   Dance.
4.   Listen.
5.   Impersonate.

Many children, through these extended experiences with movement and music:

1.   Enjoy movement and music more.
2.   Learn to express their ideas more effectively.
3.   Learn to listen more perceptively.
4.   Achieve better control of body movement.
5.   Discover characteristics of music and folk dancing of many countries.
6.   Discover characteristics of music of different periods of history.
7.   Become more aware of basic elements of music.

They also learn more about:

1.   *Melody*   Follow contour of the melodic line, through more controlled body movements.

2. *Tempo*   Develop ability to make subtle changes of tempo to emphasize expressiveness of music.
3. *Rhythm*   Use poly rhythms, syncopated movements to express individual ideas as well as acquiring a vocabulary of dance steps for folk dancing and heritage dances.
4. *Form*   Become familiar with rondo form, three-part form, variation form, and free form through individual and group movement.

Many children, through these initial experiences playing percussion instruments (see p. 64):

1. Enjoy music more.
2. Become more perceptive listeners.
3. Learn to sing in tune better as they sing with melody instruments.
4. Develop skill in playing.
5. Discover their music capacities.
6. Become interested in band, orchestra, and social instruments.
7. Become more aware of the elements of music.

They also learn about:

1. *Melody*   Direction and sequence of melodic line, scale, chordal and tonal center.
2. *Tempo*   Adaptability of the instruments to specific tempos and the need to develop skill to play in tempo.
3. *Rhythm*   Accent, basic beat and rhythmic patterns.
4. *Harmony*   Chord sequence in accompaniments.
5. *Form*   Phrase pattern: repetition contrast and length.
6. *Dynamics*   The dynamic range of the instruments alone and in combination and the need to emphasize the expressiveness of the music through this range.
7. *Timbre*   The difference in quality of the instruments and the possibilities they offer in bringing out the mood of the song.

Many children, through extended experiences playing instruments:

1. Find more enjoyment in music.
2. Discover and develop their music capacities.
3. Learn to sing better in tune, either in unison or poly phonic writing.
4. Become still more perceptive listeners.
5. Improve their playing skill.
6. Improve their ability to read music notation.
7. Continue to explore and improve their ability to improvise.
8. Discover the importance of percussion instruments in many cultures.

THE CHILD PROGRESSES ... PLAYING

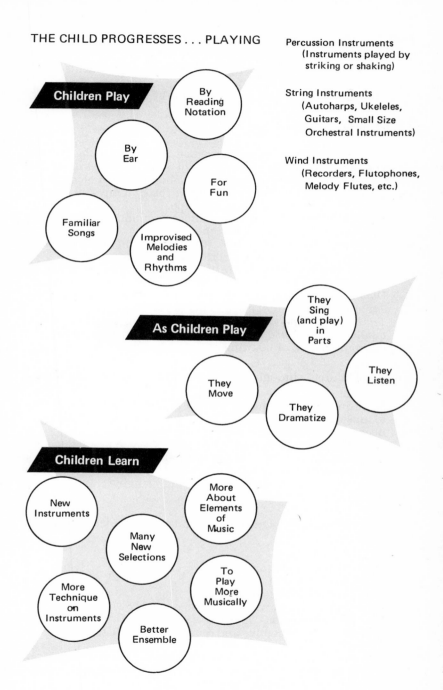

Percussion Instruments
(Instruments played by
striking or shaking)

String Instruments
(Autoharps, Ukeleles,
Guitars, Small Size
Orchestral Instruments)

Wind Instruments
(Recorders, Flutophones,
Melody Flutes, etc.)

Children Play

By Reading Notation

By Ear

For Fun

Familiar Songs

Improvised Melodies and Rhythms

As Children Play

They Sing (and play) in Parts

They Move

They Listen

They Dramatize

Children Learn

New Instruments

More About Elements of Music

Many New Selections

More Technique on Instruments

To Play More Musically

Better Ensemble

9. Recognize the relationship of percussion instruments to the expressiveness of music.
10. Become still more aware of elements of music.

They also learn more about:

1. *Melody*   Begin to emphasize musical quality of the melodic line, and further understanding of scale and rhythmic patterns of the melody as well as combinations of melodic lines.
2. *Tempo*   Develop skill in playing at faster tempos and better control when playing at a slow tempo.
3. *Rhythm*   Learn to improvise interesting and exciting rhythmic patterns alone and with others.
4. *Harmony*   Improve ability to play harmonic accompaniments, descants by ear and/or notation.
5. *Form*   Become more aware of overall structure of music, including introductions, codas, phrase patterns, and climas.
6. *Dynamics*   Acquire greater skill and feeling for using the dynamic range of the instruments to play expressively.
7. *Timbre*   Become more skillful in bringing out the musical quality of the music through the choice of instrument and/or the combination of instruments.

Many children, through these first experiences reading music:

1. Move from concept through graph or line and picture patterns to music notation.
2. Become independent readers of simple notation.
3. Notate their own compositions.
4. Become interested in learning more about reading music.
5. Become more aware of the elements of music which they have experienced listening, moving, singing, and playing instruments.

Many children, through these extended experiences in reading music (see p. 70):

1. Increase their repertoire.
2. Learn to sing and play in groups.
3. Become more interested in music.
4. Enjoy exploring a variety of music on their own.
5. Interpret music more "musically."
6. Become more perceptive and more interested listeners.
7. Enjoy all types of music more.
8. Become more aware and extend their knowledge of the elements of music they have experienced listening, moving, singing and playing instruments.

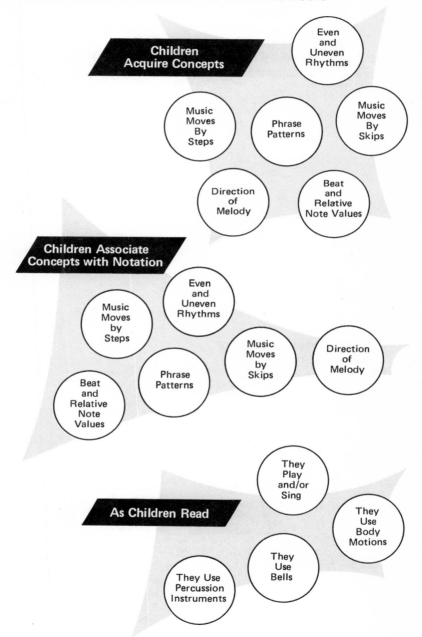

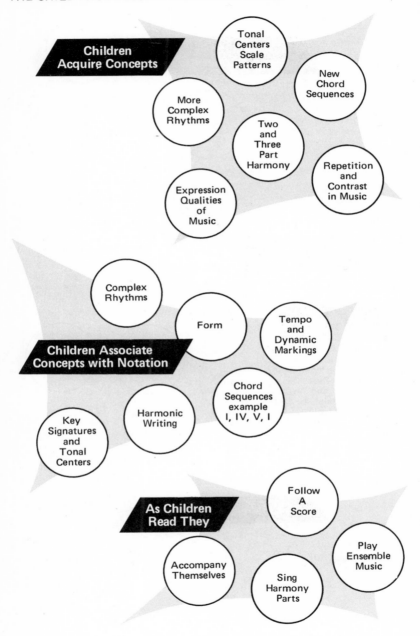

A CHILD'S INITIAL EXPERIENCES . . . MUSICOLOGY
(Beginning Research)

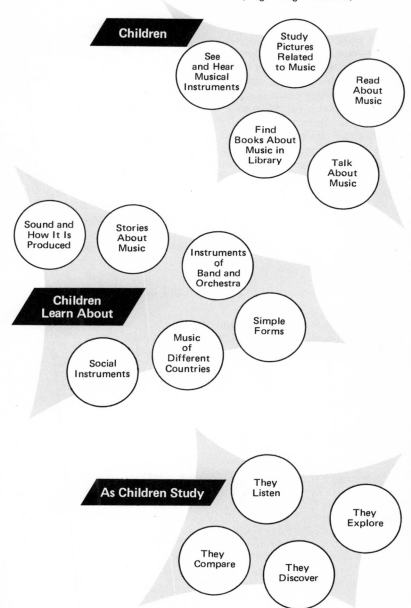

Children

See and Hear Musical Instruments

Study Pictures Related to Music

Read About Music

Find Books About Music in Library

Talk About Music

Sound and How It Is Produced

Stories About Music

Instruments of Band and Orchestra

Children Learn About

Simple Forms

Social Instruments

Music of Different Countries

As Children Study

They Listen

They Explore

They Compare

They Discover

CHILDREN CAN BE "MUSICOLOGISTS"

Musicology, as defined in *The Macmillan Encyclopedia of Music and Musicians,*[4] is "the science of research comprising the investigation of all documents relating to various phases of the art."

One aspect of the music program should be research. Children should be made familiar with the documents and literature of music. Seeking to find music related to a particular period is research. Examining records of early recorded music is research. Looking at pictures of old and new instruments while browsing is research. Finding books that answer questions such as, "What makes an opera?" "What were the operettas popular at the time of the Golden Years of Broadway?" and "Where did the G clef symbol originate?" is research. Searching through books and records by a child to find the history of his own particular instrument is research. Children should be encouraged in the science of musicology throughout their school years, and a music library commensurate to the importance of this activity should be encouraged in every school.

Many children, through these initial experiences in research:

1. Begin to ask more questions.
2. Become interested in learning about music.
3. Begin to associate knowledge with sound.
4. Listen more critically.
5. Learn to talk about music.
6. Become interested in a special area of music.
7. Begin to acquire a personal library.

Many children, through these extended experiences in research:

1. Improve their skill in searching for information.
2. Become more interested in music.
3. Increase their knowledge about music.
4. Add to their repertoire of compositions.
5. Perform better because of their understanding of music styles and elements of music.
6. Relate music to other areas of study.
7. Become more interested in particular areas of music.
8. Add to their personal libraries.

4. Albert E. Wier (Ed.), *The New Encyclopedia of Music and Musicians* (New York: Macmillan, 1938), p. 1278.

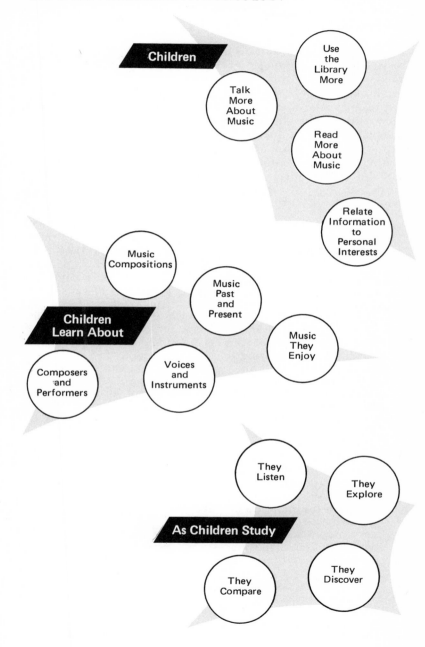

SUMMARY

A sound music program in the elementary school is one which frees children to use music to communicate in original ways. In order to accomplish this goal, certain conditions must be set so certain skills must be developed. They can be developed creatively by a teacher who works closely with a music specialist, each of whom exposes the children to many divergent experiences that promote divergent thinking and acting, that are open-ended in nature, and that result in self-satisfying, creative, original, and exciting products. Continual exposure to open-ended experiences will reinforce the fluency and quality of ideas from the children so music learning truly makes a contribution to creative development.

TO THE COLLEGE STUDENT AND THE TEACHING TEAM

1. Try to write some musical stories. Even if you cannot play a piano you will find you'll get a great deal of satisfaction in creating musical symbols for the characters of the story to be played each time they appear. Tell your story to some children and watch their reaction.
2. Take an inventory of your class and find out who plays musical instruments. Bring them to class some day and experiment with them to find all the ways you can to teach children effectively.
3. Jazz is truly one of the most creative of all music forms, especially the jam session where the music is made up as you go along. Have a jam session with the instruments you have among your friends or children.
4. If you do not play an instrument, experiment with an autoharp, a flutophone, or create some of the instruments mentioned in this chapter and make up some music. Put it on a tape recorder and evaluate it during the playback.
5. Discuss all the ways you can think of to teach the instruments of the orchestra creatively to the children.
6. Make a collection of children's musical recordings and listen to some in class and discuss many ways they may be used with children. Some suggestions: *Peter and the Wolf, Little Indian Drum, Hansel and Gretel.*
7. Make a list of all the ways music may be tied in with other classroom experiences.
8. Check a music program in your school and note how it is tied in with the rest of the day. Does the music teacher take care of the music entirely? In what ways could you improve the program?

9. Design a music center for any classroom and think of all the independent activities that could be provided in this center for before, during, and after school for the children.
10. Take some children's poems and encourage children to write them into music.
11. Find out what instruments the children in any classroom can play and ask them to bring the instruments to school and demonstrate them to the other children. Make up stories or songs to go with the music or about the instrument. Ask the children to paint the sounds of the instrument brought to school.
12. Help the children to collect all sorts of materials which provide a sound and then synchronize these sounds into an orchestra or a sound story.
13. List all the creative ways you can think of to introduce the reading of music to primary children. By what creative ways could you introduce key signatures and music symbols to young children?
14. Make up a story which has bongo drums accompaniment and tell it to some children. Encourage them to create a story using only a marimba for accompaniment.
15. After children write a poem, have them find appropriate music for a background while they recite their poems. Encourage the children to select music to serve as a background for a choral speaking exercise.

SELECTED BIBLIOGRAPHY

Bernstein, Martin, and Martin Picker. *An Introduction to Music.* Englewood Cliffs, N.J.: Prentice-Hall, 1966.

Brye, Joseph. *Basic Principles of Music Theory.* Corvallis: Oregon State University, 1965.

Elliot, Raymond. *Fundamentals of Music,* 3rd ed. Englewood Cliffs, N.J.: Prentice-Hall, 1971.

Gordon, Edwin. *Psychology of Music Teaching.* Englewood Cliffs N.J.: Prentice-Hall, 1971.

Hitchcock, H. Wiley. *Music in the United States.* Englewood Cliffs, N.J.: Prentice-Hall, 1969.

Leach, John R. *Fundamental Piano for the Teacher:* Englewood Cliffs, N.J.: Prentice-Hall, 1968.

Liepmann, Klaus. *The Language of Music.* Cambridge, Mass.: M.I.T. Press, 1953.

Madison, Thurber H. (Ed.) *Basic Concepts in Music Education:* NSSE 57th Yearbook, Part I. Washington, D.C.: The Association, 1958.

Nye, Robert, and Bjornar Bergethon. *Basic Music for Classroom Teachers*, 2nd ed. Englewood Cliffs, N.J.: Prentice-Hall, 1962.

Stransky, Leroy. *The World of Music*. Englewood Cliffs, N.J.: Prentice-Hall, 1969.

Salzman, Eric. *Twentieth-Century Music: An Introduction*. Englewood Cliffs, N.J.: Prentice-Hall, 1967.

Winold, Allen, and John Rehm. *Introducton to Music Theory: An Integrated Approach to Notation, Music Reading, and Ear Training*. Englewood Cliffs, N.J.: Prentice-Hall, 1971.

CHAPTER III

The Creative Teaching of
Music by the Classroom Teacher

Creativity in teaching can thus be judged by the quality of opportunities actually provided by the teacher for young people to have educative experiences.

—ALICE MIEL[1]

INTRODUCTION

Certain conditions must be present in order for creativity to be developed through the use of music. Also certain principles, such as those suggested in Chapter I, must underlie the teaching act. In this chapter the authors have tried to translate these conditions and principles into teaching behavior by providing a view of the type of teaching we label creative. These flashes of creative practice have been gleaned from the classrooms of creative teachers whom they have observed at work.

One of the most important conditions for the creative teaching of music is that the classroom teacher and the music teacher work as a team for the good of the children.

Teachers are no longer handicapped for lack of good music in the classroom; record players, tape recorders, television, and other audiovisual aids can come to the rescue when excellent music is needed for good listening experiences. Record players and tape

1. Alice Miel, *Creative Teaching: Invitations and Instances* (Belmont, Calif.: Wadsworth, 1961), p. 9.

recorders greatly enhance the teacher's opportunity to work creatively with music.

Before you read this chapter, try to recall whether or not you ever saw a teacher teach a music lesson which you thought was truly creative. If so, which of the elements of creative teaching suggested in chapters I and II did it contain? After you finish reading Chapter III, check your observation against it to determine whether or not elements from Chapter III were contained in the lessons. Consider what changes in your own behavior you could bring about to become a more creative teacher.

Creativity has been defined in this volume as the ability to tap past experiences and come up with something new. If we accept this definition *we must accept the responsibility of providing an opportunity for the child to acquire a worthwhile past.* This challenge is an exciting one, for it points out the importance and necessity of making each day's experiences varied, of good quality, and satisfying for the individual, thus adding pleasure to the individual's tomorrows.

A great deal of the classroom teacher's and the music teacher's time should be spent, therefore, on helping the children "acquire a worthwhile past," that is, providing experiences on which the students can build a musical life. We recently observed a classroom teacher who was doing this.

THE CLASSROOM TEACHER IN ACTION

An Experience in Light, Color, and Rhythm

Miss Hill's objectives read as follows: As a result of this experience, each child will

1. Develop an understanding of rhythm and rhyme as evidenced by his body motions, his use of light and color on the walls, his use of rhythms in his voice, and his interpretation of an assignment that combines rhythm, color, and movement.
2. Understand note value, time signatures, measures, and rest symbols as shown by his interpretation of selected pieces of written music.
3. Understand that music is inherent in movement and sound and that it is organized sound, as shown by his ability to compose and interpret music in a variety of ways.
4. Have the opportunity to create with music, as shown by the creative products from the lesson.

At the beginning of Miss Hill's lesson the children discussed rhyme. They had recently been writing rhyming verses so this was something of a review. Together they recited some rhyming poems which they liked. Next they talked about rhythm. Because they had been sitting quietly, Miss Hill encouraged some vigorous movement by teaching the children the Virginia Reel. After they had danced successfully, they went back to exploring the concept of rhythm. One child observed that you can *hear* rhyme but you can *see and hear* rhythm.

Another concluded that rhythm was everywhere. Together the class explored rhythm: one girl walked, and the class said she had rhythm; another ran, another skipped. One of the boys acted out pitching a baseball; another cast a fly rod; another bowled. Each child pantomimed some sort of rhythm. Then the children did some rhythm patterns together: They wrote their names in the air—in a big space, and in a little space.

They explored the rhythm of each other's names. By selecting certain people in the group to clap their names and by assembling the rhythms in various patterns a "sound" chorus resulted. One pattern follows:

Joe	Smith	clap	clap
Hen-ry	No-lan	clap-clap	clap-clap
Mar-i-et-ta	Ko-man-eck-y	clap-clap-clap-clap	clap-clap-clap-clap

Miss Hill observed that the children had indeed heard and seen rhythm and that now she would like them to see rhythm in another way. She asked each child to choose a partner and then she distributed flashlights to each pair of children. She asked the no. 1 member of each pair, on the given signal, to write his name on the wall or ceiling of the classroom with the flashlight so they could now *see* the rhythm of their names. Then the no. 2 member of each pair had a chance to write his name.

She then divided the group into three parts. One group showed the rhythm of *Joe Smith* along the bottom of one wall of the room; another group added Hen-ry No-lan, and the third group added Mar-i-et-ta Ko-man-eck-y. The wall danced with the repeated patterns of the names.

Miss Hill then told the class to continue with the light rhythm but to try to find a place on the walls of the room that no one else was using. The no. 2 members of each group clapped their hands so the children *saw* and *heard* the various rhythms. The entire room danced with light.

Then Miss Hill asked the children to turn off all their lights. "We have had such a good time showing rhythm that I would like to see how well you can show me other rhythms. The no. 1 people will now take the flashlights. I am going to play a record. I want the no. 1's to show me the rhythms you hear in this record—all on this wall. The rest of us will watch and listen and see how many rhythms we can see and hear."

Miss Hill put on "Stars and Stripes Forever." Immediately the wall came alive with bold, jerky marching strokes. One boy, who had a larger light than the others, just showed the accented beat at the beginning of each measure. After a while Miss Hill gave the signal to kill the lights.

"I noticed Buddy's rhythm was different from the others. Show us yours again, Buddy." Buddy showed the accented beat.

"Buddy," said Miss Hill, "does that beat make you think of any particular color?"

"Red," Buddy promptly answered.

"O.K.," said Miss Hill. "Here is a piece of red cellophane and a rubber band. Cover your flashlight with it and then show us the accented beat."

A red light jerked across the wall to the music of Sousa's march.

"Linda," Miss Hill went on, "show us your beat to this music. What color would you use to show it?" Linda chose yellow to show the $\frac{6}{8}$ time.

Colored cellophane pieces were distributed to all the children, and working alternately by 1's and 2's, they showed in color the rhythm of a series of records played by Miss Hill that included: "Stars and Stripes Forever," "The Waltz of the Sugar Plum Fairy," a rock and roll number, "Laura's Theme," "Honey Pot," and "Swan Lake."

The room was a virtual psychedelic light show of moving colors which changed to flowing, swimming colors, with certain colors becoming predominant at one time, and fading another. The children showed rhythms both by movement and by flashing the lights off and on. (See Fig. 3–1.)

Miss Hill then gave the signal to switch off the flashlights and turned the overhead lights on.

"Let's stop and see what we can learn about writing rhythms," said Miss Hill. "We have *heard* rhythm and we have *seen* rhythm, but we should know that there are ways we can write it so that other people can read it and act out the same rhythms we do. In music, rhythm is written in notes, as you know. Let's look at some notes and talk about note value."

Miss Hill had cut some whole notes, quarter notes, half notes, eighth notes, and sixteenth notes from black cardboard. Using recent learnings in arithmetic (see p. 258), she brought out the value of the notes by placing them on the bulletin board in the

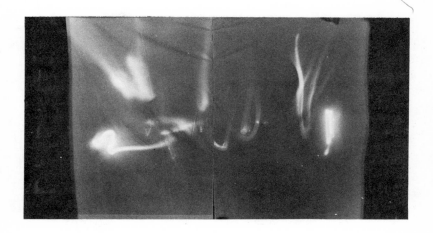

FIGURE 3–1   Miss Hill encouraged the children to make a light show by projecting the colored lights on a sheet.

manner used by the children for the clapping rhythms of the sound chorus. The children caught on to note value quickly, so Miss Hill introduced the concept of a measure of music and showed how notes were placed in a measure. She introduced the time signature showing how the top number designated the number of beats to a measure and the bottom number designated the type of note that received one beat.

Miss Hill then introduced some cardboard charts which she had prepared, showing measures of music from one of the pieces to which the children had danced or shown the rhythm (Fig. 3–2). The rhythm patterns were played with the lights and discussed. The concepts of cut time were also introduced with the measure from "Turkey in the Straw."

The children had enjoyed the afternoon of music and numbers to such a great degree that Miss Hill decided to carry it further the next day.

One of the children had written the following story in creative writing period. Identifying the musical possibilities of the story, Miss Hill printed it on a chart as follows.

A Musical Story

Once there was a big, old bullfrog whose name was George. Every day he sat on a lily pad in the pond and

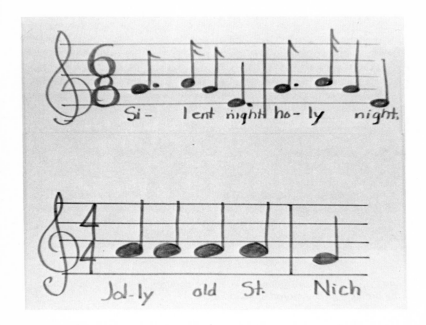

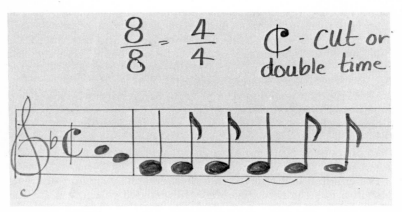

FIGURE 3–2   Miss Hill's charts for introducing time signatures.

watched his beautiful friend Airsy, the dragonfly. He wished he could be a dragonfly and flit from flower to flower and bush to bush.

Every day George would call to Airsy. "Ga-rump, ga-rump," he would say. "I want to be a beautiful dragonfly like you. How can I be one? Ga-rump, ga-rump."

But the dragonfly never paid any attention. He just flew around kissing all the flowers and buzzing to himself.

One day George said to himself, "I am tired of being an ugly, old bullfrog. I am going to find out how to become a dragonfly." And he jumped from one lily pad to another to go to seek his way in the world.

Before long, he came to a big goldfish swimming around in a shallow place in the brook.

"Mr. Goldfish," he croaked, "how can I become a dragonfly?"

"What a foolish idea," said the goldfish. "You can't be an ugly dragonfly. You're just an old bullfrog." And he swam off proudly, glad that he wasn't an ugly, old bullfrog. So George jumped on.

Before long he came to a deer bounding near the brook.

"Mr. Deer," croaked George, "how can I become a dragonfly?"

"What a foolish idea," said the deer. "You can't be a dragonfly. You're an ugly, old bullfrog." And he bounded off proudly, glad that he wasn't an ugly, old bullfrog. So George jumped on.

Before long he came to a rabbit hopping around in a shallow place near the brook.

"Mr. Rabbit," croaked George, "how can I become a dragonfly?"

"What a silly idea," said the rabbit. "You can't be a dragonfly. You're an old, ugly bullfrog." And he hopped off proudly, glad that he wasn't an ugly, old bullfrog. So George jumped on.

Before long, he came to a ————.

(This made it possible for Miss Hill to use the ending of the story over and over to accomplish her purposes.)

The children read the story together. Then Miss Hill suggested they make a musical story of it, so she asked Eddie to show her with his hands how a frog would jump from lily pad to lily pad. Eddie used the palm of his hand and banged it across the top of his desk.

Miss Hill asked one of the children who could *not* play the piano to stand by the piano and run his hands up and down the keys.

"Now," said Miss Hill, "I want Eddie to tell me on what part of the piano keyboard he would show George, the frog, jumping."

"Here," said Eddie, pointing to the bass end.

"All right," said Miss Hill, "go make your hand jump along that part of the keyboard, and we will see if we can get a musical theme for George."

Eddie soon had a deep ba-rump, ba-rump tune to represent the bullfrog.

"Now," said Miss Hill, "who can show me with his fingers how a dragonfly would fly?"

Peter was chosen, and then proceeded to the piano to select a tune at the soprano end of the keyboard to represent the dragonfly.

The children listed the characters that George, the bullfrog, was going to meet in his search. The list included a goldfish, a rabbit, a deer, a snake, and a mole. As each character was added, a musical sound was created for it.

Eventually Miss Hill encouraged the children to end their story, which they did as follows:

> "Mr. Snake," croaked George, "how can I become a dragonfly?"
>
> "What a foolish idea," said the snake. "You can't be a dragonfly. You're an ugly, old bullfrog." And he slid off proudly, glad that he wasn't an old, ugly bullfrog. So George jumped on.
>
> George jumped back to his pad. Suddenly—Crash! Down came Airsy, right on top of George.
>
> "Boy, you're lucky," said Airsy. "For you to be safe all you have to do is blend in with the color of the lily pad. I have to fly around all the time."
>
> "Really!" said George, "Then I guess it's not so bad being a frog after all!"

The story was then broken up into pieces for choral reading and was read and put on tape as a musical story.

On the third afternoon, Miss Hill decided to carry the high motivation of the children further. She divided the children into five groups and gave them each an assignment to prepare for presentation at the end of a half hour. The assignments were as follows:

Group I: Using the story we wrote yesterday, make up new music by using the instruments in this box. Another group is making up a "light" story and a third group is creating a dramatization. You will put them together in a half hour.

Group II: Using this box of props (cloth, crepe paper, scissors, paste, construction paper, colored feathers, two wigs), dramatize in pantomime the story we wrote yesterday. Another group is making up music for the story and a third is making a colored light show of it. All three groups will make their presentations at the same time.

Group III: Using the flashlights and the colored cellophane, create on the sheet in the front of the room, a light show of the story we wrote yesterday (Fig. 3–3). Two other groups will present a dramatization and a musical accompaniment when you give it together.

FIGURE 3–3   Lights tell the story of the bullfrog and the dragon fly.

Group IV: Using the flashlights, shadows, and any record you select from the pile of music in the front of the room, give your impression of a psychedelic light show on the sheet in the front of the room. (See Fig. 3–3 above.)

Group V: Using flashlights, show a scene from an old-time movie. Select music from the records in the music center.

The rendition of the story in sound, pantomime, and colored lights was a beautiful, sensitive culminating activity. The other assignments were carried out with delight and eagerness and demonstrated a great deal of creativity.

This experience proved so successful that on succeeding days the children tried other assignments, some of their own assignments. A few examples follow:

Group I: Take this record and show how various machines would work to its music. Allow the class to guess what kind of machine you are.

Group II: Use this tap dance record and pantomime a television vaudeville act.

Group III: With lights, music, and shadows behind the sheet at the front of the room, show the story of pollution in this country today.

Group IV: Using homemade musical instruments, create a flashlight story on the screen at the front of the room.

Group V: With music, which you create or select, act out this painting for the remainder of the class. Use props if you wish.

Needless to say, Miss Hill and her class had some rich, rewarding experiences as a result of her plan. Children were seen looking through music books and reading song rhythms and suggested creative activities for further group projects.

THE MUSIC EXPERT: A MYTH?

A recent survey on teacher education for the National Association of Schools of Music[2] shows that many states either allow or expect elementary teachers to carry out their own music instruction and that a majority of elementary teachers in this country are now doing so.

Recent studies have also led us to believe that approximately 80 percent of a child's intellectual development takes place by the age of eight. Yet there has always been a shortage of music teachers in the primary grades. In schools where music teachers are available it is common to find them devoting the bulk of their time to chorus, band, instrumental instruction, and rudiments of music in the intermediate grades. It would appear, then, that the belief that a skilled music teacher handles the planning of musical experiences for most of the elementary school children of America is a myth.

This in itself is not a serious problem. A serious problem has resulted, however, when teachers in training have been told they would have the services of a music expert once they were on the job and found instead no one to help them. Untrained, insecure, and often lacking musical ability, these teachers have been unable to provide rich musical experiences for their students and thousands of children have been deprived of developing their creativity through musical outlets.

Another aspect of this problem is that classroom teachers and music teachers, in many schools, have continued playing outmoded and unreasonable roles. In spite of vast acceleration in school populations, in spite of unbelievable growth in physical plant, in spite of astonishing changes in music styles, schools have done little to change or refine the pattern of organization for the teaching of music to students in the modern elementary classroom.

2. Katherine Crews, "Music Every Day. You Should, You Can, Here's How!" *The Instructor* LXXX (December 1970), p. 37.

CLARIFICATION OF ROLES

In other disciplines, a specialist diagnoses and prescribes, while trained personnel carry out his prescription. It should be thus for the specialist in the school. Attempting to teach each child in a school system is an exhausting and unnecessary experience for specialists in the creative arts, especially when classroom teachers are able to do it themselves. A more fruitful program would utilize these people as other professions utilize their specialists: to provide training and help for those who are not so highly specialized and to be a consultant when special help is needed.

A specialist can bring to a staff new ideas concerning the teaching of music. He can help teachers develop their own creative abilities by providing rich opportunities for them to explore and utilize creative materials. In some schools, staff meetings, held on afternoons of early dismissals of the children, are utilized for art, music, and physical education workshops where the special teachers teach the classroom teachers. They, in turn, go back to their classrooms and teach the boys and girls. Programs such as these deploy the energy of the specialist into areas where everyone may benefit. They are economic in terms of time expenditure and keep a school staff constantly informed, stimulated, united, and secure in the steps it takes toward meeting its objectives. Obviously such a spirit affects the children and promotes better educational programs, rich with satisfying social experiences.

In some schools, teachers invite the specialists in to help plan units of work. They sit down with the music, art, and physical education teachers and go over their plans with them, asking for suggestions for including creative experiences in their work. In this way many ideas are shared and the specialists discover where and when they will be needed to help teacher and pupils. They can also share materials with the teacher and learn from her about the children who need help.

For example, a teacher will come to a place in her plans where she has neither the ability nor the equipment to proceed alone. Rather than halt her children's progress, she seizes an opportunity for them to meet and work with new personalities, and, through careful planning, uses the specialist who acts as a consultant in helping the children solve their problems. The specialist does not necessarily take over the class, but rather works in a team teaching situation. These periods can fit into the specialist's schedule and still enable him to spend his energies where they are most needed. A class studying transportation may wish to write a song for a play and thus need the help of a music teacher for several days. After this experience, it may not need him again for several weeks. It is necessary for the music teacher to organize his program to the point at which he can apportion his time most effectively.

Very careful use of the consultant's time was worked out in one school in this way. Each consultant put a mimeographed schedule on the wall outside the door of his office, blocking each day into hour-long periods. When a problem arose in which a teacher and the children in a particular classroom felt they needed the help of the specialist, they would determine the day and the length of time they would need him and dispatch a committee to sign up for that time. If that time was not available, the next best time was chosen. The specialist was obtained when and where he was needed the most and could adjust his teaching methods to meet the needs of the group. Before each visit, the classroom teacher contacted him and briefed him on the purpose of his visit and advised him on what he could do for the children. In this way each experience with the specialist was a valuable one, fitting with the regular activity of the group and contributing toward reaching the teacher's goals.

The specalist must be careful to reserve time to visit the classroom to study the children to determine areas in which he might provide guidance and help to the teacher. This sort of relationship calls for and builds high professional attitudes among staff members. The specialist himself must be a creative person who understands and enjoys people and who will not impose himself but will apply his specialized skill, technique, and point of view when they are needed.

One of the greatest criticisms of the popular trend toward team teaching is that in many instances one teacher takes over a class for a while, and there is little or no continuity in the program among members of the team. Any administrative plan is doomed to failure when subject matter has priority over children. Real team teaching means that many people come to know the children well; the team does a better job in developing creative abilities than a single teacher can do. Otherwise, the whole idea defeats its own purpose.

Current experimentation with various organizational patterns in modern schools creates a need for flexibility of thinking in planning patterns for teaching music. The open classroom concept demands flexibility from both the classroom teacher and the music teacher. In the British open classroom the consultant role is predominant in the music teacher's planning. It is not the type of consultant role mentioned above, however. The music teacher is present all the time in the school where there are no walls to serve as physical boundaries to the mingling of many groups of children. Children pursue, to a great degree, their own interests and learn through discovery, self-teaching, and individual help. Any music experiences which are initiated come largely through stimuli presented in the environment or reports growing out of an individual or group interest.

The classroom teacher and the music teacher must work closely together here for the music teacher provides many musical experiences on the spot or begins plans for other musical experiences to be held later. In many open schools the classroom teacher, or a member of her teaching team, is responsible for the entire music program. The conventional role of the music teacher is gone—and it is interesting to note in passing that many of the protests of teachers that were considered insurmountable blocks to creative teaching have been shown to have no substance.

For instance, teachers are handling larger groups of children than before; they are not isolating them in a music room as many had felt was necessary; and music is being integrated more than ever into the total curriculum. All these changes have come about positively because people believed in the philosophy of the open school and dared be flexible enough in their thinking to discard outmoded and overly conventional plans of organization in order to make the philosophy work.

John Goodlad[3] feels the answer to the problem of art education in our schools is to make certain of the presence of art specialists in the schools. The same plan could apply to music specialists. Goodlad feels the problem is organizational in character and demands an organizational solution. He suggests that one out of ten teachers be an art or music specialist and that this can be achieved through the organizational plan of team teaching: Every team should have an art and music teacher on it. At times the music teacher becomes the lead teacher with other teachers serving in the capacity of consultants.

Dr. Katherine Crews states: "There are many ways to teach children music; teachers lacking in singing and pianist ability should realize that they have other effective equipment and abilities for the purpose. The most important of these are ears to hear, records to play, zeal to learn, and teaching abilities."[4]

It is often true that teachers feel inadequate to teach music because there *are* music specialists in the school. It is also true that many music teachers are under excessive pressures, work with crowded schedules, carry heavy programs, work with many per-

3. John Goodlad, "Advancing Art in U.S. Public Schools," in George Pappas (Ed.), *Concepts in Art Education* (London: Collier-MacMillan, 1970), pp. 274–279.
4. Ibid., p. 37.

sonalities, and must add special projects in addition to their regular assignments. Each teacher has a contribution to make and each should complement the other, concentrating on the child's experiences with music and combining their efforts to create the best music program possible. Each has much to offer but it is apt to be a sure guess that their combined efforts will turn out to be superior to the efforts of either teacher working alone.

Classroom teachers are not always certain as to what should be taught in the classroom. However, this is not unusual. Recent articles in music education publications demonstrate that music teachers themselves are not always certain as to what should be taught in the classroom. If music teachers cannot agree on what should be taught, where can the classroom teacher turn for guidance?

First of all, each classroom teacher should diagnose her own music skills as objectively as possible, determine what she is able to do musically—and then do it. Those aspects of the music program which she feels she cannot do well she can seek help for— from colleagues, children, audiovisual materials, and the music which fills her life each day.

Basically, the main emphasis in any teaching situation must first be on the child, not the subject matter, the school organization, or the materials. How can *each* person in the school help each child to find a satisfactory and rewarding way of life? This means that each teacher, both "regular" and "special," must develop an ability to adjust to the immediate situation and use his talent and knowledge to help children become acquainted with and experience music.

The story of Miss Hill and her class, at the beginning of this chapter, is an illustration of how the classroom teacher can effectively meet worthy music objectives in a unified school program. Any creative teacher can develop such a lesson.

THE TEACHER'S HELPERS

"I love music but I don't know a thing about it . . . I can't even carry a tune or play a chord." This is a familiar comment, and it is usually followed by the question, "How can I use and teach music in my classroom?"

The material that follows is written with the classroom teacher in mind, although the music teacher may also find it useful. It is the purpose of this section to help the classroom teacher find her role in the music program and to see ways she can play that role creatively.

Thanks to the invention of the record player, tape recorder, and television, the teacher is no longer handicapped in providing music experiences for children. The contribution of the teacher who surrounds her children with music cannot be overestimated. Although a teacher who sings or plays a musical instrument obviously can provide broader music experiences for students, *all* teachers can bring children and music together through the many recordings available today.

Perhaps the best reason for choosing recorded music for the children is simply because it is interesting or beautiful. Often music will speak for itself. The teacher's responsibility in this case is only to enjoy the experiences with the children. Today emphasis is being placed more and more on the importance of esthetic experiences for the individual. These experiences can occur at all age levels depending on the atmosphere in which the material is used and the manner of presentation. Can we let music speak for itself without always feeling a need to teach specifics? Do we need to move with the music? Or make up a song to the melody, or play percussion instruments with it? There is a need and a place for moving, writing lyrics, playing instruments, but also for the joy of listening just because the music is beautiful.

Children are surrounded with reading materials and hear speech long before they learn to read or to speak. They mimic the vocabulary with which they are surrounded. Recognizing this fact emphasizes the importance of providing the children with a vocabulary of sound. All teachers can easily help each child acquire this vocabulary of sound, and it could be the most important music experience of all.

It has been noted that listening is a skill—perhaps one of the most difficult to learn. Since we are continually surrounded by sound, we often learn to tune it out. The teacher should be aware that learning to listen can be a long, slow process for some children, and she must be satisfied with small gains. She must believe each experience is a valuable one and worth the effort. If we believe we can help children live enriched lives by meeting their need for musical experiences and help them to develop a sensitivity and love of the esthetic aspects of music, then we must make it possible for them to hear the music. For many children it is a simple matter of exposure.

There are many ways to surround children with music in the classroom and make them aware of beautiful and interesting sounds. No attempt to teach specifics is necessary here, but neither should they be ignored. The teacher, recognizing the importance of incidental learning, might call attention to a lovely melody, a toe-tapping rhythm, or a special vocal or instrumental solo passage. Perhaps the technique of disc jockeys who have been so highly successful in promoting individual recordings could be applied to the classroom. It is simply repetition, asking the children to choose a musical selection to be played sometime during the day or to choose the records for the week. These suggestions imply students have heard a reasonable number of recordings from which to choose. Giving each student an opportunity to make his own favorite record list is perhaps one of the best ways to encourage him to discover music for himself. This experience can be a challenge to the teacher as well as the student, at many age levels. Since there are no regulations that determine the degree to which students of specific ages must or must not enjoy certain musical compositions, both the teacher and the student have complete freedom to explore the vast library of materials available.

The freedom of "real" listening experiences can also be creative for as the individual hears music he can have a new and exciting experience. There is a difference in the *degree* of listening ability of each child. The more involved he becomes in listening, the more creative the experience is, in that the music becomes a part of him. This points up the necessity for careful selection of materials by the teacher as well as the importance of the teacher's attitude toward music as reflected in her enjoyment of listening.

The Record Player and the Tape Recorder

The answer to the need for good and special music to play in the classroom may be found in the extensive use of the tape recorder and the record player, both of which may be used in a multitude of ways.

Recordings may be used simply to create a pleasant atmosphere for the children. This may mean sharing a school or personal collection, and it assumes the availability of a record player or a tape recorder. If one figures the number of hours a record player can be used and considers the wide range of machines available, it is reasonable to consider this equipment as a necessary part of the school budget. A wide range of recordings is available. For example, several albums of the RCA Victor Adventure Series will provide many hours of pleasant and worthwhile listening for a nominal sum. The local library is often a storehouse of good records. (See Chapter X.)

There is little evidence available on listening preferences of the child of the seventies, so there is great opportunity for experimentation by both teacher and children. A simple project such as choosing the records children like to hear while resting or eating or painting or before starting a reading lesson could prove to be a valuable experience. Finding the record that makes them feel lazy or helps them rest or makes them want to get to work is another possible project. It is good to find a recording which seems appropriate for the day or even one which will make them feel better on a gloomy day. There is really no end to the many ways music might be used to create a pleasant atmosphere for the students.

Students are learning many songs from the radio and television, so they are accustomed to learning through simple repetition, with the songs themselves serving as the motivation factor. There are many recordings available today, including folk songs sung by recognized artists in their field, as well as the albums which accompany the basic song series. Students and the teacher may have the enjoyment of learning new songs and singing them with accompaniments which include instruments not usually available in the classroom.

Many of the recordings are so irresistible that the "nonsinger" may soon be humming along and singing with the recording. The atmosphere of a classroom can sometimes be changed by taking one or two minutes to sing a favorite song. Releasing tension or creating a special mood might be accomplished through a "sing" of a few minutes.

A teacher who has a tape recorder available might record the students' singing of their favorite songs and use this in place of a record. Recording a collection of their "mood" songs is fun. The tape can be made while the music teacher is in the room to provide the accompaniment for the students, or a parent might enjoy taping an accompaniment for the group.

The Body: A Musical Instrument

Can you sit absolutely quiet and not move a muscle as you listen to a fast polka, a waltz, or any strongly accented tune? It is extremely difficult not to react physically to music in some way. Children dance to music and seem to make music as they dance (Fig. 3–4). A very small child responds in many ways to a variety of musical sounds. While visiting with friends, a three-year-old girl was observed dancing in the corner of the room to her favorite "dance record." In this case, although the child chose to be close to the adults, she was not to be observed, so we were careful to watch only out of the corner of our eye. The dancing was fun, rhythmic, beautiful, and obviously giving great pleasure to the dancer, who was completely involved before the dance was over,

FIGURE 3–4   *The body: A musical instrument.*

not realizing she had a delighted audience enjoying the experience with her.

Naturally we cannot have twenty-five to thirty-five children dancing at one time in a classroom and really give them an opportunity to be "sent" by music. There are just too many distractions. It is possible, after children have become acquainted with a selection, to rotate the dancers (or those who enjoy moving to music), letting a small group at a time move, or encouraging individuals to share different sections of a composition.

Educators often debate the effectiveness of free movement as opposed to directed movement. Teachers have been heard to object to children marching in a circle or a straight line, suggesting that children move as they wish and go where they choose, instead. "Do what the music tells you to do" is a frequent directive made to the group. Other teachers have emphasized the parade technique and use of similar directed movement over free movement. These are extreme examples of philosophy and illustrate the differences in thinking. Why do we assume all children enjoy and learn better in one way than another? What we really need to consider is both approaches in a classroom.

One teacher included both approaches in working with pre-school-age children in a demonstration class. Free response was best illustrated in this group by the inclusion of "pillow talk" (see Fig. 3–5). Each child sat on a pillow, listened to the music and used arms and body to react to the music without moving from the pillow. Their eyes were closed (except for the usual peeker) and the reaction of the children to the music was amazing. At first they tended to follow a pattern. The shy child hid by wiggling his fingers between his legs, while the more outgoing child reacted with bigger, more observable motions. These exceptions in the class did change, and it was not long before most of the groups were reacting and appearing to enjoy themselves without fear of expressing themselves as individuals.

It was interesting to note that some children who did not choose to participate watched the others and were critical of their motions, as evidenced by several comments. "She's going too fast for the music," observed one four year old, while a five year old commented that one classmate was going "way high up" with the music. Short contrasting selections are especially good for the first session of "pillow talk."

In addition to this free response, the children clapped hands together, moved together, and walked or marched together as they tried to feel the beat of the music. One child showed how he would walk with his grandfather on a hot summer day. All the children walked in this manner or played a percussion instrument to the rhythm of the motion. Sometimes contrasting pieces were played and the class chose that most like the motion or the teacher picked up the pattern on a piano, bells, or drums. A single approach did not seem to excite creative response as much as a combination of the two.

Using Motion or Visual Aids to Describe Music

Another approach for motivating children to really listen to music, both for pure enjoyment and to discover some of its basic elements, is to guide them to convey something about the music through a device, a motion, or a visual aid. This is different from asking a student to show how the music makes him feel. Asking a student to show what he hears in the music is more basic, as in many cases he will be describing the element of music which causes him to react as he does. For example, listening to a slow,

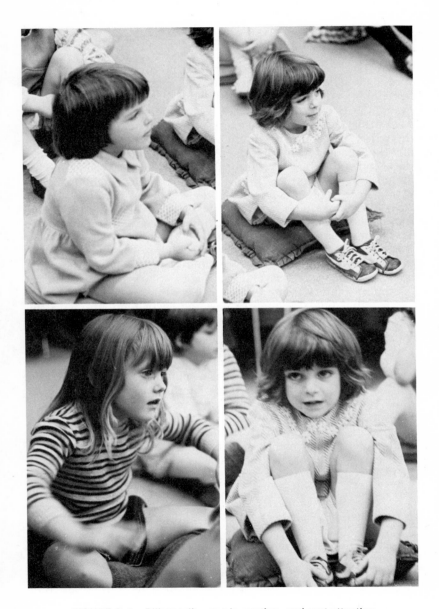

FIGURE 3–5   Pillow talk—music, motion, and rapt attention.

soft selection might make a child feel sleepy but showing what he hears would probably be illustrated by something involving a tempo—a slow motion or a soft chant indicating a degree of volume. The illustration the student chooses might include the feeling "it makes me sleepy," but the emphasis would be on the music, which is the cause of the individual's reaction. He discovers why he reacts a certain way and illustrates it in some manner.

Trying to find many different ways to express these elements can be a challenge to groups as well as to individual creative activity. For example, how many ways can we illustrate "Waltz on Ice" by Prokofiev? (See Fig. 3–6.) First, let's listen for the form or the design of the selection. It has three melodies and they are played in this sequence after an introduction:

Melody 1
Melody 2
Melody 1
Melody 3
Melody 1
Coda—an added ending

Let the children find how many melodies there are and then find some way of showing each one. One class decided to use their

FIGURE 3–6   Hand puppets represent the three medolies in "Waltz on Ice" by Prokofiev in the "Watch and Listen" television series.

hands in a skating motion for melody 1. They sat motionless unless they were reacting to this melody. Later they moved their hands and arms up and down for melody 2, and another time added a rolling motion for melody 3. In this case all the children moved all the time.

Another class chose motions for each melody but different groups chose their favorite melody to interpret. The interest shown by the entire class as each group brought their ideas to life was interesting.

One class chose to illustrate the same music by using percussion instruments, being careful to play exactly with the beat of the music. The strong beat or accent was played in melody 1, the three beats in melody 2, and the rhythm of the tune for melody 3.

A class that enjoyed moving might "dance" the form by changing motions for each melody. A variation of this might be the whole group dancing melody 1, with small groups or solos dancing melody 2 or 3, and everyone coming in on the coda or ending for a "grand finale."

Puppets are an excellent medium for illustrating form and rhythm in music (see Fig. 3–6). These were used in the "Watch and Listen" television series created for young viewers of the magic Toy Shop over WHEN-TV in Syracuse, New York. A doll made on a mitten and worn with two fingers "skating" beneath the skirt illustrated melody 1. A clown made in similar fashion skated melody 2, and a snowman made of styrofoam balls on a stick twirled to melody 3. These were not only fun to watch but fun to use when they were given to children.

One student created a visual for the music by making one pipe cleaner skater with a pink skirt representing the first melody and a gentleman pipe cleaner skater representing the third melody. Still another idea is to paint a design to illustrate each melodic pattern.

All these ideas are effective only if there is repeated listening so the music really becomes a part of the individual. These activities can be shared with other classes, parents, or friends. All children may participate and since the selections are short several may be included. Experiences of this kind may be expanded and extended to many other music compositions. All ages can participate at their level. It is interesting and exciting to see how children of different ages choose to describe the same music.

Combining Stories and Rhythm

Choosing key words in children's stories and using them to help children "feel" relative note values can be easy and fun. The stories following—"A Trip to the Farm" and "Halloween Guests" —were used in classes of four and five year olds, and the response of the children was excellent. In one class the "rhythm" word was spoken in a pattern as the story was read. For example, Jack-O-Lantern reads as four, even quarter notes; Black Cat as two half notes. One class began to chant the words and the children found the notes on the bells and eventually added other percussion instrument sounds. "A Trip to the Farm" provided an opportunity for adding many animal sounds.

Sometimes it is helpful to establish a steady beat by tapping lightly on a drum or clapping softly and then chanting or singing the words of the poem or story to this steady pattern. Children enjoy clapping or tapping their feet to this steady beat as they chant the words (see Fig. 3–7). Once a steady 1—2—3—4 beat is established, the rest seems to be easy in the average elementary classroom.

Another way to vary this experience is to let children clap one of the rhythms while the others guess if it is Swish, Black Cat, or

FIGURE 3–7 *Stick puppets can greatly enrich music appreciation, as seen in this picture where an impromptu performance is in progress using the piano as a puppet stage.*

one of the other words. Since there are several, the game might be started by asking the children if the pattern clapped is "pumpkin" or "meow." Eventually, children discover all the words that are clapped alike as well as the ones which are different. Bells and percussion instruments can be substituted for piano to add variety.

Fun to Take a Trip to the Farm

As I walked into the barn I heard some cows and they were going MOO, MOO. *Upstairs in the hay loft were some little kittens. The mother was afraid I was going to hurt her little family, so she said* MEOW, MEOW. *The little kittens were crying* MEW, MEW. *I heard a lot of noise out in the yard and what do you think I saw there? Little pigs who were hungry too. They were going* OINK, OINK, OINK, OINK. *I was glad when the farmer fed them. The next thing I heard was a strong sound:* QUACK, QUACK, QUACK, QUACK. *Could you guess what was making that sound? A duck, of course. Then I saw some little chickens and I heard them going* PEEP, PEEP. *Last of all I saw an old rooster strutting across the yard going* COCK-A-DOODLE-DOO, COCK-A-DOODLE-DOO. *I didn't know there were so many kinds of sounds on a farm, did you?*

1. *cow—MOO*   𝅝   5. *duck—QUACK* ♩ ♩ ♩ ♩

2. *cat—MEOW*   𝅝   6. *chick—PEEP*   ♪♪♪♪ ♪♪♪♪

3. *kitten—MEW* ♩ ♩   7. *rooster—COCK-A- DOODLE-DOO*

4. *pig—OINK* ♩ ♩ ♩ ♩   ♩. ♪ ♫ | ♩ ‖

This could lead into a discovery of sounds in the room, the school, in the city or around the house.

Halloween Guests

It was a dark and windy night. It was Halloween. I was all curled up in a big comfortable chair in front of the fireplace. It was warm inside but outside the wind was howling and making strange sounds: aooo—aooo. *The porch light was on, and there was a lighted* jack-o-lant-ern *made out of a big, fat* pump-kin *on the porch.*

I listened carefully as I hoped someone would come to visit me. Soon I heard voices and my doorbell rang. Now who do you think was standing on my porch? It was a black cat *that went* meow. *That's right—a* black cat *that went* meow. *I gave the* black cat *some* can-dy *and curled up in my chair again. In a few minutes the door bell rang. This time it was a long, loud ring. I hurried to the door and there stood two* wit-ches. *They were all in black with high peaked hats, and of course they had brooms. After all Halloween witches have to have broom-sticks to ride on, don't they? I wonder what you think these witches were doing. That's right, they were sweeping my porch*—swish *went the brooms*—swish, swish, swish. *Of course they got their candy, and I went back to my chair.*

This time I almost fell asleep in my big chair in front of the warm fire. It seemed I heard a soft noise on the porch. I listened and listened. I just had to see who was on my porch. I got up very quietly, went softly to the door, opened it gently, and there stood two little white *ghosts. What do you think they did when I opened the door? They went* boo *as loud as they could and ran right away.*

Follow-Up

Let's see how much you learned about my Halloween guests.

1.   How did the wind sound?
      1   2   3   4

2.   What was on my porch?

Jack-o-lan-tern
      1 -2- 3 - 4

3.   What was the jack-o-lantern made of?

Pump   kin
1-2   3-4

4.   Who came to see me?

Black cat
Wit-ches
White ghosts
Broom-sticks

5.   What sound did the black cat make?

𝐎
Meow
      1   2   3   4

6.   How did the broom sticks go?

𝐎
Swish
      1   2   3   4

7.   How did the white ghosts scare you?

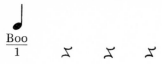

This activity is another means of helping children to develop their rhythm capacity and to feel the relative note values, therefore it is important to keep the beat very steady and the note patterns in relationship to the basic beat. A variation of this activity is to ask the questions and clap the pattern used by the child who answers or combines words used in the story to develop a chant, adding appropriate sounds to dramatize and give meaning to the experience.

Analyzing Music

Have you tried cutouts fastened to straws or pencils to be moved rhythmically and serve as guides to the rhythm of music? They may be introduced by the teacher and then used by the children to study a musical selection, or they can be created by the children to describe their favorite musical selections. This experience emphasizes listening, analyzing the music to determine the most appealing or most dominant element, and synchronizing movement with music.

One teacher introduced Kabalevsky's "March" and "Comedians Gallop" with cutouts taped to pencils to illustrate the contrast in the two sections, the rhythm changes, and the form of the music. A horse galloped with the recurring melody, and a little mouse scampered all around during the xylophone solo. The children seemed to feel the steady beat of the march and the excitement of the gallop as they took turns with the stick puppets. Perhaps the best evaluation of this experience was reflected in the statements, "I liked that!" and "Let's listen to that next time."

Part of the success of this lesson was that the teacher had made careful preparations. She had chosen music with a strong rhythmic appeal, listened to it repeatedly, worked out the presentation and through practice became thoroughly familiar with the music. Her confidence as a result of this preparation plus her enthusiasm for the music and for her presentation created a worthwhile music experience for all. This experience provided an exceptional opportunity for individual involvement, which is so important to the student and too often omitted.

Discovering Contrasts in Music

Painting rhythms on a wall with a flashlight as in Miss Hill's lesson can be a fine learning experience. (See p. 79.) Contrast a composition with a strong, healthy beat such as a march to that of a composition which has a steady, softer beat. For example, listen to Sousa's "Stars and Stripes Forever" and Bach's "Air on the G String" picturing the beat of both on the wall with a flashlight. Each gives the listener a feeling of four, but the choice of instruments and the difference in tempo, dynamics, and melodic line in each composition tends to cause the student to create a different design for each.

Children may enjoy creating a free design of their own favorite composition. Sometimes the melodic line may be the strongest influence on the listener; sometimes it is the rhythmic pattern. The *shape* of the melody may be illustrated by this technique: As the melodic line rises, the light may climb to the ceiling or even play on it and drop to the floor with a descent. The rise to the ceiling may be smooth and steady or may jump from one level to another. Letting the music guide the light as the child listens can be fascinating for the designer and the observers.

Using flashlights to show the form of the music can be colorful. Place colored paper or cellophane over the end of the flashlight and then use a different color for each section of the music. Adding color to the design, which will reflect the tempo, melody, and beat or rhythm, could give an excellent description of the elements of the music as well as serve as a motivating force for concentrated listening. One student used red for the first section of a composition, white for the second section, both red and white for the third section, and ended by superimposing the white on the red for the final tone. Not only did this student become aware of the construction of the composition, but through repeated listening to the piece gave evidence of enjoyment and feeling for its musical quality.

Anderson's "Syncopated Clock," which has such an interesting rhythmic pattern, would be an excellent composition to listen to and "design." One flashlight could keep a steady motion while another could move to the syncopated rhythm. This could be used each time the main melody repeats, with an alternate pattern and colors for the alternating melody.

Designing the melodic line and the accompaniment of Saint-Saëns' "The Swan" can be exciting. This leads to the use of two flashlights and is especially good to show the pitch line, the phrasing, the contrast of the melodic line and the accompaniment.

The possibilities of designing music with flashlights are limitless. It must be remembered, however, this *can* become a device that could be more important than the listening experience. If creating interest in music and guiding students to become better acquainted with it through awareness of its elements is the teacher's objective, then continuous emphasis must be placed on the relationship of the design to the music.

Children may design the compositions in individual ways so one student may respond to the rhythm, another to the melody, and so on. Designs are not wrong or right, but it is possible for the children to lose the music and become so intrigued with the pattern that there appears to be no relationship between the two. Usually this means the children are not really hearing the music. If this happens, one might ask the students to tell what there is in the music that calls for the kind of design being produced. Another approach is to discuss the design in the same way. Can we find music to go with this design, or, using percussion instruments, can we create music to accompany this design? It is helpful to chart the important characteristics of the pattern and then plan the music to reflect these ideas.

One class worked out a pattern for the melodic line of "The Swan" by showing the pitch changes and phrases. This took concentrated, repeated listening and practice by individuals. Each wall of the room was used for practice. Finally the class chose the one they felt best described the music. Each student had an opportunity to show his design before one was selected as the most effective. Here it is important to remember that an activity may not appeal to all children, so there should be no pressure—only encouragement and opportunity for participation. The teacher then asked the students what else they heard in the music that seemed important. One child brought out that the music was fairly soft and the group agreed this could be illustrated by the use of a soft color. Any soft color was acceptable to the group, but in this case a soft rose was chosen. Another child heard a part which "moved" more. This was the water-rippling accompaniment which was worked out and finally combined with the melody. A worthwhile follow up to this experience would be to have each child select his favorite composition and create a design to show the class. Some of the compositions which might be suggested:

Bach-Gounod	"Ave Maria"
Bach	"Air on the G String"
Tchaikowsky	"Andante Cantible"
	"Lara's Theme" from *Dr. Zhivago*
	"Londonderry Air"

Also, use popular songs of the day.

It would be advisable to include compositions with contrasting moods to keep the class interested. Good programing, whether for a symphony concert or a day in the classroom, usually includes variety and this is especially important when working with children.

SUGGESTIONS FOR THE CLASSROOM TEACHER'S MUSIC PROGRAM: PRIMARY GRADES

The child beginning school is concerned with himself and his immediate world. The kindergarten is his second home; the teacher is his second mother. He is active and his attention span is short. He is interested more in *doing* than in the *result* of his doing. Music is natural to him and manifests itself in the rhythm of all he does. He likes to experiment with sound and with his body and to repeat things he has learned. Repetition plays a great part in his learning. Music should be present from time to time throughout his day.

Primary children enjoy the following activities that lay a foundation for forms of creative expression. (Also, see the charts and outlines in Chapter II.)

Learn by Rote to Sing
1. Songs about home, school, neighborhood.
2. Songs with special phrases to help child find his singing voice.
3. Excerpts from songs that older children sing.
4. Nonsense or fun songs.
5. Songs with actions.
6. Songs that suggest movement and dramatization.
7. Songs that children make up about everyday experiences.
8. Songs of the seasons and special days.

Move to Music
1. That suggests walking, running, skipping, galloping.
2. That suggests dramatizations in singing games.
3. For free and individual interpretative response.
4. Clapping.
5. That allows child to respond at his own tempo.
6. That suggests animal movements: the lumbering of an elephant, the waddle of a duck.
7. That suggests mood: show happiness, show loneliness, etc.
8. That suggests abstractions: show water, be a wheel, etc.
9. That encourages original dance patterns.

Play

1. Simple instruments to accompany songs.
2. Sand blocks for train songs.
3. Rhythm sticks for clock songs.
4. Rhythm band instruments.
5. Bells.
6. Mouth organs.
7. Drums to accompany creative dances.
8. Musical games.

Listen

1. To teacher or a visitor play the piano, violin, or other instrument.
2. To others sing a beautiful song.
3. To learn a new song.
4. To dramatize a story to music.
5. To begin to establish good listening habits.
6. To children's records.
7. To radio programs.
8. To musical television programs.

Develop

1. An awareness of up and down in music.
2. An awareness of high and low.
3. An awareness of loud and soft.
4. A feeling of steady rhythm.
5. An interest in music.
6. A knowledge of instruments.
7. Their own creative songs and dances.

Explore and Discover

1. Different sized bells for different tones.
2. The piano and its possibilities (big and long strings—low tones; smaller, shorter strings—high tones; finding tunes).
3. The possibilities of making different sounds on a drum (big and small drums; sides and rims as well as heads to play on).
4. The possibilities of melody instruments for creating as well as accompanying songs learned (tone blocks, melody bells).

Use the Body with Music

Dance with scarves, capes, ribbons, bells (use for creative rhythms and dramatizations).

Play Simple Instruments

1. Autoharp.
2. Ukelele.
3. Rhythm instruments—sticks, sand blocks, drums, etc.
4. Simple melody instruments—tone blocks, etc.

5. Piano and a good phonograph.
6. Flutophone.
7. Marimba, xylophone, bells.
8. Mouth organ.

Making musical instruments at all grade levels can help children become more observing and aware of different kinds of sounds. Such an activity can grow out of a unit on "Sound" (see Chapter IX), where children listen to all kinds of combinations of materials to produce new sounds and to discover which materials carry sound and which do not. All kinds of small objects (thumb tacks, paper clips, pebbles, macaroni, rice, sand, glass) can be enclosed in hollow containers (boxes, tin pie plates, gourds, paper plates, old balls) to test for new sounds (see Fig. 3–8). Sound stories and musical compositions may be invented from the products of such experimentation. In activities such as these, children learn through discovery and create with what they discover.

The following list is a springboard to the many ideas children will have, once they begin to invent with sounds.

Clicking Instruments

1. Rhythm sticks—doweling of small diameter cut in twelve-inch lengths; hard wood is best.
2. Wood blocks—sections of old baseball bat.
3. Temple blocks—sections of old bowling pins.
4. Claves—paired resonant sticks; six-inch sections of old broomsticks.
5. Coconut shells—split coconut shells; two paper cups stuck together.

FIGURE 3–8   Ten year olds enjoy making their own instruments.

Ringing Instruments

1. Triangles—horseshoes or large nails, suspended.
2. Chimes—silver spoons of different sizes, suspended; resonant curtain rods.
3. Gong—length of iron pipe; old brake drums; strike cymbal.
4. Cymbals—resonant metal covers; brass trays.
5. Tambourines—heavy cardboard pie plates with bottle caps (sanded smooth), roofing disks, or sea shells attached near the rim.
6. Jingle sticks—jingling metal disks fastened loosely on a stick.

Swishing Instruments

1. Maracas (shakers or rattles)—gourds with seeds or pebbles inside; various containers with chalk, gravel, peas inside (mounted on handles, if desired); medicine bottles with rice; clam shells with shot; old light bulbs covered with papier maché (when dry, break glass by rapping sharply on table).

Booming Instruments

1. Drums—any hollow container covered by a sheet of rubber, plastic, paper, or leather.

One kindergarten teacher demonstrated a wise use of the percussion band. The children listened to a recording with a good rhythm. The percussion instruments were placed where the children could choose any particular one. The teacher played sections of the music and asked individuals in the group to play their instruments as the music suggested. In this way she obtained a variety of rhythms from the children. The group learned from each other that there were many ways of interpreting music and using instruments. Some accented each note with bells and tambourines, some struck the beat with cymbals and triangles, others hit only the afterbeat with drums and rhythm sticks. The teacher then suggested the entire record be played and each child would play his instrument as he had done individually. The concert that followed was much more beautiful and creative than the more common accented bang of instruments when the beat is set by the teacher. A change of instruments promoted further discovery and exploration and new effects.

The concert was beautiful because the children had had an opportunity to listen to the music, create a special part with their instrument, and then had the fun of putting them together. Sometimes the percussion instruments may be used to help children discover the accent, basic beats, or rhythm of the melody. Children may choose instruments best suited to each part and have fun moving from one rhythm to another avoiding complete repetition and also getting the swing of the music.

Percussion band instruments may be used for many other purposes than the toy orchestra. Each instrument, if it is a good one, is worthy of exploration by itself. The drum, for instance, should be used alone a great deal—instead of a piano, perhaps. Drum rhythms created by children can be utilized for certain kinds of rhythm steps which the piano does not inspire. Use of these instruments is not confined to the lower grades. Third- and fourth-grade boys created a group of Inca and Aztec dances using a drum rhythm of their own creation with unusual effect when danced in costumes and masks. They had learned that most savage tribes used the rhythm of the drum as their chief source of music.

The creation of music, begun in the nursery school and kindergarten, should be continued through the child's school life. Children can soon learn their melodies and record them so that others can play them. Using a marimba, xylophone, or tuned glasses, children can easily learn to make up tunes and record them with numbers. After each child has had much experience with composition of this type, the group may create a song for a school program, and the teacher may utilize this opportunity to teach children how to record music with notes and measures so anyone can read them, just as she teaches them to write their stories so that others may read them. Some first-grade teachers have done this simply and with a great deal of success. The time for presenting written music must not depend on a grade level—it happens when the children have had a rich experience in composition and recording in a simple fashion. It may come at any age. If it is taught with meaning and in the framework of the child's own experience it is understood.

One fifth grade which had a rich musical background wrote and filmed a motion picture on the history of their community. The class then started to write a song for the introduction to the film, but became so interested in composing music that they not only wrote songs for the entire film but wrote orchestrations for the songs as well. Members of the class who played musical instruments met with the music teacher and set the songs to a musical background for the film.

If children at an early age play simple instruments with success, they will desire to continue their explorations of instruments. At first the percussion instruments answer the need; then the simpler instruments such as the flutophone, recorder, mouth organ, marimba, ukelele, and guitar become a challenge. In the intermediate grades the instruments of the band and orchestra claim the attention of the child. Children who start to play these instruments need instructors who will guide them toward successful experiences. Each instrument is unique and demands a special approach adapted to its design and acoustical properties.

The teacher helps the child establish a relationship with the instrument; he gets the "feel" of it, he finds out what he can do with it and is given simple exercises which provide successes for him from the start. Much of his earliest work with instruments should be "ear" training; he need not be bored with monotonous and meaningless drill if each lesson contains melodic material and is rich with variety and crowned with a sense of achievement. If he understands and loves his instrument he will practice. Some of his practice will be with the work he, himself, has written and recorded. The compulsion of the intermediate grade child to master skills shows in his ability to master a musical instrument when he is properly motivated.

Success is necessary if this motivation is to be continued. Too many unresolved failures may cause a child to abandon his instrument. Music experiences should give pleasure and satisfaction to children at all times.

Things to Do with Rhythm Instruments

1. *Make up a story and use percussion instruments for sound effects.* Example: The alarm clock (triangle) awakes us in the morning. The clock (gong) strikes eight. Mother calls, "Are you sleeping?" (Sing the song to the accompaniment of the clock ticking [wood blocks]). On the way to school we hear a train (sand blocks) and horses (coconut shells). Such a story is another way to teach the appropriateness of individual percussion instruments.

2. *Practice some drum talk.* During this activity, the drum plays the rhythm of words or names. One variant of this consists of the teacher beating the rhythm of words or parts of a familiar song on a drum, and the children answering by playing instruments or clapping the rhythm of answering words. Examples for primary grades:

Teacher drums:	"Mary had a little lamb."
Children:	"Little lamb, little lamb."
Teacher:	"Mary had a little lamb."
Children:	"Its fleece was white as snow."

3. *Make up a story around one instrument* (the drum is especially good for this). Then play records of stories which use one

instrument. Example: "Little Indian Drum," Young Peoples Records.

Other Activities

Children can be stimulated to make up their own songs to accompany simple dramatizations. Ronald's song is a good example of this (Fig. 3–9).

Many children will have older brothers and sisters who can play musical instruments. Invite them to the classroom to perform. Better yet, invite parents who sing or play a musical instrument. Invite the Boy Scout bugler to play for the children and tell about his bugle.

Singing games are excellent to develop rhythm and to help children feel music: "Looby Lou," "Farmer in the Dell," "Mulberry Bush," "Go In and Out the Window," and many others may be replaced in the intermediate grades by "Brother Come and Dance with Me," "Here I Come, Where From?" jump-rope songs, and folk games and dances.

As children walk, skip, jump, or march, introduce a rhythmic pattern to show them how motions would look when expressed musically. For instance, a walk step might look like Figure 3–10. A skipping step might look like Figure 3–11. These experiences can form a base for reading music later on.

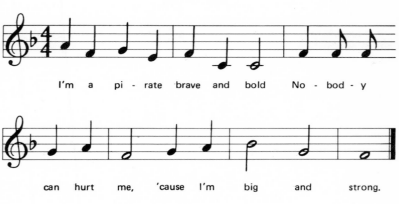

Ronald's Song

I'm a pi - rate brave and bold No - bod - y

can hurt me, 'cause I'm big and strong.

FIGURE 3–9

FIGURE 3–10   A walking step.

Music can aid the child in adjusting to new situations; it can help children to release hostile and negative tensions in positive ways. As a medium for promoting good mental health, it belongs in the category of the sociodrama and other sociodynamic devices explored by Katherine Crews.[5] A book by Lydia Fern Tallmadge, William H. Tallmadge, and Francis M. Wilson called *Sing Trouble Away* (New York Teacher's Library, 1790 Broadway, New York, N.Y., 1957) contains songs and accompanying suggestions for helping children release tensions through music.

Sing each child's name for roll call and have him respond by repeating the tune or making up one that goes with yours.

Children enjoy listening to special records about single or grouped instruments. Some records of this nature are listed in Chapter 10.

SUGGESTIONS FOR THE CLASSROOM TEACHER'S MUSIC PROGRAM: INTERMEDIATE GRADES

As children study various parts of their own country and other countries, they obtain original, authentic songs from each area and sing them. Music helps to develop the "feeling" for a country. Recordings of folk music the world over, from Irish shanty songs to African Veldt songs, can now be obtained. Some excellent examples are:

"Going West" (Young Peoples Records)
"Chisholm Trail" (Young Peoples Records)
"Christopher Columbus" (Young Peoples Records)

FIGURE 3–11   One skipping step.

5. Crews, "Music Every Day."

"Yankee Doodle and Other Folk Songs" (Young Peoples Records)
"Maypole Dance" (RCA Victor)
"Turn Me, Turn Around Me"—Czech folk song (RCA Victor)
"Wheat"—Czech folk song (RCA Victor)
"Cshebogar"—Hungarian folk song (RCA Victor)
"Tantoli Swedish" (RCA Victor)
"Dance of Greeting"—Danish folk song (RCA Victor)
"Ancient and Oriental Music" (RCA Victor)
"Early Medieval Music Up to 1300" (RCA Victor)
Records from the United Nations

Reading music is no problem when children have written their songs in symbols. The sequence in reading words is: experience, verbal symbols, printed symbols, then the writing. (See p. 222.) In music it is the same. The child experiences, he sings his experiences, the teacher prints it with music symbols, and he reads it. Then he is ready to read the music symbols of others. Just as he is given phonic training so he can become independent in his normal reading activity, he is given help in understanding and using new music symbolism as he encounters it in his reading of music.

Part singing may well be preceded by choral speaking where children talk lines of words with sounds to get the "feel" of putting together different sounds at the same time. Soon rounds can be introduced; children can experience part singing first by using their own songs or poems, and by chanting different tunes at the same time in their dramatizations, or by using sound stories. (See p. 231.)

Children in the intermediate grades enjoy experimenting with musical instruments. They can go beyond the realm of the tuned glasses and flower pots and make stringed instruments by stretching rubber bands with varied thicknesses and tensions over the open end of cigar boxes, or stringing wires or cat gut over frames. Children in these grades can make respectable wooden marimbas, glass or metal xylophones, and various kinds of drums. Often these instruments can be made in association with a science unit on the topic of sound. Intermediate grade children enjoy making up songs to accompany cheers for their favorite basketball or football teams.

Mr. Clark, a music consultant, used as many opportunities as possible to help children in his classes understand that life around them could be translated into musical expression. The children at each grade level used appropriate experiences to create music. They wrote songs constantly about everything, through group experiences and individually. Some of the topics Mr. Clark used were:

A Spooky Night	The Harvest Song
Thanksgiving Is Coming	Fun in Winter
Gobbley Gobbley	I Make a Snowman
Fall	I Like Winter
Spring	Robin Redbreast
Winter Song	Beautiful Rainbow
Snowflakes	When Santa Comes
The Wind	A New Pet
The Hoptoad	We Make Valentines
Be My Valentine	Policeman Bill
A Funny Clown	The Five Little Fish
The Fisherman's Song	The Aeroplane
We'll Sail for a Whale	Happy Boys and Girls
Dolly's Sandman	The Football Game
Ann's Trip	Oil on Puddles
A Ride on a Horse	

Here are some sample songs written by his classes and by his individual students. (See Figs. 3–12 and 3–13.)

Mr. Clark's pupils explored each musical instrument carefully once they reached the third grade. They learned to identify the instruments and their sounds. The unique sounds of each instrument led the children to write songs about them. Here are some written by groups and individuals. (See Fig. 3–14, p. 116.)

When a special event came around, Mr. Clark tried to catch the flavor of the children's interest by finding songs that went with the particular occasion. After the children in the sixth grade sang "Take Me Out to the Ball Game," they wanted to write their own

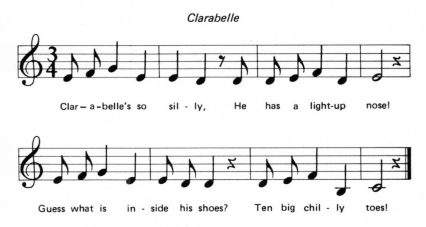

Clarabelle

Clar—a—belle's so   sil - ly,   He   has   a   light-up   nose!

Guess what is   in - side his shoes?   Ten   big   chil - ly   toes!

FIGURE 3–12   One of Mr. Clark's students wrote "Clarabelle."

The Fall Song
by Mrs. Abbey's Second Grade

The leaves are dif-ferent col - ors The leaves are fal - ling down,

When - e - ver I go out The leaves are on the ground!

Autumn Weather
by Patricia Suters, Grade 2

I like the au-tumn wea-ther, the days are crisp and cold.

I have to wear a swea - ter, the leaves are red and gold.

FIGURE 3–13

songs about baseball. They decided they would use the tune of "Take Me Out to the Ball Game" because they were so fond of it. They called their creation "The Series Song" with half the class rooting for one team and half, the other. "The Series Song" appears on pages 116–117.

The Big Bass Fiddle
by Mrs. Smith's Third Grade

I'm a big bass fid - dle and you play me

on my strings, you can play me ver - y low.

The Retreating Flutophone
by Robert Woodruff, Grade 4

The re - treat - ing flut - o - phone, saw some men and

it went home, the re - treat – ing flut - o - phone went right home!

FIGURE 3–14

The Series Song
Tune: "Take Me Out to the Ball Game"

The Yankees are a good ball team
But the Dodgers are sure to win

Our pitchers are better than Yankee ones
Campy and Snider are hitting home runs
And it's root, root, root for the Dodgers
If they don't win it's a shame
So it's one, two, three more home runs
And the game is won!

Take me out to the Yanks now
For they're the highest in ranks
Buy me some peanuts and red hot franks
We'll watch the series, the Dodgers and Yanks
Root, root, root, for the Yankees
For they're the very best team
So it's six, seven, eight, nine, ten
And the Yanks are winning again!

MRS. SLOPER'S *Sixth Grade*

Mrs. Fund often used recordings to help develop musical appreciation or musical interpretation. One of her favorite devices was to play a record and give these simple instructions: Write whatever the music makes you think of. Here are some second-grade impressions (from "Young Persons' Guide to the Orchestra")— Makes me sleepy . . . a happy day . . . sad . . . someone died . . . makes me dance . . . someone in love . . . a birthday . . . makes me fly in the air . . . makes me float . . . very happy.

"I love music. It is loud and soft. It has drums and instruments. It can be real soft and sometimes makes you sleepy . . . it will remind you of many things. It will make you think you're beautiful. It will go slow and then scare you by going fast all of a sudden . . . and it will play real loud and the sound like it stopped but it just gets real soft. It will make you sleepy forever. Now while the harp is playing with that loving piano, the band will play so soft you'll cry when you sleep. . . ."

SUMMARY

The concept that the music experiences of the elementary school child are under the guidance of a music specialist is largely a myth, as few schools employ a music specialist. Among those who are employed, many do not work with all teachers, and few work directly with all children.

In order to provide valuable music experiences for children, the role of the classroom teacher and the music teacher must change. The classroom teacher can broaden the music program by incorporating music experiences into other areas of the curriculum and can assume the responsibility for teaching those areas of music of which she is capable.

The road to this new role has already been paved with helpers for the classroom teachers: materials abound in the form of text books and printed matter; recordings, record players, and tape recorders can be used to greatly enrich a grade teacher's program.

Movement and music provide a perfect combination for the development of music appreciation, rhythm, and harmony. The environment of any school abounds in visual aids that can be used to enrich music teaching, or, better yet, with materials that provide children with an opportunity to create musically, such as stick puppets, story books, poems, paints and flashlights. The creative approaches possible in the teaching of music are limited only by the imagination of the teacher.

TO THE COLLEGE STUDENT AND THE TEACHING TEAM

1. Even if you are not trained to play the piano, sit before a piano keyboard and experiment with the sounds. See if you can make sounds to accompany the following:
   a. a swimmer
   b. a ballet dancer
   c. soldiers marching
   d. water dripping
   e. a ping pong ball
   f. children skipping
   g. rain falling
   h. a thunder storm
   i. a deer leaping
   j. children playing leap-frog
2. Plan a color show for children and determine all the ways you can use music to add to the color effect.
3. Write some musical stories for children but leave them open-ended. Present them to the children to find out how they will use music to finish the stories.
4. Brainstorm all the ways you could use flashlights to teach music other than the ones mentioned in this chapter.
5. Try the following exercise with some children:
   a. Play several pieces of music with contrasting rhythms or tempo and have them make the rhythms on the wall with flashlights.
   b. Ask them what color a certain section reminds them of; then another; and another. Provide a cellophane disk for

the children to cover their flashlights and encourage them to show many beats and rhythms in one composition by using rear projection on a sheet suspended in the classroom over which the various colors can dance and move in harmony.

c. Encourage them to add shadows by standing near the sheet or by holding appropriate objects near the sheet. Movement can also be added to gain interesting effects.

6. Select a classic such as "Peter and the Wolf" to play for your children. Instead of telling them the story and introducing the themes in a conventional manner, however, introduce the characters, suggest that a theme play for each character and then play the music allowing the children to construct their own story from the music.

7. Create as many *musical* sounds as you can without the help of conventional instruments. Weave them into a musical story or operetta.

8. Brainstorm all the ways you could use puppets (and other visuals) to teach music.

9. Make a list of children's classics in literature which might be used for the development of music appreciation.

10. Problems for discussion:

a. The creative teaching of music as it is defined in this chapter means making music fun. But, it does not insure that children are learning the fundamentals of music.

b. There is evidence available to show that children are not learning music rudiments under the present methods of teaching.

c. Creative teaching and incidental teaching are the same thing.

d. Creative teaching requires too much time on the part of the teacher to be effective.

e. The illustrations of the lessons in this chapter were founded on the principles of creative teaching as discussed in Chapter I.

f. The teachers described in this chapter all set physical, psychological, intellectual, and emotional conditions for the creative teaching of music.

SELECTED BIBLIOGRAPHY

Austin, Virginia. *Learning Fundamental Concepts of Music: An Activities Approach.* Dubuque, Iowa: William C. Brown, 1970.

Andrews, Gladys E. *Creative Rhythmic Movement for Children.* Englewood Cliffs, N.J.: Prentice-Hall, 1954.

Cheyette, Irving, and Herbert Cheyette. *Teaching Music Creativity in the Elementary School.* New York: McGraw-Hill, 1969.

Colwell, Richard. *The Evaluation of Music Teaching and Learning.* Englewood Cliffs, N.J.: Prentice-Hall, 1970.

Gelineau, Phyllis. *Experiences in Music.* New York: McGraw-Hill, 1970.

Hood, Marguerite. *Teaching Rhythm and Using Classroom Instruments.* Englewood Cliffs, N.J.: Prentice-Hall, 1970.

Luck, James. *Creative Music for the Classroom Teacher.* New York: Random House, Alfred A. Knopf, 1971.

Marsh, Mary Val. *Explore and Discover Music.* New York: Macmillan, 1970.

Mynatt, Constance, and Bernard Kaiman. *Folk Dancing for Students and Teachers.* Dubuque, Iowa: William C. Brown, 1969.

Nordholm, Harriet. *Singing in the Elementary Schools.* Englewood Cliffs, N.J.: Prentice-Hall, 1966.

Nye, Robert, and Vernice Nye. *Music in the Elementary School: An Approach to Music Methods and Materials,* 3rd ed. Englewood Cliffs, N.J.: Prentice-Hall, 1970.

Pace, Robert. *Piano for Classroom Music.* Englewood Cliffs, N.J.: Prentice-Hall, 1970.

Raebeck, Lois. *New Approaches to Music in the Elementary School.* Dubuque, Iowa: William C. Brown, 1969.

Stringham, Edwin John. *Listening to Music Creatively.* Englewood Cliffs, N.J.: Prentice-Hall, 1959.

Vernazza, Marcella. *Making and Planning Classroom Instruments.* Belmont, Calif.: Fearon Publishers, 1969.

Winslow, Robert W. *Music Skills for Classroom Teachers.* Dubuque, Iowa: William C. Brown, 1970.

CHAPTER IV

Music for Its Own Sake

If we could have devised an arrangement for providing everybody with music in their homes, perfect in quality, unlimited in quantity, suited to every mood, and beginning and ceasing at will, we should have considered the limit of human felicity already attained . . . !

—EDWARD BELLAMY[1]

INTRODUCTION

In the child-centered approach to teaching music is there ever a time when music is taught just for the sake of helping children learn about music? When and why? What roles do children play as young musicians? Can appreciation in music be developed in children? We have seen how the child can play many diverse roles as a composer. Are there any reasons or benefits for the child to play the role of the performer?

The title of this chapter may cause the reader to think that the authors have abandoned the child-centered philosophy of the teaching of music. This is not the case. If one objective of the elementary school program is to provide opportunities for children to discover and experiment with music in all its forms, and if individual differences in children's talents and interests in music are to be respected, a special section of this text must be devoted to the role of the teacher(s) in accomplishing these objectives.

The classroom teacher and the music teacher will be conscientiously planning experiences such as we have described in this book. Such experiences will help each child to build his own personal feelings and understanding of music and will result in his

1. Edward Bellamy from *Looking Backward* (Boston: Houghton Mifflin, 1931).

own private appreciations and tastes. The teachers will also plan experiences above and beyond the class experiences for those individuals who show a particular interest in music and a talent for it.

This aspect of music development requires at least a basic knowledge of music and the components of music education that help the listener build his own values and provide him with a criteria for judgment in evaluating the work of others as well as the ability to judge his own work. This aspect of music also furnishes the child with a knowledge of music symbolism and music notation, to serve as a tool for his own creative purposes.

We have often referred to the need to put convergent learnings to use and have illustrated this concept with classroom situations (see p. 5 and p. 82). Such experiences will place the child in the role of the listener, the performer, and the composer, and each role will help develop him as a person and as a musician.

WHAT MUSIC WILL BE TAUGHT

The facts, knowledges, and skills essential for music literacy are included in the outlines of the music program in the elementary school in Chapter II. An expansion of these understandings is developed here for the benefit of the classroom teacher who may feel more comfortable if she has them before her.

It is important to point out that this material can and should be taught creatively. It is also important to point out that *all* children will not learn these facts. A correlation exists between intelligence and the ability to symbolize. Slow learners who have difficulty symbolizing will have difficulty learning music symbols. Although they are important, these learnings become secondary to the child's enjoyment and interest in music.

The 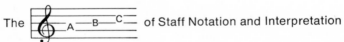 of Staff Notation and Interpretation

Music notation is another form of communication. The development of the system makes it possible for man to preserve and pass on his musical ideas. The great works of the past are available to us through the use of this system, and new works are notated for current and future interpretation. Most music is notated through the traditional patterns although some contemporary composers working with tapes, electronic sounds, and unusual use of instruments are creating new ways of notating their ideas. However, this is a new field and demands special study. The information included here may be helpful to teachers and children who have an interest in learning more about music.

Five lines and four spaces (*a staff*) are used as a basis for notation. ≡≡≡ These are useless, however, until a clef sign is placed on them. The most common clef signs are the *treble clef* 𝄞 or **G** clef sign and the *bass clef* 𝄢 or **F** clef sign. When they are combined they are known as the *great staff.*

The C between the staffs is *middle C.*

Notice the treble clef crosses the second line or **G** four times. The other lines and spaces on the staff (called *degrees*) follow the pattern of the alphabet from this letter. The dots which are a part of the bass clef sign center around the fourth line, which is F, and the other degrees of the staff follow the alphabet sequence. Short lines known as *leger* lines are used to extend the pitch range of the staff.

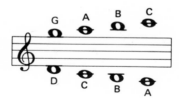

Staff notation related to the keyboard of the bells or piano.

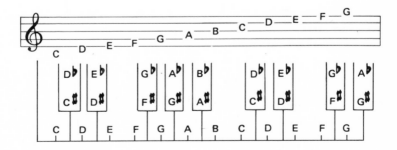

Most of the music used in the classroom is based on the major, minor, pentatonic or modal scale patterns. These scale patterns are a sequence of whole steps and half steps. *Sharps* (♯) which raise the pitch of the tone one-half step and *flats* (♭) which lower the pitch of the tone one-half step are used to keep this sequence. A half step is best illustrated by checking a piano keyboard and listening carefully. For example, play C, then the black key to the right of C. This is the sound of one-half step (from any key or tone to its nearest neighbor). The black key above C is known as C♯ or d♭, an *enharmonic* tone, two names for the same pitch. At one time there were two different sounds, one for C♯ and one for d♭ but since the time of Bach one sound or pitch is used for both. Play C, then d and you will hear the sound of one whole step.

It is the sequence of whole and half steps that determines the difference in sound between major, minor, pentatonic, or modal scales.

Check the notation of several songs and you will notice they sound comfortable when you sing the last tone, but unfinished if you stop before the last tone. This tone is usually the first tone of the scale used to notate the song.

Row Your Boat—Last

The song is played only on the white keys, keeping a major scale pattern.

The same song may be played

This time F must be changed to F♯ to keep the scale pattern. Pick out a few tunes using the flats and sharps, then try playing them without the flats and sharps and your ears will soon help you understand why they are used.

The arrangement of flats and sharps at the beginning of the music is called a *key signature*. This makes for efficient notation and ease of reading. This tells you what sharps or flats to sing and play and the scale the music is based on. We say, for example, the song is in the key of C when there are no sharps or flats used in this scale.

The second example of "Row Your Boat" is based on the D scale and two sharps are needed to keep this sequence, F♯ and C♯, so we find these in the *key signature*   Key of D Major.

Children's songs are usually written in the following keys. That means they are based on scale patterns requiring the flats or sharps in the signature to keep the correct sequence.

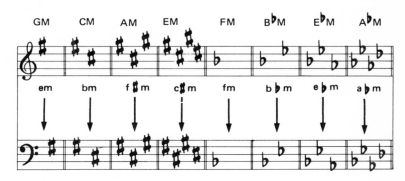

The capital M is used to identify a *major key* and a small m to represent a *minor key*. Each scale has its own sound as the sequence of whole and half steps is different for major and minor scales. To train the ear and develop sensitivity, hearing the various scale patterns is important. Classroom teachers will find the music teacher of great help in explaining scales and their relationship to the tonality of a song.

The sharp farthest to the right is the seventh tone of the scale. To find the name of the scale (key) go up one-half step to the eighth tone which is the same as the first. C♯ is the sharp farthest

to the right in this key signature 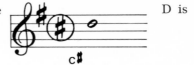 D is

one-half step above C♯. The scale using two sharps starts and ends on D. The name of this key is D.

The flat *next* to the one farthest to the right in the key signature is the fourth tone of the scale and the name of the key.

Key of E♭

Sometimes a composer wishes to change a tone which has been played flat or sharp before or is part of the key signature. A *natural sign* cancels a sharp or flat. For example, B♭ flat becomes B natural.

The placement of the note on the staff tells us the pitch of the tone but the duration of the sound must be interpreted through an understanding of the *time signature* (2/4, 4/4, 6/8) at the beginning of the music and relative note values.

Notes are not absolute but are relative as illustrated in the figure below. The note itself does not indicate its exact duration but rather the relationship of one kind of note to another in space of time. Fast marches and slow lullabies, for example, may both he notated using quarter notes (♩) and eighth notes (♪). The tempo or pace of the music is determined by the style of the music and indicated by the markings at the beginning of the music, such as fast, slow, allegro, adagio, etc. Regardless of how fast or slow the music is performed the duration of the notes must be relative, a quarter note (♩) twice as long as an eighth note (♪) and half as long as a half note (♩).

Another way to acquire a feeling for the time relationship of notes is to play or sing a familiar tune as though it was written in notes of one time value. This is difficult! It is also helpful to notate patterns by dashes of relative lengths.

Notes used to indicate duration:

Relative note values

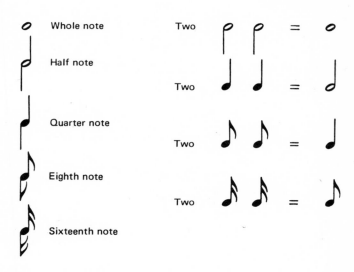

Time Signature

The *top number* of the time signature indicates the number of counts or beats in a measure (3/4 = three beats in a measure, 5/4 = five beats in a measure).

The bottom number of the time signature indicates the kind of note which equals one count or beat (4 ♩ = 1, 8 ♪ = 1, 2 ♩ = 1).

These examples may help.

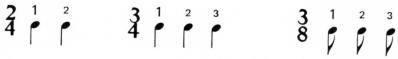

A *measure* is a group of beats, the first of which has an accent. The groups are marked off by bar lines:

Music is rarely made up of sounds of equal duration. Different kinds of notes are used to indicate the length of the sounds and this arrangement of long and short sounds creates a *rhythm* or *rhythm pattern*.

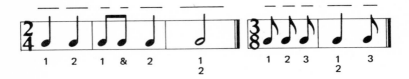

A dot adds one-half the value of a note. For example:

$$\quartnote = 1 \rightarrow \dottedquarter = 1\frac{1}{2}$$

$$\eighthnote = 2 \rightarrow \dottedeighth = 2$$

$$\halfnote = 3 \rightarrow \dottedhalf = 3$$

Examples

The *and* sign (&) is used to divide one beat into two equal parts 1 = 1&.

This information should be introduced to children when they are aware of the basic concepts of pitch and rhythm and where it is necessary to the understanding of the music.

Primary children will have little use for knowledge of these notations but many older children become curious about these markings which they discover on a page of music and will ask about their meanings. As soon as children begin to read music, these notations become important and can be taught along with the other music symbols.

Other symbols used in notation:

Repeat Signs

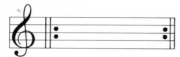

Repeat the sections between the bar lines.

Repeat to the beginning.

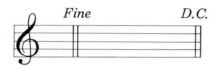

D.C. stands for Da Capo (Repeat to the head or beginning, continue playing to the word Finé [ending]).

D.S. (Dal Segno) repeat to the sign and play to the end.

Children can be made aware of tempo markings through lessons such as those taught by Miss Hill where the teacher, in notating the music for various rhythms, can point out to the students that sometimes it is necessary for the composer to communicate a little something extra to the performer by way of a memo written on the music itself.

Tempo markings are used to indicate the pace of the music, which is important in its interpretation.

> Largo—slow and broad
> Andante—walking tempo
> Allegro—quick
> Presto—very fast

Terms indicating change of tempo

> Retard—gradual slowing of speed
> Accelerando—gradual increase of speed

Dynamic markings relate to the range of volume of the music.

pp —pianissimo—very soft

p —piano—soft

mp —mezzo piano—moderately soft

mf —mezzo forte—moderately loud

f —forte—loud

ff —fortissimo—very loud

Terms indicating change of volume

crescendo   <   gradually louder

descrescendo   >   gradually softer

Many songs published today substitute the English vocabulary for the foreign terms.

Notation in the Primary Program

We have already read about two intermediate grade experiences in which music facts were taught meaningfully and creatively (p. 5 and p. 81). Let's look at a primary situation which shows how a teacher may creatively begin such a program.

A kindergarten teacher had a little boy who brought a beautiful colored leaf to school one day. He showed the leaf to the rest of the class and the group discussed it. They noted and identified its color and its shape; they talked about the reasons for its change in color and the change of seasons. The teacher guided the discussion into the life story of leaves: how they were buds in the spring; then the warm sun and soft rain helped them grow and burst through their shells. They talked of how the leaves unfolded, spread out to the warm sunlight, and how they hung trembling on the branches. They talked of how storms tossed the leaves about and how the sun's heat made them limp. And then came the fall, and the leaves changed in color and finally came fluttering to the ground where they lay covered by the winter's snow, or where they were raked up—or brought to school by a little boy to his teacher.

As the discussion progressed, the teacher suggested they play out the story, so various children pretended they were leaves. One little boy curled up on the floor, then began to uncurl, and then stretched—and stretched—and stretched. He was the bud opening into a leaf in the warm sunlight. Teacher and children admired this interpretation, and then the teacher asked that he do it again. This time she turned to the piano and accompanied his movements with piano rhythms. The children all clapped as his actions were put to music, and the boy concluded his little play.

Then the teacher asked who else would like to play something about a leaf. A little girl stood up and, holding her hands above her head, pitched and tossed her body about. She was the leaf in a summer storm. Teacher played some storm music to go with her movements. Other children played they were rain falling on the leaves; some were the leaves falling to the ground; others curled up like the leaves under the snow. One creative idea led to another and the teacher accompanied the children's rhythms with appropriate music.

Finally she introduced a song about leaves, and the children learned to sing it. While they were still expressing enjoyment over the song and talking about it, five-year-old William said, "I have a song about a leaf." Teacher asked him to tell the group, so he sang:

The   lit - tle   leaves   are   grow - ing   on   the   trees.

FIGURE 4–1   William's song about the leaf.

"Isn't that lovely!" said teacher. "Let's all sing William's song." So she picked out the tune on the piano, and they all sang it. Karen said, "I could sing a song, too." "Good," said the teacher, "that goes right along with William's song. Let's sing them both together." So they sang both lines of the song.

Other lines were added until the song was complete. Teacher then picked out the song on the piano. "I guess I'd better write down our song," she said, "so I can play it again and won't forget." She took some lined paper from the piano and made the notes on the staff. "This is the way you write music," she said.

Other experiences of this nature produced similar songs until a book appropriately titled "Our Songs" and with a gay cover painted by a child sat on the piano. The book was used daily when the children sang their favorite songs.

These children were living creative experiences in a relaxed, creative atmosphere. The rhythms were created first; the music served to show how the feeling and action could be interpreted by more than one medium. The products were creative, and the children took a thorough part in the creative act. They had not been inhibited in their thinking by the demand to fill a set pattern; they had not been forced to be a "listening" and "following" audience— each one listened, thought, acted, led, and produced. Moreover, each child was experiencing basic understandings of music notation.

SPECIAL METHODS FOR MUSIC TEACHING

Several outstanding contemporary musicians have developed special techniques for teaching children music. Although each has included many ideas that can be adapted by the classroom teachers, special study is necessary in most cases for the understanding and application of these approaches. Music educators express conflicting opinions as to the value of many of these approaches in our American schools. A careful study of each school of thought is necessary, therefore, before a teacher can decide which, if any, will be most valuable for her classroom.

Workshops on a regional or national level offer the best introduction to each of these approaches. Some school systems have set up classes that explain both the philosophy and the approach, and a teacher is wise to avail herself of any such opportunity to learn about any approach before adapting it to her classroom.

No attempt has been made here to analyze and debate the values of these methods. Rather, the authors have attempted to draw attention to those strategies which are based on the creative principles of teaching as listed above. Reference material presented in the bibliography or visits to schools using these various approaches will furnish the reader with a more substantial picture than we have presented here.

One of the most popular of the current creative approaches is the Orff method. Carl Orff[2] believes that children learn through active participation in musical experience and that they are motivated to continue through successful experiences. Orff recognizes the fact that various aspects of the child's musical development must occur simultaneously and that creativity must be encouraged at all stages of complexity. As soon as a child can reproduce two tones, mechanically or vocally, he should be encouraged to

2. Carl Orff, *Music for Children* (Germany: B. Schott, distributed in U.S.A. by Belwin-Mills Publishing Corp.). Also, see books listed in bibliography at end of chapter.

produce "new" music utilizing these tones through rhyme, instruments, or movement.[3]

Orff realizes that the music instruction and experiences of the past have limited children's musical development, hindered free expression, and stifled their interest. He, therefore, begins his music program with the children themselves, their voices, their movement, their rhythm and gradually introduces experiences of musical complexity.

In addition to songs, Orff employs rhymes and jingles to stimulate children's responsiveness to tone qualities or words and to the natural relationship between poetry and music. Orff uses instruments in many creative ways. He insists on two qualifications: good tone quality and sturdy construction. Orff recommends a music corner and both group and individual activity is encouraged. He has also made a recording which demonstrates the beautiful music he gets from children and it is available for classroom teachers' listening.

The Kodály system expresses another philosophy and is being stressed in many parts of the country. Although the children in the Kodály approach move to music from the beginning of their training so that they feel the rhythm pattern, the meter, the beat, and the phrases of the music and show these by clapping, stepping, and turning, and although they learn to write music early in the program, much of the Kodály method is rigid, lockstep progression and allows for little creativity.

Mary Helen Richards has written a text, *Threshold to Music*[4] which adapts the Kodály ideas for use in American schools. Mrs. Richards has devised five sets of charts and other materials to promote her philosophy. However, the strategies here allow for little creativity.

Another current revival is the Dalcroze system. This method emphasizes rhythmic movement, solfege, and improvisation in developing young musicians. In some concepts it is creative but these instances are limited.

The Manhattanville Music Curriculum Program is another approach to the music experiences for children. This program, like the others, requires serious study before it can be effectively introduced in the classroom.

The artistic and educational rationale of the program includes discovery, conceptual learning, the music of our time as logical places to begin, and includes the importance of total experience.

3. Sylvesta M. Wassum, *Music for Children*, Manual (New York: Angel Records, 1958).
4. Mary Helen Richards, *Threshold to Music* (San Francisco: Fearon Publishers, 1964).

The curriculum is both concept- and process-oriented and should be considered a style for learning, to be used only as a guide. The curriculum is spiral, including cycles or levels of learning and strategies or plans of action. The heart of each strategy becomes the framework for operation. Student and teacher evaluation play important roles in the program.

Recently, television demonstrations have been presented on the Suzuki method for teaching violin. Although Suzuki believes that all children are born creative and that the environment plays a major role in developing or repressing natural musical abilities, his methods are centered around drill and allow very little room for the child's total creative development.

When teachers set about to investigate these various strategies for developing music expression in children, they will be surprised to discover that they have been using some of the ideas from each system in their own work with children—for example, the use of movement, of rhythmical chanting, playing instruments, and using dramatization. All these activities play a part in the planned activities of these programs but each in a manner unique to the basic philosophy of the approach. To understand how they contribute to the development of the objectives of each program, the teacher will need to study the program in detail.

A CONCEPTUAL APPROACH TO MUSIC

The emerging philosophy of current elementary music education is a conceptual approach. Concepts in the categories of melody, rhythm, harmony, form, tempo, dynamics, tone color, and style should be developed in the school music program. These concepts are not to be taught separately but are identified for the purpose of providing an outline for any necessary logical, sequential lesson planning.

In an article in *The Instructor*,[5] Dr. Katherine Crews defines the concepts as follows:

Rhythm consists of groups of sounds and silences of varying lengths, usually controlled by a recurring pulse or beat. All music has rhythm. We find that the beats group themselves into sets, usually of twos and threes; and that they form various patterns, sometimes even or smooth, sometimes uneven or jumpy.

Melody is a linear succession of tones, i.e., a tune. We learn that the tune may stay on the same sound or move up and down,

5. Katherine Crews, "Music Every Day. You Should, You Can, Here's How," *The Instructor* LXXX (December 1970), p. 37.

in small steps or large steps called skips or leaps. When two or more tones are sounded at the same time, the texture of the sound is changed and either polyphony or harmony exists. There is polyphony when two or more melodies are sounded together as in a round, and harmony when simultaneous sounds move together in chords. (Another definition of melody is that it is a combination of pitch sequence and rhythm.)

Form is the construction plan of music. We begin to learn about form by recognizing that melodies are grouped into phrases which may sound alike (repetition), almost alike but either higher or lower (sequence), or different.

Tempo refers to the speed at which the musical notes are sounded, fast or slow.

Dynamics means the degree of loudness and softness of the music.

Tone color is timbre or tone quality, discovered by listening to the way different voices and different instruments sound. It is the unique characteristic of a particular instrument which enables the listener to distinguish it from others.

Harmony is the relationship of chords and their progression or movement from one to another. Harmony adds depth and perspective to the music and enhances the melodic line.

Style is the result of the combination of all these elements.

These concepts become understandings to children through planned activities in listening, singing, moving to music, and playing instruments. The experiences in this volume have been included because each contribute in some degree to the development of one or more of these concepts. They are also included because they present music as a potent force in the communication process and the life style of man, not as an isolated skill to be learned as a task or chore.

THE PERFORMER AND CREATIVITY

In Chapter II one of the objectives for teaching music in the elementary school was stated as follows: To provide opportunities for children to discover and to experiment with music in *all its forms* and to select for themselves that which best meets their growing needs. The fulfillment of this objective requires the teaching of music for its own sake.

Assume you have just heard a fine performance of one of your favorite musical compositions. Now ask yourself how creativity was involved in this experience for you, the performers, and the composer.

We could agree the musical idea, which was original with the composer, was creative. He combined talent, inspiration, and scientific skill to notate the idea. Like composers of all periods in history, he used the materials of his era, but also explored new ways of combining new musical sounds to express his ideas. The Baroque composers placed the emphasis on the combination of sound to create certain forms of music popular at the time. The Romantic composers stressed the need for emotional and imaginative expression, while the Moderns are exploring new combinations of sound through the use of electronic instruments and new tonalities. Although every composer is influenced by the times in which he lives, each individual composer must make selections from the materials available; he must explore new materials and then create a composition reflecting his style and musical ideas. He *creates* music. It must be remembered that the composer cannot always bring his creation to life; he is dependent on others' creative ability to perform. And if his creation is to be completed and communicated to others there must be an audience to receive it. Composers, for instance, often write music which they cannot perform. Songs, are often written by men, but sung by high sopranos. A Beethoven symphony, to be enjoyed, must be "created" (recreated) by an orchestra.

What is the role of the performer who did not write the original composition but did bring it to life? Can this contribution be considered a creative experience? A performer must have the knowledge to interpret the notation, be familiar with the style of the composition, and have the talent and skill to produce the sounds. We might ask why one performer succeeds musically and another one fails; or why one orchestra is considered superior to another one; or why one group of children thrills an audience because they make beautiful music. It is probably because one creates a musical experience while the other makes only sounds—using the notation provided to make music, bringing the symbols to life. In this case the music seems to belong to the performer who creates the sound. Even in large musical groups, each note played or sung contributes to the total effect.

It is interesting to compare a performer's approach with the steps involved in the creative process as identified by Mary Lee Marksberry in *Foundation of Creativity*[6] and reviewed as follows:

1. *Period of Preparation.* The creator becomes involved with and identifies the problem at hand. The performer selects a composition which will be appropriate for a specific occasion. This in-

6. Mary Lee Marksberry, *Foundation of Creativity* (New York: Harper & Row, 1963).

FIGURE 4–2   The child as a performer.

volves a knowledge of many compositions, the realization of the abilities of the soloist or the group, and a consideration of the occasion and the audience.

2. *Period of Incubation.* The creator lives with and is surrounded by the problem. The music must be studied in relation to the performer's technical ability, and the difficult sections analyzed and rehearsed with appropriate practice techniques and continual work to discover the real meaning of the music.

3. *Period of Insight.* All parts of the problem seem to be clear. The performers feel comfortable and familiar with the music as all the parts of the composition come together. A soloist moves easily from one selection to another. In a group performance, the members have an insight into the relationship of the parts, one to another, and all to the total effect.

4. *Period of Illuminaton or Inspiration.* Ideas or answers seem to come; this may also be classified as the moment of discovery. The tempo, the dynamics, the quality of tone, individual solo passages in a chorus or orchestra, a harmonics sequence, and a special percussion effect all lead to the exciting discovery of new meaning in music. A soloist finds a way to give new quality to a lyrical melody or a conductor discovers the vitality of an interesting rhythmic pattern. The music begins to live and to communicate.

5. *Period of Verification, Elaboration and Perfection, and*

Evaluation. The product is tested for its worth; tension is eased. The excitement of performance cannot be described accurately in words. It can be heard in the music, however. All the preparation and the experience of the past come together to create for a moment in time an indescribable experience with music.

Naturally, all musicians do not follow an exact pattern in their preparation for performance, but the creative process appears to be present in varying degrees as soloists or groups prepare and present their music.

THE YOUNG LISTENER AND CREATIVITY

Let's consider the listener. Listening is a completely individual experience. (See Chapter II.) Each person listening hears what he is capable of hearing or perhaps what he is interested in hearing. An audience is frequently made up of many age groups with a variety of backgrounds represented. The room is frequently filled with one sound, but there is no proof that each person is hearing the same sound. To one listener the rhythm might be the most appealing part of the music; to another the mood or the emotional content; and to still another the construction or manipulation of the sounds might be most interesting. A melodic line might be employed because of the voice or instrument being featured, because of past association, or just because it is beautiful. To some the music might inspire an extramusical idea, a picture, a poem, or a story. Perhaps it will serve the listener as an esthetic experience, something experienced and valued for its own sake. This, to many listeners, might be the most important contribution music can make, although indefinable and immeasurable. Throughout all listening experiences the child must be allowed to take from the music what it has to offer. The teacher should never impose her values and interpretations on him.

Music, then, calls for a composer, performer, and a listener. In addition to these three categories, there is sometimes an arranger who creates a new score that may suit the needs of a particular instrument or group. One composition may be played on a piano originally, orchestrated for a large or small instrumental group, or placed in a choral setting. Sections for the music may be arranged in small ensembles or for vocal or instrumental solos with piano accompaniment. "Clair de Lune" by Debussy is an example of one composition which may be heard in many instrumental combinations. Beethoven's *Ode to Joy* from the Ninth Symphony is heard in many versions including a contemporary setting by the Lausson

Trio. The music may be a simple transcription which adheres carefully to the musical content or a more elaborate setting including the reworking of the selection with the addition of material and modification. In either case, the arrangement creates a new sound.

Many times informal listening experiences may serve as motivation for becoming better acquainted with a particular musical selection. At other times the selection may be enjoyed more after the students have become familiar with the music through other approaches.

Building a record library is a necessity for a good listening program. ("Live" music would be ideal but impractical and unrealistic in the classroom.) Children will probably spend more time listening to recordings than in any other form of music activity in their school years. Each year improved collections are published. The music teacher can make helpful selections. The distribution of the records is a problem which must be solved within the framework of the school. The music teacher in one school system in the Midwest felt the listener's experiences so worthwhile he became a roving minstrel of records, circulating a variety of them once a month. In one school in upstate New York, records were placed on tables at several locations around the room and in the corridor. They were changed occasionally. The school library is another good, safe place which is accessible to both teachers and students. Record distribution is a problem unique to each school and must be worked out to make it convenient and desirable for classroom teachers to share listening experiences with the children.

The teacher who loves music can play almost any selection to a class and some will find it appealing. (No one should be offended if all the class does not accept a recording as a favorite.) It is interesting to note changes in listening skills throughout the year if the teacher has the desire and patience to continue sharing music she loves in an informal way with her children.

It is generally recognized that children have short attention spans. Realizing this, we must be patient and willing to provide many opportunities that could help children develop an interest and skill in listening. It is most important that each child be free to enjoy the music in his own way. As was stated above, each member of a concert audience may hear something different in each selection. Children should be allowed this privilege. There are times when children need to be guided to listen for specific things in music, but there must be times for just listening. Enjoying listening to music with your children is basic to all other music experiences. All teachers can enjoy and contribute to this part of a child's learning if they enjoy music, have a repertoire of selections to share with the group, and believe that children and music belong together.

Listening, as a learned skill is basic to all communication and to the development of language arts skills (see Chapter VII, p. 222). It has been here implied that all listening is not the same. There are four types and categories of listening, all of which can be applied to listening experiences in music.

1.   *Marginal listening* is the type of listening that we do when we listen to more than one thing at a time. The group of children discussed earlier listened to music and expressed the music through an art medium. Soon the art product became the main focus of attention and the listening was marginal.

2.   *Attentive listening* occurs when all persons involved in the listening act have their eyes and ears focused on a center of interest, such as children listening to a teacher for instruction or watching a television program. An example of attentive listening is demonstrated in the lesson which resulted from Miss Parker's trip to the zoo.

3.   *Analytical listening* is a concentrated type of listening such as when children are told to listen for special directions or to listen to a speech to select specific points from it. An example of analytical listening is shown in the lesson with Mrs. Hill and the flashlights when the children were asked to translate beats of music into colored light and identify the *shape* of a melody as mentioned on page 80.

4.   *Appreciative listening* is listening purely for enjoyment. The listener is in a relaxed, comfortable state and is generally listening to something of his own choice. When children choose records or radio programs for listening they are engaged in appreciative listening.

Each type of listening requires varying degrees of concentration on the part of the children. The teacher needs to realize that not all situations require the same degree of listening or the same type of environment. In his book *Adventures in Communication,* James A. Smith[7] lists some pointers for teachers in teaching listening in the language arts. These lists appear to be important in teaching listening of music as well.

1.   Be sure the physical conditions are properly set up. Remove all distractions that you possibly can—both noise and movement. Make sure that all chairs face the right direction so

7. James A. Smith, *Adventures in Communication* (Boston: Allyn and Bacon, 1971), pp. 105–141.

FIGURE 4–3   Mr. Rinehart asks the children to listen for the number of times the main theme is repeated in "Pavonne."

that eye strain and uncomfortable sitting positions are erased. Place materials to be used in a prominent place and remove materials which are not to be used. Make sure each child is comfortable and that he can see well.

2. Speak in an animated and interesting manner, as though you yourself can hardly wait to tell the children what you have to say.

3. Make sure your speaking speed does not exceed the children's listening speed.

4. Help children make up rules for good listening.

5. Help the children to understand what they have heard, much the same way you would check comprehension in a good reading lesson. Ask children questions as: "What did Bill tell us about?" (selecting a main idea); "What was the first thing that happened to Bill?" etc.

6. Praise the children often for good listening. When you give directions and they are carried out well, motivation for listening is enhanced when the teacher says, "Good. I am proud that you did such a good job! It shows that we all listened well!"

7. Be a good listener yourself. Teachers so often only half listen to a child as their eyes roam around the room taking in all the other children at work. Develop the habit of looking directly at the child when he talks and respond specifically to him.

8. Avoid needless repetition, especially in giving directions. It is better to say, "Do all of you understand that?" than "Listen once more and I'll say it all over again." The child who thinks he has it correct (and most of them will) will not listen the second time. This discourages good listening.

9. Avoid needless demands of pupil attention. Instead try using interesting gimmicks and devices to gain immediate attention.

10. Allow the children to talk. Remember that most teachers talk too much!

11. Help children eliminate bad listening habits. Make a list of the poor habits you notice in your children. One teacher's list looked like this:
   a. Children are distracted by playthings on or in their desks.
   b. Children "fake" attention—they are really daydreaming.
   c. Children interrupt with unrelated thoughts.
   d. Children look out the window or at the clock.

12. Do not place too much emphasis on "regurgative" materials. A basic goal in education today is creativity. To foster creative listening, seek to develop an attitude of mental alertness in children. Attitude or "set" toward listening is important. Much of the time that children are required to listen is for the purpose of reproducing what they hear. More emphasis should be placed on encouraging them to *think about* what they hear. Avoid overuse of these reproductive sets and plan conditions for creative thinking.

13. In the teaching of listening, teachers should be sure that the children realize that there are varying degrees of attention required for different kinds of listening. Children can be helped to listen properly if they are told at the onset of each lesson just how important the listening for that particular lesson is, how they can best listen to get from the lesson what they should, and the guides or directions for the particular kind of listening needed for the lesson.

Part of the task of the teacher is to set the mental and physical conditions necessary for listening in each new lesson throughout the school day.

Some ideas which emphasize music and develop listening are:

1. Sing commands or directions for a change. This is especially effective in the lower grades.

2. Also effective is singing the child's name for roll taking. The child sings back to the same tune or a tune that completes the tune. For example, the teacher sings to the tune of "Frere Jacques":

"Are you here?
"Are you here?
Mary Brown?"

and Mary sings:

"Yes, I am."

3.   Call children by their first names by singing the names such as "Yoohoo, Henry Adams. Are you here?" and have each child respond in a singing sentence such as "Yes, Miss Wilson, here I am." The response should be a blending tune to Miss Wilson's question. Different tunes can be sung to each child. Tape this. Sometimes results are delightfully creative.

4.   Begin the period by playing records or playing a variety of musical sketches on the piano. Have children listen for music that is alike or different. Use some of these ideas for comparisons:

Alike in rhythms
Alike in tones
The same musical instruments to get an effect
Fast–slow
High notes–low notes
Clapping–tapping
Rhythm patterns
Folk music–classical
Jazz–popular
Spanish rhythms–Japanese rhythms

5.   Listen to and interpret music with simple rhythm instruments.

6.   Musical chairs is a good marginal listening game.

THE YOUNG COMPOSER AND THE CLASSROOM TEACHER

We have already noted how the classroom teacher and/or the music teacher can help a child learn to compose. (See p. 5 and p. 16.) Helping children technically might be the responsibility of the music specialist, but there is much to composition besides the technical skill.

The desire to create or compose a composition should be encouraged. A child may sing a little tune while playing with blocks or holding a doll. The teacher who says, "I like your tune," has often made a contribution to the child's confidence. Sometimes the tune can be shared with classmates, and other times it is enough just to be recognized. A secure child who is able to share a tune with classmates might encourage others to create original melodies. Often this experience can be expanded by suggesting other topics for compositions. For example, the teacher says, "Mary made up her song about her doll, and John made one about our rabbit. I wonder if someone could sing about our new bird?"

The use of the piano, bells, and percussion instruments to initiate the noises of rain, wind, animals, birds, and other sounds about us might encourage children to compose. (See pp. 107–108.) Chopin's "Raindrop Prelude," Debussy's "Clair de Lune," and other compositions were inspired by nature. Children could be made aware of their world by encouraging them to describe that world with music. Even daily activities may be described in sound: For example, the use of drums or bells to show the difference between music that makes us sleepy or wide awake.

Such experiences can be included when children are learning to tell time or learning about the sun and the moon in science lessons.

A drum may be used to create a composition of different moods, depending on the musical idea in the mind of the child, and the teacher may notate the compositions rhythmically by the use of dashes. Suppose a child sings, "Rain-drops, rain-drops, falling down." With an even tempo this could be notated by the use of long, even dashes below or above the words. Since each syllable is equal in time to the others. (See "Halloween Guests," p. 100.) However, if he sings it with another rhythmic pattern this should be indicated with uneven dashes. For example: Rain drops, Rain-drops, fall-ing down. If the last syllable is held, make the line under the word *down* twice as long as the others.

The bars on the bells are often lettered so if a tune can be played on this instrument it is possible for an inexperienced teacher to notate the pitch of the melody. Let's assume the child has used the bells to play the first line of the song about the rain.

The teacher can easily observe the bars which are played and combine the pitch names with the rhythmic patterns.

Rain	drops,	Rain-drops,	fall -	ing	down
G	E	G	E	F	E	D

Another way of notation on a song which is even more helpful is to show the pattern of the melodic line.

There are many ways to guide older students to compose in an informal way. Those who sing easily may improvise a descant or alternate melody to a favorite song. Students interested in instruments may choose to improvise a counter melody on their instrument.

Older students may wish to notate their songs themselves. Here again, creating the opportunity for them to do so and offering encouragement and an attentive ear is important. Children who have played bells, piano, or any melodic instrument may find notation easier than those who have not. Those who have used autoharps, guitar, or the ukelele may enjoy adding an accompaniment, perhaps through the old trial and error method.

Creating melodies and rhythms for classroom dramatic presentations can vary from simple sound effects to a complete musical score depending on the talent and interest of class members and the teacher team as shown on page 245. The need to create a particular mood for a scene often offers a fine opportunity for students to explore the world of sound. Contemporary musicians have shown us the way to include a variety of sounds in music compositions beyond the traditional musical patterns. Our ears are filled with new noises which come over the airways by radio, television, recordings, and as background music for motion pictures. Students (as composers have always done) will select and use the sounds which make musical sense to them.

When thinking of the student as a composer, it is important that each teacher contributes to the experience in an individual way. The teacher who does not have time, the interest, or skill to provide complete notation experience should realize the value of simply saying, "I like your song; could you sing it for us?" or "How about singing another song?" This may be a good time to ask for help from the music teacher who could show how a song looks in musical notation. Imagine the joy of a child who can see his song notated by dashes or by colors or in the traditional manner. He will also take great pride in hearing or performing something he has written alone or as a group activity. (See Fig. 4–4.)

Some classes enjoy writing group songs for special occasions. (See p. 115.) This creates an opportunity to combine talents to achieve one objective. An excellent way to motivate this activity is to encourage students to compose a song for their room or for a special holiday or dramatic activity. The teacher must be careful in guiding this project to be sure all children have the opportunity to contribute and that no one is embarrassed because he cannot or does not choose to make suggestions. This is often a

FIGURE 4–4   The child as a composer.

time-consuming activity, but it is a high point for students. OUR song can be edited for all age groups. The music teacher may be needed to complete this project.

It is important for composers of all ages to be aware of many kinds of sounds, including contemporary concert music. Playing a variety of recordings makes a contribution to the classroom program. Otherwise the children hear a limited number of musical styles. The recordings listed at the end of this chapter and in Chapter X may be helpful in making selections for the school record library.

THE YOUNG PERFORMER AND THE CLASSROOM TEACHER

How can the classroom teacher and/or the music teacher help the young performer? Again, it is the attitude of the teachers which is important. Teachers must believe in the performing act and empathize with the experience.

We share many things in the classroom so why not include talent, a picture, a story, a song, or an instrumental selection? Imagine the thrill of a child whose teacher makes it possible to share the playing of a clarinet with his classmates. John has had only a few lessons, but he demonstrates how the clarinet is blown, how a reed must be placed carefully on the mouthpiece, and how the pitch of the tones are changed by covering the holes with the fingers. In October, John can play only four different tones but as times passes the number increases and soon John can play a tune, even a tune the class can sing. Contrast this relationship with another John whose teacher doesn't ever ask about his precious instrument and doesn't even seem to care.

"What about time schedules?" the teacher asks. "And what about the child who cannot or does not choose to play an instrument?" Time for everything is a basic problem. Perhaps if we become more concerned with individual differences and have less demands on our time for so-called bookkeeping chores there will be time to devote to each child.

The child who cannot or does not choose to play a musical instrument may be guided to find pleasure in another's performance. Proportionately very few people play ball, but many enjoy watching a ball game. In music some may choose to perform while others prefer listening. This means continual awareness for something of interest in all children and encouragement of each one to excel in his field of talent and interest while respecting and enjoying the talents of his classmates.

FRINGE BENEFITS FOR PERFORMING GROUPS

Superior leadership and skill are necessary for a successful performance, as well as cooperation of all staff members and parents. The dedicated classroom teacher who not only permits the students to take special lessons, but who shows an interest in the students' accomplishments and encourages them; the administration which works to make the program possible and functional; the parents who provide a practice time and place and transportation for extra rehearsing; the students who do the work; and the individual who uses his skill and inspiration to direct the program, all play important roles in the final performance. Although the object is making music, the example that the performance offers in cooperative effort is a valuable experience for students. The discipline in individual practice, rehearsals, and performances is easily observable in most groups and is another fringe benefit.

Performing groups offer the students the opportunity of belonging. Even the nonperformer often enjoys belonging to a school with a fine performing group. The term "our" band is probably heard more frequently than "their" band. The groups contribute to school as well as community spirit and all take pride in their accomplishments. This occurs only if there is agreement on sound educational goals by all members concerned, including the community. Performing groups, it must be remembered, are only *one* aspect of a good music program.

SOME PROBLEMS CONCERNING PERFORMANCE

Some teachers have asked: Is performing for others exploitation or showing off? Is performance a justifiable experience for children? Who should perform? When should children perform?

Many adults remember the fright of a recital or the boredom of listening to their friends playing a recital piece. Children of today who are well prepared enjoy performing in a recital if the proper atmosphere is created. Radio and television may be broadening our adult lives, but they are also eliminating some worthwhile experiences with and for children. How many times have you heard a child in any kind of performance outside the classroom in the last five years? Performance is necessary to bring music to life. Symphonies, orchestras, choirs, chamber music, pop groups, vocalists, and others cannot exist unless they are given the opportunity to be heard. The school affords a good practice ground for such experience.

The emphasis in our public school music progam has been on performance for a good many years. The importance of this part of the program provides an opportunity to develop students' individual talents and also provides pleasure for the listeners. The quality of performance differs from school to school just as it does in any area of study. In many schools across the country, performing groups vary from vocal ensembles to large choruses, from chamber music groups to concert bands and orchestras. This varience in performing groups makes it possible for performers and listeners alike to become acquainted with many types of music.

The classroom teacher who realizes performing can be a creative experience has much to offer the students. As stated above, the composer may write the music but the performer must bring it to life. Even small children have the ability to create a quiet mood while singing a lullaby to a doll or a feeling of joy as they sing about a circus parade. Guiding children to really understand a song and communicate the feeling doesn't take technical skill; it does take a desire to help children have a true musical experience. This can be applied to performance in vocal or instrumental music as well as in movement.

In one demonstration of movement, scarves were used by small children to interpret music: a robust march, a delicate minuet, a fast gallop, and a slow barcarole. The children showed no difference in their movements in any of these selections. They simply waved the scarves. This certainly was not a creative experience in music. One wonders whether the children even heard the music. Have you ever tried to walk to a Sousa march or dance the twist to a Strauss waltz? Doesn't it seem to be more difficult to move against the beat than with it? The teacher should not insist on specific movements when children are interpreting music through performance, but should guide children to show the sound of the music with feeling. Often questions or comments such as the following will be helpful: "Can you tell what kind of music John is listening to by the way he moves?" "Is it fast or slow?" "Is it loud or soft?"

"Can we tell what a child is hearing?" you ask. Try the twist with the waltz pattern and the question will be answered. It is the nature of music to communicate, and the performer only emphasizes this communicative value.

The student who performs vocally needs to communicate a feeling or mood with words and music if he is to have a creative experience. He may try different tempos, decide whether the song should be sung loudly or softly, look for places which could be sung by a solo voice, choose percussion instruments which will add to the musical effect and enhance the meaning and provide a creative performance.

Instrumentalists must create a mood or musical idea without the aid of a verbal text. Playing songs to students often is an excellent way to help them become aware of the musical quality of performance. "How can you play this song so we will understand the meaning of the text as we listen?" is a good question to help students "make music talk." Although the young musician is limited technically, it is amazing how the quality of performance can be improved when there is inspiration from his teacher and his friends.

One of the most important contributions a teacher can make in the area of performance is providing an opportunity for children to gain confidence and experience. Every teacher who has performed remembers practicing for months and then that fatal day arrived with accompanying butterflies and shaking knees. "Nerves" cannot be eliminated and many artists admit the need for stimulation which "nerves" create in order to perform at their best. Knees may shake and the lips tremble, but the performer learns to play or sing, either in spite of this feeling or because of it. There is nothing wrong with stage fright so long as it is recognized as a natural phenomenon and explained to the child. The teacher can help the students perform better if many opportunities are provided for performance and the experience becomes a way of life and not a "life and death" special event. It is generally more difficult for the older beginning student to perform for his classmates and it will take more skill on the part of the teacher to include him in classroom activities. Playing the songs that classmates can sing takes the attention away from the soloist, and it is an excellent way to get all to participate. Some guidance from the music teacher might be needed as many songs are fairly difficult for beginners to play and many instruments need special music if they are to be used with piano. There are many current song books which include material easily adapted to classroom use.

The instrumental teacher is often happy to assist by providing the correct music for the students. This helps the students to perform, and it adds to the strength of the large instrumental group.

Another way the classroom teacher can help is in the discovery and encouragement of talent. In most situations the music teacher is with the children such a short time it is impossible to identify talented children. In some primary grades it is the responsibility of the classroom teacher to conduct the music program which means the music teacher does not even see the children. This is also true when the music teacher acts as a consultant who may not work directly with children. Although many instrumental music programs are not started until the intermediate grades, some schools are exploring the use of instruments with younger children, adapting the experience to the age of the child. The work of Orff and Suzuki have a strong influence here.

Performing groups are organized primarily in intermediate grades, although some schools involve younger children. Again, the classroom teacher can be most helpful in identifying talent and creating interest in the groups. Taking children to rehearsals of these groups and encouraging students to attend concerts is very important.

Classroom teachers can create opportunities for children to perform within the framework of the classroom schedule. In early grades students may be encouraged to include solos as part of the sharing time activity. A song often takes less than sixty seconds to sing. Beginning instrumentalists may play very short tunes. Putting the instrument together before "sharing" starts is one way to save more time for music.

Assembly programs play an important function in many schools. Those which are based on sound educational principles are an important experience for students who participate or those who observe and listen. They are most beneficial to the *performing* musician, for they act as a motivating force for improvement and give confidence and recognition to him if he is carefully prepared. Preparation is extremely important if a student is to have a successful experience in performing in public. Performing for classmates during rehearsals may help him. Often tape recording a rehearsal will produce positive results when teacher and children evaluate the tape. Repeated taping has value, but unless there is real understanding on the part of all as to the purpose of the taping, it can be detrimental. Hearing oneself if properly prepared and with the right attitude can be a valuable experience.

Encouraging vocal and instrumental ensembles within the room is an excellent way of guiding students toward performance. There appears to be a great desire on the part of individuals to belong to a group or gang. This desire can be used to create all kinds of ensembles at many age levels. Using a group to sing the verse of a song as others join in on the chorus may be a beginning. Students who play the piano in a duet might create interest for the individuals involved and provide pleasure for the listeners.

It is often the piano student who is neglected in the classroom. The lessons are after school, the parents pay the bill, and the classroom teacher is not aware that the child plays. These students need encouragement as well as opportunity to share their talent with others. The special music teachers can be most helpful here in providing music for groups. Ensembles of instruments within a room are not always possible since all instruments cannot be combined to give the greatest satisfaction, so sometimes there may be a need to borrow a clarinet or trombone player from across the hall.

Have you ever thought of playing recordings of outstanding soloists for the children? Let's take John as an example. He practices the clarinet faithfully, attends rehearsals, performs when he is asked, and really tries to play well. How many times has he ever heard a fine clarinet player? Has he heard anything played on a clarinet besides that which comes over the air? What about asking the music teacher to suggest recordings for John?

Of course including vocal literature for those who are most interested in singing is also a good idea. Check to discover soloists on the staff and in the community and invite them to be guest artists for your children. This is a delightful way to help the young performer and often a real joy for the guest. Many teachers perform well but often are not invited to perform in their schools.

Another way to add interest for the young performer and classmates is to include a study of the history and/or acoustics of instruments in research projects. (See p. 260.) This will depend on the age and interest of individuals and will give the individual an opportunity to know more about the instrument of his choice on an intellectual plane. A true artist is often aware of all information regarding his instrument and its history. The science of voice production will be of special interest to students who enjoy singing.

There are those who believe everyone should be included in the chorus and all children should play an instrument. There are others who believe the performing group should be organized for students with superior skill and interest. The conflict appears to be milder in schools in which the general music program is strong. Here all students have an opportunity to participate in music to the best of their ability. Such experiences not only provide all children with a musical background but in general tend to improve the quality of the performing groups.

This, after all, is what the objectives of a good music program should be. All parents contribute equally for the right to give their children sound musical experiences in school. The authors take the stand that a program in music, properly administered, will help develop each child's creativity and his music expression. A properly administered program is not one in which all the funds for music are directed to the use of a few talented ones, to the loss of the greater group. The mistake is made when music educators assume that a school program will be "either/or." It *must* be both. Just as the average child has the right to be exposed to a rich musical program with many opportunities in the elementary school, so does the talented child deserve the right to be challenged and helped with his unique ability. The policy of the school in a democracy should be equal opportunity for all.

Should children not avail themselves of the opportunity to be in a performing group, no stigma should be attached to them. Just as children do not spend all their time in the same way because of talents and interests, different children do not choose to engage in performing groups. Their choices should be respected.

Very young children realize and respect each other for a variety of reasons. One child seems to move more gracefully than others, another child can outrun the rest of the class, while still another may be the organizer. As we watch children cast a play, we recognize the variety of talents in the room. Again, the attitude of the teacher is most important. One teacher invited the members of the class who sang in a select chorus to teach the rest of the class the songs they learned in rehearsal, and when the concert was given, all took pride in the fact that students from their class enjoyed the concert more because the music was familiar. In another school, students in the advanced reading groups in a second grade learned to play melody flutes. One teacher let these students demonstrate their progress to the class each week, and it was a special day for all when the class sang with the young performers.

Again, it should be stated that the quality of the general music class must provide an opportunity for all students to have satisfactory experience in music at their level of ability so no child is deprived of a basic music background. Not being chosen for organized groups, whether a dramatic group, sports team or a music group, can create great tensions for children. Careful planning by the teacher can create an atmosphere which will guide the children to take the experiences in their stride. The emphasis must be on the individual differences, with a continuous effort to help each child discover his strengths or talents and enjoy the talents of others. With the proper attitude between the teacher and the children, each child can participate in special activities without feeling hurt, when individual talents do not permit membership in a particular group. This attitude is not easy to achieve, but it is possible when there is concern for each child.

IMPLICATIONS FOR CHILDREN

How then can we help children have creative experiences as composers, performers, listeners, and, perhaps, arrangers? We must recognize the importance of individual differences not only in capacities but also in interest, taste, and experience. We must consider, too, the question of the sequence of music experience for children. Which should come first—a child's original composition or listening experience? free response to music or structured response? Must children's experiences be one *or* the other? Can we prove that *each* child in the classroom will be attracted to music in a similar way? Should all children be expected to be composers, performers, listeners, or arrangers? Is it not possible that a teacher might use a drum or the piano to pick up the rhythm of a child moving across the room one day and another instrument on another day? Is it possible that some children might gain more by one experience than another; or even more important, by both? Is the learning experience so defined that we must offer the child only one approach in our classrooms?

We need not label children as composers, performers, or listeners only. It is possible to create classroom situations in which each child who so chooses may have an opportunity to experience all areas of music. It is possible that some children might hum a new tune or create a chant naturally while others prefer singing a song learned previously, and still others enjoy listening. We often decide what children should do in music without giving them enough different experiences which might make it possible for the individual to choose intelligently. Some experimentation shows that some children create original rhythms or melodies without a rich musical background, while others need a vocabulary of sound with which to work. In the meantime, perhaps we can develop a program which is so varied and appealing that each child may find the joy of involvement in at least one area of his choice.

Teachers differ, too. One classroom teacher with an unusually lovely voice might offer children a different experience from the teacher next door who does not sing well but is at home with recorded concert music and can share her love of music through recordings. One teacher tends to stress performance; one listening. Although it is important for children to have a variety of experiences, teachers should be encouraged to share their special strengths with their classes. With this in mind, various musical experiences with children are discussed in this text, hoping to encourage teachers to select ideas that can be adopted or expanded for children as composers, listeners, performers, or any combination of the three areas.

It is important for the teacher and the specialist to know each child in the classroom and to build a program of music experiences on this knowledge. Each teacher may wish to teach music her own way, but all teachers should teach with these criteria in mind:

Each teacher should try to:

1.   Create an atmosphere which will encourage children to explore sounds alone and in combination. These experiences for children will involve creative learning and creative teaching. The application of the skills taught and the degree of "feeling" for music by each child will be the best way to evaluate such a program.

2.   Provide an opportunity for each child to acquire a repertoire in music; songs, concert selections (recorded and live) and movement (both free and structured).

3.   Help children acquire skills which will allow each individual to produce music for his own pleasure and to share with others.

4.   Provide an opportunity for ensemble experience, both vocal and instrumental and in combination.

Self-Inventory for Classroom Teachers

1.   Do I enjoy listening and singing and let my enjoyment show so children are aware music is important to me?

2.   How many songs do I know I can introduce to my children, either by singing myself or using recordings?

3.   How many recordings of concert music do I know which I feel children "need" to hear?

4.   Does my room indicate I have an interest in music (books, pictures, instruments, sound)?

5.   Am I including music which goes beyond the classroom in my daily program?

6.   Am I including music which originates in other classroom experiences or integrates with them?

7.   Am I including a wide variety of music types (contemporary, ethnic, classical, folk, rock, popular, etc.) in my listening experiences?

Self-Inventory for Music Teachers

1.   Am I introducing children to all areas of music?

2.   Am I encouraging children of many degrees of talent by providing each with satisfying experiences in music?

3.   Am I aware of the areas of study in each classroom and "feeding" them with related material?

4.   Am I aware of the talent and interests of my classroom teachers and assisting them in every way possible?

5.   Am I using my musical talents to the greatest advantage possible for the benefit of all?

SUMMARY

Because of its importance in the life style of man, music deserves at times, to be taught as an entity unto itself. Special methods for teaching music have been devised through the years and each have had a unique effect on current music practices. Popular among music educators today is the "conceptual" approach.

Unique problems with which the classroom and music teacher must deal in teaching music for its own sake are: methodology; how to deal with the child as a performer; how to develop each child as a listener; how to stimulate and develop the child as a young composer; and how to help the child, especially the talented one, become interested in searching for knowledge about music.

Unique methods may be applied for each facet of the music program mentioned in this chapter but the most basic contribution the music and classroom teacher team can make is to provide opportunity for children to play these roles and to give support and enthusiasm to the child in each capacity.

TO THE COLLEGE STUDENT AND THE TEACHING TEAM

1. Some questions for discussion.
    a. The music program in the school should be designed largely to develop talented children.
    b. The performer, in terms of the fiddle player in a symphony orchestra, does not play a creative role.
    c   Methods such as the Orff and Kodály and others mentioned earlier in this chapter are very restricting to children and can be very uncreative.
    d. A child who performs before a group should not perform until he feels no nervousness.
    e. Every elementary school child should play a musical instrument as part of his music education.
    f. Children, in order to develop a taste for good music, should be made to listen to recordings as a part of every music program.
2. From the many good modern musicals, select songs which might well be incorporated into a music program in the elementary school. "Do-Re-Me" from the *Sound of Music*, "The World Is Coming to a Start" from *Purlie*, "If I Were a Rich Man" from *Fiddler on the Roof*, and "The Age of Aquarius" from *Hair* are but a few. How would you introduce these

songs? What would be your objectives? How might you use them to avoid criticism from some school patrons?

3. If you are teaching, assign some of the musical shows to your children for listening pleasure. The day after the show, discuss it with your children and try to analyze the music values and standards through a discussion.

4. How would you use a television show to develop appreciation listening skills with children? A sensitivity to instruments, awareness of time, rhythms, harmony, interpretation, etc.? Design a sheet for children to use as a guide to develop any one of these aspects of music.

5. If you are teaching, try using music in other subjects in the curriculum as much as you can for a week. Use listening, singing, choral speaking, and direct instruction. Use music:
   - As a motivator
   - For background accompaniment
   - For relaxation
   - As a correlation with a subject
   - As a summary to a specific teaching situation

6. Assess the "talent" in your room by having a Friday afternoon talent show or a concert. Find those who play an instrument, those who dance, or sing. The children who do none of these things well enough to want to appear can work together to create songs, skits, or a dance to present for their part of the show.

7. Learn to play a simple instrument such as a mouth organ, a flutophone, an autoharp, or a marimba. Learn it by exploring the instrument and picking out simple tunes of your own. When you are comfortable with the instrument, get help with some specific skills. Do you think children would like this approach? Is it more motivating than "practice" pieces on the piano?

8. Take a nursery rhyme, a children's story, or a story of your own and tell it by using the piano to make accompanying sounds. Use the low notes to make animal noises, high notes for rain, etc. You will be amazed at how the piano can help even if you have had little or no training. Try to create musical stories to tell to the children and notice their reactions.

9. Compile a file of recordings for various purposes: for dramatization, for rhythms, for folk-dancing, creative interpretation, for music appreciation, etc. Contact your local music store for resources.

10. Try writing a short play in your class. Perhaps you may want to use music in it. What skills are needed to be able to write a play? Do you have them? Did you follow any of the steps in the creative act mentioned in Chapter I when you wrote your play? What opportunities for creative development does the presentation of the play afford? Pin-

point the time in the total act of play producing when creativity may be nurtured.

SELECTED BIBLIOGRAPHY

Arnoff, F. W. *Music and Young Children.* New York: Holt, Rinehart, and Winston, 1969.

Austin, Virginia. *Learning Fundamental Concepts of Music: An Activities Approach.* Dubuque, Iowa: William C. Brown, 1970.

Barlow, Howard, and Sam Morgenstern. *A Dictionary of Musical Themes, the Music of More Than 10,000 Themes.* New York: Crown Publishers, 1948.

Barnes, Robert A. *Fundamentals of Music: A Program of Self-Instruction.* New York: McGraw-Hill, 1964.

Carlson, James C. *Melodic Perception.* New York: McGraw-Hill, 1965.

Castellini, John. *Rudiments of Music.* New York: W. W. Norton, 1962.

Clough, John. *Scales, Intervals, Keys, and Triads: A Self-Instruction Program.* New York: W. W. Norton, 1964.

Colwell, Richard. *The Evaluation of Music Teaching and Learning.* Englewood Cliffs, N.J.: Prentice-Hall, 1970.

Dallin, Leon. *Foundations in Music Theory.* Belmont, Calif.: Wadsworth, 1962.

Darazs, Arpod, and Stephen Jay. *Sight and Sound: Visual Aid in Melody and Harmony.* Oceanside, N.Y.: Boosey and Hawkes, 1965.

Elliot, Raymond. *Fundamentals of Music,* 2nd ed. Englewood Cliffs, N.J.: Prentice-Hall, 1965.

Fleming, William, and Abraham Veinus. *Understanding Music.* New York: Holt, Rinehart, and Winston, 1960.

Finkelstein, Sidney. *How Music Expresses Ideas.* New York: International Publication, 1970.

Gary, C. (Ed.) *The Study of Music in the Elementary School: A Conceptual Approach.* Washington, D.C.: Music Educators' National Conference, 1967.

Gelineau, R. Phyllis. *Experiences in Music.* New York: McGraw-Hill, 1970.

Gordon, Edwin. *Psychology of Music Teaching.* Englewood Cliffs, N.J.: Prentice-Hall, 1971.

Grant, Parks. *Music for Elementary Teachers.* New York: Appleton-Century-Crofts, 1960.

Hargiss, Genevieve. *Music for Elementary Teachers.* New York: Appleton-Century-Crofts, 1968.

Hartsell, O. M. *Teaching Music in the Elementary School.* Washington, D.C.: Music Educators' National Conference, 1963.

Hartshorn, W. C. *Listening to Music in the Elementary School.* Englewood Cliffs, N.J.: Prentice-Hall, 1966.

Hitchcock, H. Wiley. *Music in the United States.* Englewood Cliffs, N.J.: Prentice-Hall, 1969.

Howard, Bertrand. *Fundamentals of Music Theory.* New York: Harcourt Brace Jovanovich, 1966.

Kaplan, Max. *Foundations and Frontiers of Music Education.* New York: Holt, Rinehart, and Winston, 1966.

————, and F. J. Steiner. *Musicianship for the Classroom Teacher.* New York: Rand, 1966.

Kendall, J. D. *Talent, Education and Suzuki.* Washington, D.C.: National Education Association, Department of Audiovisual Instruction, 1966.

Kendall, John W. *Listen and Play.* Evanston, Ill.: Summy-Birchard, 1961. (Adaptation of Suzuki method.)

Knuth, A. S., and William E. Knuth. *Basic Resources for Learning Music.* Belmont, Calif.: Wadsworth, 1966.

Kodály, Zoltan. *Choral Method: Let Us Sing Correctly.* New York: Boosey and Hawkes, 1952.

Lehman, P. R. *Tests and Measurements in Music.* Englewood Cliffs, N.J.: Prentice-Hall, 1968.

Madison, Theodore (Ed.) *Basic Concepts in Music Education.* Washington, D.C.: National Society for the Study of Education, 57th Yearbook, 1958.

Music Educators' National Conference. *The Study of Music in the Elementary School—A Conceptual Approach.* Washington, D.C.: M.E.N.C., 1967.

Nye, Robert E., and Vernice T. Nye. *Music in the Elementary School,* 2nd ed. Englewood Cliffs, N.J.: Prentice-Hall, 1964.

Orff, Carl, and Gunild Keetman. *Music for Children* (adapted by Doreen Hall and Arnold Walter). Mainz, Germany: B. Schott's Söhne (available from Associated Music Publishers, One W. 47th St., New York, N.Y. 10036), 1963.

————. *Schulwerk: Music for Children Series: Teachers Manual.* New York: Associated Music Publishers, 1960.

Ottman, R. W., and F. D. Mainous. *Rudiments of Music.* Englewood Cliffs, N.J.: Prentice-Hall, 1970.

Portnoy, Julius. *Music in the Life of Man.* New York: Holt, Rinehart, and Winston, 1963.

Ratner, Leonard G. *Music, the Listener's Art,* 2nd ed. New York: McGraw-Hill, 1966.

Richards, Mary Helen. *Threshold to Music*. San Francisco: Fearon Publishers, 1964.

Salzman, Eric. *Twentieth-Century Music: An Introduction*. Englewood Cliffs, N.J.: Prentice-Hall, 1967.

Suzuki, Shinichi. *Nurtured by Love, A New Approach to Education*. Jericho, N.Y.: Exposition Press, 1969.

Tellstrom, Theodore. *Music in American Education*. New York: Holt, Rinehart, and Winston, 1971.

Thomas, Ronald. *Manhattan Music Curriculum Synthesis*. Elnora, N.Y.: Media, 1971.

PART 2

The Nurture of Creativity Through the Teaching and Use of Music

AN OVERVIEW

If the development of creativity in children is to be an objective of the elementary school, caution must be exercised that all areas of the curriculum contribute to its growth since it cannot be taught as a subject or skill. In Part 2 of this volume, the authors have selected material that may be used to develop creativity in children through the application of the creative principles stated in Chapter I and the knowledge of children and their relation to the music principles in Chapter II. The authors have been guided in their selection by the following criteria.

1. *Novelty.* New ideas have been selected that stimulate children and the materials selected will provide children with new experiences, affording them the opportunity to learn new skills and to apply them in divergent ways to produce unique, creative products.
2. *Principles.* Each illustration or suggestion, if properly used within the framework of the teaching principles presented in chapters I and II, will develop the powers of creativity and will set conditions for creative teaching. If improperly used, however, many of the illustrations on the following pages can defeat the goal of developing creative power. The variable in each case is the teacher: Her method will make the difference.
3. *Functionalism.* A first rule of all art expression is that it must be functional, that is, it must serve the purpose for which it has been made. A beautiful office building loses much of its beauty if it is so poorly designed inside that the offices are small, improperly lighted and equipped, or poorly organized. The materials on the following pages were selected because they may be integrated with the total school program to make learning more functional—or, they may be used for children's sake, to make life more beautiful and more livable.
4. *Generality.* The following illustrations were chosen because they are general enough to be presented in many ways and to be adapted to many age levels.

CHAPTER V

Music Through the Creative Arts—in Music and Movement

> . . . *Movement is the very essence of creative rhythmic expression. This form of creativity differs from all others because the body is the instrument of expression. Awareness of this sensitive instrument is one of the first steps in exploration in a rhythms program.*
>
> —GLADYS ANDREWS[1]

INTRODUCTION

Closely allied to a rhythmic "sound" program is a rhythmic "movement" program. It is practically impossible to listen to some music without responding physically: tapping the feet, swinging the shoulders, clucking the tongue. Through rewarding experiences with bodily rhythms, teachers can build a keen sense of rhythm in sound. Movement education, as it is being developed in this country today, is the base of many other learnings.

Pantomime is one kind of movement which communicates. Think of the great pantomimists of our time: Red Skelton, Marcel Marceau, Dick Van Dyke, Sid Caesar, and others. Think of any one of their famous pantomime acts. Do they communicate? Could their movements easily be set to music? Music *is* often used as a background to pantomime. Music and bodily movement are inseparable (see Fig. 5-1).

1. Gladys Andrews, *Creative Rhythmic Movement for Children* (Englewood Cliffs, N.J.: Prentice-Hall, 1954), p. 26.

FIGURE 5–1   Music and dance are inseparable.

MUSIC AND MOVEMENT

The Nature of Rhythms and Dance

Rhythms, properly used, can lead to another form of creative outlet—the dance. Communication can take place among people
through bodily movement as well as through verbalism. Rhythms
are sometimes encouraged in the kindergarten and first grades
and are then forgotten until the child reaches adolescence and
desires to participate in social dancing. This is unfortunate for
the years between kindergarten and junior high are the growth
years, when the child needs help in moving gracefully and re-
assurance that he is handling his body correctly. Many times his
awkwardness is accented rather than diminished when he takes
dancing lessons and is forced into a "one-two-three" pattern. Children cannot handle such instructions with ease because the movements of their growing bodies are difficult to control.

The dance, in order to be creative, must be considered in different terms from those commonly affiliated with it in the past.
We are not talking about a dancing school type of class in which
all children do the same thing at the same time and follow fixed

patterns of movement predetermined by the dancing teacher. This type of experience may have a place in teaching dancing, but not at the onset; it should come after the children have had the opportunity to create and dance their own dances. Once they have experienced free dance movement, have established a relationship to space, and have mastered the concept of patterns in dancing, and understood the need for specific music for specific dances, learning a fox trot, a waltz, or tap dance is a fairly simple pattern.

Dancing has its roots in the distant past. All people everywhere have danced to express feeling and to communicate ideas. Dancing is a natural expression of the inborn creative drive of every individual. It plays a more dominant role in our own civilization with each passing year.

A dance is a movement put to a pattern. It is a form of expression and can be employed as a means of developing creativity. In an accepting, permissive atmosphere, the dance may be utilized to develop divergent thinking processes. Originality may be fostered, individuality can run rampant, and those characteristics and qualities of creative people may be encouraged in a legitimate manner. The dance also provides ways for expending excess physical energy and emotional tensions.

There are other reasons why the dance should play a more important part in the elementary school curriculum than it currently does. Dance has crept into our culture more than we realize. Children witness dancing every day on television, and now children dance socially at an earlier age than ever before. Dancing is an integral part of our musical shows. The dance portion of these popular productions has become so important that the choreographer is given top billing with the producer. With both transportation and communication media becoming more refined, both rural and urban children are seeing more of these productions each year. Children exposed to classical dancing such as the ballet and those incorporated in the opera witness the importance of dancing in our society. With such emphasis placed on dancing as a communicative device, and as an esthetic form, children need to know about it, to understand it, and to use it for their own communicative and creative development.

Common to rhythms and to dance is music—or at least, rhythmic sounds put to a beat. Because of the necessity of music in primitive or sophisticated form in order for rhythm and dance to exist, rhythms and dance provide a natural and exciting way for teachers to teach music in the classroom. It also provides another means for developing creativity through problem-solving situations. In order for music to be explored and taught through the use of dance media, however, certain conditions must be set.

Conditions Necessary to Promote Rhythms and Dance

1. *Physical conditions.* The major material needed, of course, is the *children* themselves and the space in which they may experiment. Simple props may be helpful. In the primary grades, soft colorful scarves, ribbons, and balloons will encourage free expression through bodily movement. In the intermediate grades other props usually found in the school environment also serve as a stimuli for dance expression: a football or basketball, a swing, rollerskates, jump ropes, and similar materials. A good supply of recordings and a record player are almost essential. A piano, a drum, or simple instruments that the children themselves can play are also a necessary part of the program.

Ideally, a gymnasium is the best place to work out dances, but the movable seats in the classroom can be pushed out of the way so a central space is available. On warm days, the lawn outside the school, or a flattened mound near the school is ideal. In this instance, an old plug-in or a new battery-powered record player is a valuable asset. The joy of using dance as a means of creative expression, however, lies in the fact that little or no equipment is really necessary except the children themselves.

2. *Social-emotional conditions.* A certain type of classroom atmosphere is essential if children are to feel uninhibited to express themselves. The "air of expectancy" is of primary importance here. Each child must feel he is an accepted part of a congenial group.

An atmosphere of permissiveness must exist in the classroom, where children may feel free to explore bodily movement without fear of embarrassment. In the kindergarten, the children can be encouraged to create rhythms for which the teacher creates music.

The dance program is closely allied to the music program, but in the dance program the movement and thought are often primary, and the music is sometimes relegated to a secondary position, and the listening is marginal. The music accompanies and enriches the creative idea—it is not always the dominant factor.

At times, music as such is not necessary for rhythmic movement. In one class attempts were made to produce interpretive movements without the use of the piano. Four and five year olds were encouraged to take off their shoes and socks and to free themselves of inhibiting sweaters and belts. They then sat in a circle on the floor with the teacher. She held out her hands and said, "Let's see all the things we can do with our hands!" All the children held out their hands and manipulated them in a variety of ways. Some spread their fingers, some wiggled them, some waved their hands in the air. One boy clapped. The teacher let each child demonstrate what he could do with his hands, and the others imitated him. When clapping was introduced, the teacher asked if they could think of other noises they could make with their hands. Some ran their fingers rippling on the floor. Some spanked the floor, some snapped fingers, and some beat a rhythm on the floor or some part of their body.

When the possibilities of hand movement were exhausted, they went through a similar experience with the use of their feet. Children wiggled their toes, bent their feet sideways, they stood and stamped, galloped, walked, and ran. Each shared his idea with the others. The teacher next said, "I like the sounds we made with our hands and feet. Let's take Bobby's sound for a minute and see what we can do with it. Now everyone listen while Bobby makes a sound with his hands."

Bobby proceeded to make a galloping sound with his fingers on the floor. "I wonder what movements we can make up to go with Bobby's sound? Does anyone want to try while the rest of us make the sound?" Each child had an opportunity to interpret the sound in his own way. Some raced around the room, others galloped, some swayed from left to right, and some just imitated the others, as was to be expected.

Eventually other sounds were introduced, to both accompany movement and be interpreted by movement. One child worked out a rhythm on the drum, and the other children interpreted the rhythm with their bodies. The bell-like note of the triangle and the jangling of the tambourine provided new experiences and new opportunities for interpretation. Finally, the piano was introduced to accompany some of the movements the children were making. After much experience of this nature, children interpreted some piano music.

A series of experiences of this kind, utilizing rhythmical noises rather than music, helps the child to concentrate on his own ideas and his own body interpretation (Fig. 5–2). Children discover what they can do with their arms, legs, and trunks. And they explore the possibilities of putting these movements into patterns.

Poise and fluent body movement can be developed in children who are not under constant pressure to conform to adult ideas. Much of the clumsiness which growing children exhibit is due

FIGURE 5–2   *"This is me dancing," says Linda.*

to the restriction modern living places on their experimentation with changing physical growth. The running, jumping, tree-climbing, swimming, leaping, and tumbling of children are the natural ways they develop grace of movement. If our culture limits children in the pursuits of these activities, the school can help provide an "artificial" means for meeting these needs by sub-stituting experiences for children through physical education and dance experiences. Much release of tension and pent-up bodily energy can lend therapeutic values to such experiences.

After the child has learned to interpret sound and music, and to create pattern and rhythm, he will enjoy learning dances that other people have created. In the primary grades, simple dances such as "Looby Loo," primary folk dances, and song dances such as "Brother, Come and Dance with Me" are enjoyed by most children. Their own creative representation should not be dominated by the traditional dance forms, however.

Children soon learn that a dance is merely movement put to a pattern. They will make up movement of their own to which to add music, and they will learn to interpret music with movement. Sometimes the two can be combined, such as in a Mexican hat dance in which a group pattern is followed, then during the dance each individual at one time breaks away from the circle of dancers and develops his own individual interpretation of the music.

Children in the intermediate grades will enjoy the folk dances of other countries as well as their own. The Virginia Reel, square dances, and the minuet all have a place. One fifth grade, studying the Inca culture of Peru, came across some authentic music and ceremonial dances of the Incas. They interpreted the music as they felt it would be danced, and made costumes and props to go with their dances.

Group dancing starts in the early grades and becomes more important to the child as he develops and looks more to his peers for approval and prestige. By the time he reaches the inter-mediate grades, this phase of his development is at its peak. This time is opportune for teaching group dancing. Group interpreta-tion through dancing can be as creative as individual interpreta-tion and can have its product an experience in social cooperation and expression. Such group work can help provide a means for boys and girls to bridge the awkward gap between the sexes at this age. This is perhaps the best time for modern and social dancing to be introduced.

A group of fifth- and sixth-grade girls worked on the interpreta-tion of dance music in the following way. The two grades num-bered off into five groups. A pianist played a selected piece of music and the combined groups all listened. Each group tried different steps and movements to interpret the music. They frequently returned to the piano and asked for the music to be replayed; then they would go back and work out more ideas. A time limit was set for this preliminary planning when the pattern of dance was worked out. As soon as each group felt it was ready, the participants announced to the teacher that they had their interpretation prepared and seated themselves around the edge of the auditorium until all groups were ready.

The teacher called on Group I to give its interpretation. Each member took his place in the center of the circle, and the pianist played while the ideas were presented. After the first attempt, the dance was evaluated. The audience picked out especially good points and indicated the weak points and where the pattern was too long or repetitious. Then the group went through it a second time with some changes and then seated themselves to watch the interpretations of the other groups. This procedure was followed until each of the five groups had presented its dance and had been evaluated. Then again the groups went to different sections of the gym and started to polish their dance. After a period of time each group again presented its finished product.

These experiences were, of course, preceded by discussions at the beginning of the term as to what constitutes a dance. These children approached experiences such as these with enthusiasm. Often a different composition was played for each group and an interpretation worked out through the same procedure as that presented above. Later, these children worked in reverse: They made up a dance pattern and then sought to find appropriate music to accompany their dance.

A group of fifth- and sixth-grade boys worked with their music and gym teachers to create a football dance. The gym teacher had taken them to see a group of male dancers. The boys took the dramatic movements of the football game and assembled them into a pattern while the music teacher and some of the students who could play the piano worked out music to accompany the patterns. The result was highly imaginative.

The boys utilized the graceful movements of the run and the kickoff, the flowing sweep of the forward pass and the patterned movements of the line up. Comic relief provided contrast with exaggerated movements of the huddle and the touchdown with a great deal of individual interpretation in tumbling and turning somersaults. So effective was this dance that it was given as an assembly program for other children and parents to enjoy.

The same group combined with the girls and created an Indian village dance with the pattern of the dance styled after life in an Indian village as they had studied it. Peaceful music provided the mood for the opening of the dance where the squaws sat in a circle occupied in carrying out the many village activities to patterned movements. One pounded corn, one wove a blanket, another sewed buckskin, and another scraped a deerhide. Then the peace of the village was broken by a messenger who brought the news that the braves were returning from war. The braves entered in full war dress with stories of their conquests, which each told through gestures. A war dance followed to celebrate the victory. The dance ended with the women calmly pursuing their tasks while the braves went off to hunt as the day ended.

After many interesting experiences of this kind in which individual and group imagination have a chance to operate, children of this age often become interested in social dancing and in special kinds of dancing such as ballet, acrobatic, and ballroom dancing. Dancing provides unique opportunities for social as well as creative development.

3. *Psychological conditions.* In addition to the social security a child feels in being accepted in a congenial group and the joy of working in a permissive atmosphere, there are other psychological securities each child needs in order to feel free to act uninhibitedly and to be able to express his own creative ideas with his body. As we have seen from the above illustration all suggestions for bodily interpretation must be accepted. No child should be made to feel his contribution is silly or subject to rejection before it is tried.

It should be understood that a creative dance is a new one, made up from original ideas of the children or a combination of the dances they already know put into new patterns. At the onset of the experience, the product is an unknown quality; all children should be encouraged to work through the creative process to a creative product. A highly motivating force is necessary to accomplish this objective of involvement. Several ideas are presented on the following pages because of their high-intensity motivational force.

Esthetic release must come from the finished product. Completed products need not be refined except in those instances when they are to be presented to other people. Once again in this instance we utilize the principle of deferred judgment to develop creativity. In the refinement of the dance the principles of elaboration, alteration, expansion, and others may be applied.

4. *Intellectual conditions.* Aside from the highly motivational, tension producing force which must be a challenge to the intelli-

gence of the child, certain other intellectual conditions must be set. Children should understand the place of the dance in the cultures of the world. In the intermediate grade program children can learn the dances of each country as part of their social studies program. These dances can be learned and danced, as they were in the social studies unit on Mexico described on page 249.

Children should know what these dances do for the people of a particular culture or what they try to communicate. They must also know that these dances are the classical dances of the country and as such constitute part of the folklore of that country. By and large, the learning of these dances does not develop the creative powers of the children learning them. However, they do serve the purpose of showing them a multitude of ways that thoughts and feelings can be put into movements and from these movements they may create new patterns of movements on their own. The children should also understand that the success of performing a folk dance or a classical dance such as the ballet lies in learning it so well and copying the movements of the original dance so accurately that each dancer's movements are highly synchronized with the others. This is a far cry from the creative dance in which they put their own ideas for movement into new patterns. The former develops the convergent thought processes; the latter develops the divergent thought processes. The contrast in the two processes may be likened to the two kinds of workbook exercises in reading in which one exercise instructs a child to draw something exactly like a given picture in the book and to color it exactly as that picture is colored, while the other asks the child to draw something he saw on the way to school.

Creating a dance is a problem-solving process. The creative result is a pattern of movements and both the process and the product can be creative. Performing an existing dance is a problem-solving process, but neither the process nor the product is creative. Both concentrate largely on imitation.

5. *The teacher's role.* The development of creative rhythms and creative dance lend themselves wholeheartedly to the principles of creative teaching described in Chapter I. As in all teaching for the creative development, the role of the teacher in a dance program is to provide many situations for all kinds of dancing. A good school program of this nature is one in which the physical education teacher, the music teacher, and the classroom teacher work closely together to work out a serious, developmental program rather than a fragmented one. Procedures used in the classroom and in the gymnasium should be closely related

to the child's normal growth and development. The dance program, to accomplish its creative objectives, must be carefully planned and not confined to gym periods alone.

In assuming a team role for the development of creativity in children, the physical education teacher and the classroom teacher assume new responsibilities for the physical education program for boys and girls. Much of the militaristic, dogmatic teaching of physical education exercises, games and dances can be replaced by helping children understand how they may grow through creative activity. The objectives of recreation, balanced living, and mental hygiene are more directly accomplished than they are through current physical fitness programs.

In teaching for creative results through the use of rhythms and dance, the teacher can build strong, positive tensions in children that will be released through expended physical energy. Once the children have become involved in the process, the teacher shifts her role from that of the leader to that of a supporting and guiding role, helping the children develop their own ideas toward a solution to their own problems. Children are helped to think for *themselves.*

As often as possible, teachers will relate the teaching of dance to the other areas of the curriculum. In later chapters in this volume suggestions are made as to how dance might be related to each area of the curriculum. It is important, too, to remember that by using the dance as a media of expression, creative qualities and powers may be developed in individuals as well as in groups. As in music, there should be a continual program of experience in dancing that will serve as a stimulus and a background for movement interpretation and creation.

The teacher must provide many experiences in the various areas of the school curriculum which can be translated into patterned movement. The subject matter of the dance is basically derived from the current interests of the children. Almost any experience can be translated into a dance expression: a football game, a holiday, a trip to the zoo, a nursery rhyme, or a piece of popular music. If the subject appeals to teacher and pupil, it can be used (Fig. 5–3).

Developing Creativity Through the Use of Rhythms, Dance, and Music in the Primary Grades

A well-planned program for developing creativity through the use of rhythms, dance, and music should result in more creative

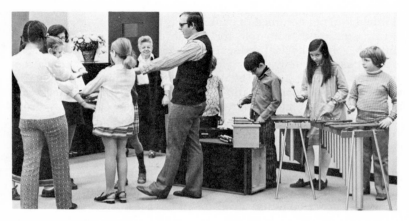

FIGURE 5–3   *Grade students create the music, while college students create the dance.*

individuals, better-adjusted individuals, and individuals who possess greater esthetic appreciation and enjoyment. Some ideas for creative interpretation follow.

1.   To explore rhythmic movement with children, give them these directions:

> Make yourself round.
> Make yourself as tall as possible.
> Move only one part of your body.
> Make your body be as quiet as possible.
> Reach as far as possible.
> Be as short as you can; or as tall.
> Tremble like a leaf.
> Slink like a cat.
> Crawl like a snake.
> Wiggle like a worm.
> Be a grasshopper.
> Be a rabbit.
> Be a bear.
> Walk like a spider.
> Chug like a train.

After explorations of this type the teacher may ask the children to find music to go with these movements. For instance, find music which makes you feel round; which makes you feel tall;

which sounds like a trembling leaf, a crawling snake, a grass-hopper hopping, or that makes you want to skip.

This of course means that the teacher will need to keep a sup-ply of records or tapes handy in the classroom so that children can listen to music much of the time. Access to a tape recorder or record player with earphones is valuable, for several children can listen at once to different selections.

In one primary grade, after an experience such as this the fol-lowing results were obtained:

For music which made her feel round, Debbie selected Rimsky-Korsakov's "Flight of the Bumblebee."

For music which made him feel tall, Alvin chose a theme from Grofé's "Grand Canyon Suite."

For music which sounded like a trembling leaf, Marcia chose the Tchaikovsky waltz from "Swan Lake."

For a crawling snake, Jimmy chose "Turkey in the Straw."

And to Gary, grasshooper music was best illustrated by Haydn's "Clock Symphony."

For skipping music Phyllis chose "Country Gardens."

2.   At the beginning of the child's school experience, the teacher can suggest children dance the following patterns:

> Their interpretation of musical recordings of many moods and tempos.
> A happy dance.
> A sad dance.
> An angry dance.
> A wild dance.
> Dance like a rabbit, a skunk, or a cat.
> Dance like an automobile, a bicycle, or a train.
> Play one musical instrument and make up a dance peculiar to it.
> Make up rhythms or a dance showing work on the farm: the plowing, the cutting of the grain, etc.
> Create a dance of men working on the railroad.
> Create a story about spooks and Halloween night.

The logical next step, of course, is to select music to accompany the dance, or better yet, go to the piano or a marimba, a mouth organ, a drum, a flutophone, a recorder, or a simple chord organ and play a tune to accompany the dance created. Accessible re-cordings and tapes help here. If the teacher does not know how to write music, she may record the tunes by numbering the ma-rimba, or the keys on the organ, or by sticking different colored stickers on each bar or key struck and reconstructing the melody with colored chalk on the chalkboard as the children create it. (See p. 3.)

3.   More complex dance suggestions for upper primary grades are:

> Dance a trip to the zoo, the circus, etc.
> Dance a recess period using movements of the playground.
> Plan a dance that tells about a day in a lumber camp, in an Indian village, in Disneyland, etc.
> Put your favorite story to a dance dramatization.
> Make up cowboy dances using ropes and ten-gallon hats.
> Make up dances about sailors and the sea.

4.   Plan rhythms and dances that include all the following movements: bouncing, turning, twisting, swinging, hopping, walking, jumping, running, leaping, stretching, pulling, pushing, bending, shaking, trembling, and squatting. Here again, select or create music to accompany the movement.

5.   Working the above in reverse is also fun. Find music labeled "bounding music," or "walking music," or "crawling music," etc., but do not tell the children what it is labeled. Play it and ask each child to respond to it, with motion. Do not insist that he walk to walking music, however. His own interpretation is a personal and valuable aspect of his own growth and development. The child's concept of walking may be legitimately different from the composer's simply because he is a child.

6.   Select music that will help the children to explore tagging, catching, volleying, dribbling, batting, bouncing, skipping, chinning, galloping, sliding, kicking, throwing, whirling, and doing a cartwheel.

7.   Favorite poems and stories can be used to create rhythmic movement which can later be put to music and dance.

8.   Action songs and movement give children opportunity to work out creative patterns. Many poems lend themselves to this sort of activity also, such as: "The Duel," "The Sugarplum Tree," and "The Owl and the Pussycat," all by Eugene Field.

9.   Children can tell stories of their own experiences or the experiences of others through dance. They can relive an airplane flight, an Easter egg hunt, a treasure hunt, or decorating the Christmas tree through rhythms which may be worked out into a dance pattern. Or they may enact Indian ceremonials, the westward movement, life in a factory, an ancient ritual, or almost any

other experience in which their imaginations may be set free to interpret material they have read.

Good listening experiences in music can be introduced here in the search for appropriate music to accompany the movement of the story. For instance, the westward movement provides an opportune time to introduce Ferde Grofé's "Grand Canyon Suite."

10.   Playground equipment and gym equipment such as balls, bats, sticks, hoops, jump ropes, hurdles, etc., can be used to work out musical dramatizations. Rolling the ball down the line of children, each of whom must jump over it will create one rhythm to which music can be added. Throwing the ball from person to person creates another rhythm; throwing the ball as high as possible creates another. Soon children can find a variety of movements to dramatize and use in a pattern. They can explore music to accompany these movements, or the teacher can create music. Various bouncing, turning, clapping, and catching patterns can be developed into new games or songs.

11.   Cut small strips of paper and write directions such as those given below on each of two pieces. Fold the papers and put them in a hat or box. All the children draw a paper and read their own but no one else's. The teacher calls on a child, who stands and dramatizes the idea on his paper. As soon as another person recognizes the dramatization, he joins the first child. All the children try to guess what the two are doing, while the teacher trys to select or create music to accompany the children in their movements.

Sample directions: Be a pingpong ball in the middle of a game; be a monkey swinging from a tree; be a typewriter; leap like a frog; play a game of baseball; be a yo-yo; be a scooter; walk a tight rope; be a bowl of jello; row a boat; be a steam shovel; grow like a flower; be a grandmother or a grandfather; be a man walking on stilts; be a boy crossing a busy street; be a policeman directing traffic.

After the children have dramatized some of these simple basic movements, more complicated divergent thinking powers may be developed by the application of elaboration, modification, or other creative ideation techniques mentioned in the first chapter. For instance, instead of the simple directions above, elaborations such as these may appear on the papers: Be a top with the wind blowing; be a frog jumping from lily pad to lily pad; swing like a pendulum in a grandfather clock at midnight; be a yo-yo that breaks; be a scooter with a fat boy riding on it; walk a tight rope carrying three chairs balanced on your nose and hands; be an egg beater beating a thick batter for fruitcake, and so on.

Other ideas for elaboration can read: Be a top with snow falling on it; be a top in the spring, in the mud, in the sunshine. The children themselves can suggest various conditions under which a top functions and these could be translated into creative movements. Children can learn to tell simple, original stories through this technique, thereby expanding their creative powers (Fig. 5–4).

12.   Take the children to the playground, a park, a wooded area, or a meadow near the school and have them explore the environment. Use the materials they find as an idea for a rhythm dance, or as a part of it.

Miss Nichols' first grade made up a dance using sticks which they tapped, crossed, and touched. Miss Smith's third graders watched ants making an anthill and then imitated the movements in a dramatization for which they played some original music. Mr. Arnold's fourth grade watched the second graders on the playground and used their movements in climbing the jungle

FIGURE 5–4   Creating the music; designing a dance.

gym, swinging, teetering, and riding the merry-go-round in making up a dance for a spring festival depicting school life.

13.   When a child is reluctant to join the group, materials can often be used persuasively, and he forgets himself—balls, balloons, scarves, hoops, his use of the drum to keep time with the group activity, and his decision as to whom to give it to next.

Developing Creativity Through the Use of the Dance in the Intermediate Grades

1.   Intermediate grade children will respond to stimuli such as these:

> Plan a dance that shows machinery working.
> Plan a dance based on ancient tribal rituals.
> Dance a street scene: children playing, women marketing, etc.
> Make up an athletic dance about baseball, basketball, etc.
> Show a meeting of the United Nations through a dance pattern.
> Make up a dance around a meeting of the Olympic games.
> Dance a tire being pumped up.
> Divide into small groups and have each group pantomime a scene.
> Dance a part of your favorite television show.
> Put your favorite sidewalk games into a dance.
> Learn a dance of another country and incorporate it into some creative dancing.
> Dramatize through dance the launching of a rocket.
> Make up movement to go with old-time movie music.

For each of these dances, appropriate music must be selected or invented. Also, following a class period in which dances are created, the teacher has an excellent opportunity to introduce worthwhile listening and/or appreciation lessons for new kinds of music or the works of composers new to the children. How much more exciting this is than to have the music teacher enter the class room, gain attention from the children, and then proceed to announce, "Today we are going to study about a man named Franz Josef Haydn," especially when the children have never heard of him. The motivational conditions mentioned in this book so many times are well met when the children dance the launching of the astronaut and the teacher says later (or on the following day if she needs time for preparation) "Your dance reminded me of some music I know and like. I'd like to know if you think this music goes as well with your dance too. Why don't I play it and you can tell me what you think. Then I can tell you about the man who wrote it." Then she introduces the appropriate music and the composer and the children listen for a purpose.

2.   Use the cheers children work up for basketball and football games. Have some children chant the cheers while others work out rhythms to go with them.

3.   For the teacher who cannot play the piano, a good drum can be used to tap rhythmic motion. The drum can be used as an introduction to rhythm band playing. The drum can also be explored as an instrument capable of many communications itself.

4.   Children in the intermediate grades enjoy charades. Have them work by groups and give them a charade to dance out around any given subject. They can select music to accompany their dramatization or create music with drums, piano, xylophone, flutophone, mouth organ, or any simple instrument as they go along.

5.   Pretend you are your favorite dessert and dance it out (ice cream melting, fluffy desserts shown with light steps, and fruit shown by shapes, etc.). Dance how it feels to be sad, happy, ugly, or silly. Pretend you are your favorite toy and act it out through rhythms.

What music can you find that best accompanies your dramatization? Create sounds to show ice cream melting, fluffy desserts, water boiling. Create music to accompany the actions of a steam shovel.

6.   Children enjoy chants. Often choral speaking can be combined with rhythms to result in some interesting dance creations. Part of Mrs. Frederick's sixth grade chanted Sandburg's "Chicago" while the rest of the class danced it with simple props. This resulted after a study of large cities in the United States.

7.   Listen to the things children say before class. Select a particular catchy phrase and have the children work it into a chant. Create a rhythm to go with this chant.

Mr. Elferd heard his children repeating a phrase, "Oh, knock it off!" before school. In the middle of the morning when he felt the children needed a break, he wrote the phrase on the board. He discussed what it meant, and then the children made a list of all the places where it would apply. The children then stood in a circle and while the children in the circle chanted the phrase using various tempos, other children put some of the situations to a rhythm in the center of the circle. Some television-commercial songs can be used in this manner.

8.   Children can chant poems and songs while classmates enact them through rhythms. Many kinds of chants can be used for this purpose such as working poems, sea shanty poems, poems of the cowboys, congo chants, spirituals, oriental chants, and chants which use instruments such as paddles, sticks, and bells.

9.   Dramatize musical ideas: a melody, a rhythm, a G clef, a staff, the notes of a staff, etc.

When intermediate grade children have used their bodies to create various rhythmic patterns they will find it easy to sense the feelings and the story of the folk dances and the popular dances of America. Dances they will enjoy will be square dances, the Virginia Reel, the schottische, the two step, the conga, the jig, the mazurka, the cha cha, the fox trot, the bunny hop, the Lindy hop, the stomp, the jitterbug, and the many diversified patterns of modern rock and roll.

SUMMARY

The creative arts program in the elementary school, more than any other area of the curriculum, can provide the several types of conditions necessary in order to develop the creativity of elementary school children because tradition allows it, and the purposes of teaching the creative arts are better understood by members of the teaching profession and the lay public.

In recent years, movement education has become popular as a part of the creative arts program, not solely as a means of developing the creative urge in children but as a means of developing coordination, of building perceptions, of developing understandings, and even as a base for teaching reading.

Movement is basic to rhythm and to music. No proper program in music will attempt to exist without movement. Movement is most closely allied to music in the forms of rhythms and dance. Dancing plays such a vital and common part in our everyday living that it should be included in the music program of all elementary schools.

Certain physical, socioemotional, psychological, and intellectual conditions must be present in order for a worthy program in movement and dance to be developed. The classroom teacher plays a vital role in setting these conditions and in fostering the program by the role she plays in it. Through her guidance, the program can be a well-planned series of experiences and another way to develop creativity in children.

TO THE COLLEGE STUDENT AND THE TEACHING TEAM

1. Make a collection of children's musical recordings. Listen to some of them in class and discuss *many* ways they may be used with children. Some suggestions: "Peter and the Wolf," "Little Indian Drum," "Hansel and Gretel."
2. Make a list of all the ways music may be tied in with other aspects of the elementary school program.
3. Check a music program in your school or some other school and note how it is tied in with the rest of the day. Does the music teacher take care of the music entirely? In what ways can this situation be improved?
4. Design a music center for any classroom and think of all the independent activities you can that could be provided for the children in this center for before school and during the lunch hours.
5. There is an enjoyable film about helping children to dance freely which you will want to see. Send for it at: California University, Los Angeles, California (*Dance Your Own Way*, 10 min., color, 1958). Notice the part that music plays in inspiring children to dance.
6. Find out what instruments the children in any selected classroom can play and ask each child to bring his instrument to school and demonstrate it to the other children. Make up songs or stories to go with the music or about the instrument.
7. Ask the children to paint the *sounds* of each musical instrument brought to school.
8. Help the children to collect all sorts of materials which will produce a sound and then synchronize these sounds into an orchestra or a sound story.
9. List all the creative ways you can think of to introduce the reading of music to primary youngsters. By what creative ways could you introduce key signatures and music symbols to young children? Then make a list of all the ways you can think of to help children create dances.
10. Try to write some musical stories. Even if you cannot play a piano, you will find a great deal of satisfaction in creating musical tunes for the characters of the story to be played each time they appear. Tell your story to some children and watch their reactions.
11. Every dance the world over is rooted in tradition. Divide your class into committees and have each committee investigate

the origin of the folk and popular dances that appeal to you. Their reports will be more interesting if they can play appropriate music and demonstrate a part of each dance. After the reports are finished, discuss ways you can use this technique and this knowledge with children.

12.   Here are some films you will enjoy seeing in class. These films will add to your own knowledge and will show some creative uses of music in the classroom:

> *Design to Music*, 5 min., color (International Film Bureau)
>
> *Children's Concert*, 42 min., black and white (Encyclopaedia Britannica)
>
> *Hearing the Orchestra*, 13 min., black and white (Encyclopaedia Britannica)
>
> *The Symphony Orchestra*, 14 min., black and white (Encyclopaedia Britannica)

13.   In many musical shows the element of surprise is used to produce a very creative effect. In *The Music Man*, for instance, the number "Seventy-six Trombones" was produced without a single instrument on stage. It stopped the show. In *Sound of Music*, children were used to create the "Do-Re-Me" number, and it also stopped the show. Think of moments you have experienced in the theater that you felt were extraordinarily creative. What made them creative?

SELECTED BIBLIOGRAPHY

Andrews, Gladys E. *Creative Rhythmic Movement for Children.* Englewood Cliffs, N.J.: Prentice-Hall, 1954.

Doll, Edna, and M. J. Nelson. *Rhythms Today.* Morristown, N.J.: Silver Burdett, 1965.

Findlay, Elsa. *Rhythm and Movement, Dalcroze Eurhythmic.* Evanston, Ill.: Summy-Birchard, 1971.

Hood, Marguerite. *Teaching Rhythm and Using Classroom Instruments.* Englewood Cliffs, N.J.: Prentice-Hall, 1970.

Humphreys, M. Lois, and J. Ross. *Interpreting Music Through Movement.* Englewood Cliffs, N.J.: Prentice-Hall, 1964.

Monsour, Sally, M. C. Cohen, and P. E. Lindell. *Rhythm in Music and Dance for Children.* Belmont, Calif.: Wadsworth, 1968.

Murray, Ruth Lovell. *Dance in Elementary Education.* New York: Harper & Row, 1963.

Mynatt, Constance, and Bernard Kaiman. *Folk Dancing: For Students and Teachers.* Dubuque, Iowa: William C. Brown, 1969.

Nye, Robert G., and Vernice T. Nye. *Music in the Elementary School: An Activities Approach to Music Methods and Materials*, 3rd ed. Englewood Cliffs, N.J.: Prentice-Hall, 1970.

Saffran, R. B. *First Book of Creative Rhythms*. New York: Holt, Rinehart, and Winston, 1963.

Sheehy, Emma D. *Children Discover Music and Dance*. New York: Holt, Rinehart, and Winston, 1959.

CHAPTER VI

Music and Dramatics, Literature and Art

Music must take rank as the highest of the fine arts—as the one which, more than any other, ministers to human welfare.

—HERBERT SPENCER[1]

INTRODUCTION

Drama, poetry, and art have been referred to as music without notes. From a base of sound and visual rhythms as described in the chapter on movement, there grows an appreciation of the more sophisticated rhythms of gesture, words, line, color, and form. Before you read this chapter, think of all the ways that music plays a supportive role to each of the other creative arts, and of all the ways you can use the other creative arts to build an appreciation of music in young children.

MUSIC AND DRAMATIZATION

Familiar Song Charades

"All right," said Mr. Randall, "will everyone please take the slip of paper I put on your desk and write the name of a

1. Herbert Spencer, *Essays on Education: On the Origin and Function of Music* (Totowa, N.J.: Littlefield, 1963).

song we know or one we have learned that can be drama-
tized." The children hurried to their seats and scratched their
heads in thought. Soon papers were collected, put in a hat,
and shuffled. Then each child drew one.

"Ellen, you're first," said Mr. Randall.

"I'll need help," said Ellen.

"O.K. Choose someone."

Ellen chose Betsy. After a brief consultation, Betsy
crouched on the floor holding her hands above her head so
the fingertips touched, making a point like a roof. Ellen then
skipped around her, making her hands rise and fall above
Betsy while her fingers danced in a pattering motion. After
a couple of guesses, one of the boys said "Raindrops Keep
Falling on My Head," and that was it. Ellen and Betsy
were then asked to confirm the guesses by singing the song.

Collin was next. He pretended he was picking fruit from
a tree, then sat and devoured the fruit in pantomime. Soon
he began to rub his stomach and twist his face in agony.
It didn't take the children long to guess his song was "Little
Green Apples." Collin then asked the class to join him in
singing his selection.

Next came Jenny. First, she made the motion of spooning
sugar onto cereal. She then sat on the floor and pretended
to be putting her thumb in a pie like little Jack Horner.
Then she danced on tiptoe, making her arms flop like wings.
It took a while, but the children finally put the three motions
together to read, "The Dance of the Sugarplum Fairy." Of
course, Jenny could not sing her song.

Presenting musical experiences from a child's background in
the form of charades is the simplest form of dramatization,
but it introduces an essential element of drama: pantomime.
It also assumes that children are having many incidental and
planned musical experiences each day of their lives. In this
case songs were identified (Fig. 6–1) and children were afforded
a good reason for singing.

CREATIVE PROBLEM SOLVING WITH MUSIC

On another day, Mr. Randall placed some cards he had made
before his class. One was a blue square on a white background,
one was an orange free form, one looked like an explosion of
fireworks, and another was a red heart and a black circle.

"Sometime today," said Mr. Randall, "I'll want you to find or
create music which tells about one of these cards. It can be any

FIGURE 6–1   Song charades.

music you know, any you find in the room, or any you have at home. At three o'clock, we will stop whatever we are doing and see what we have."

All day long, during their free time, the children hunted for appropriate music to accompany each card. At three o'clock they shared their conclusions. Among the favorites selected by the children were these: For the blue square, Charlie had chosen Verdi's *Anvil Chorus* and Maria had chosen Strauss's *Blue Danube*. For the orange free form, Ellen had chosen Liszt's *Hungarian Rhapsody*. For the fireworks explosion, Peter had chosen the song "Fireworks" from the musical *Do Re Mi*, while Henry had chosen Sousa's *Stars and Sripes Forever*. For the heart, Debbie had chosen the theme from the movie *Love Story*, but Mike had selected Liszt's *Liebestraum*. For the black circle, Toni played Haydn's *Clock Symphony*. The black ring had reminded him of a clock.

On succeeding days, Mr. Randall repeated this activity, with variations. One day he displayed photographs he had taken, on another day he used magazine pictures, and on another day, he mounted objects on cardboard, such as a paperclip, a paper party parasol, a bell, a fork, and a piece of lace. One time he used pictures of five different flowers, and on another day he used four clippings of famous cartoons.

This activity not only gave evidence of the wide background of musical experience being provided for these children, but it also encouraged them to review the musical selections they knew and stimulated them to search for new material.

The Nature of Creative Dramatics

Creative dramatics affords another means of developing musical expression in elementary school children. Because dramatization is closely allied to reading, literature, and the language arts, the authors have used it a great deal in other volumes of the series. Something remains to be said, however, regarding the creative teaching of dramatics as it relates to the fulfillment of a good music program.

Too often the teaching of dramatics in the elementary school has been confined to the interpretive function rather than the creative function. Children enjoy dramatizing nursery rhymes, stories, and poems when they are very young. Most of the learning of the child takes place in his early years, through the basic element of all dramatization: mimicry. Mimicry, a form of interpretation, can be creative in many respects but if mimicry and interpretation are employed excessively as the main utilization of dramatics, the chances for developing creative powers through this medium become narrower as the child progresses through his school years.

Like art, music, and dance, dramatic power is developmental. Mimicry, interpretation, and creative dramatics develop in the child according to the experience supplied by the school, and according to the skills he masters in his general physical, intellectual and social-emotional development. Contrary to much of the literature in the area of dramatics, the development of each of these forms of dramatics is not a sequential process. Each may be developed independently to promote skill and creativity in the child into the high school and college years. It is true that each plays a more prominent role in the life of the child at various stages of the maturation process, but each can be continued and developed throughout his life.

From the beginning of life every human enjoys "play acting" and imitating life around him. By mimicking life in early years, a child learns to behave like the adults and age-mates around him. This joy of imitation is often squelched in children at an early age and seeks its legitimate outlet in role playing throughout life. Children play roles in their games, in their play, and in mocking their peers. Later, when this is frowned upon, the children continue to imitate in their games, in school play, and in behaving like people they admire. High school and college students give vent to this creative drive by appearing in plays and joining dramatic clubs where they can pretend they are someone they are not. Adult choice of profession or vocation is often determined by our ability to identify with a role we see others playing and which appeals to us.

We play dramatic roles every minute of every day—and the roles change considerably. A young, female, college freshman may play the role of a campus coed from 8:00 A.M. to 9:00 A.M. She changes her costume, her behavior, and even her mode of speaking at 9:00 A.M. when she assumes the role of the student teacher. At 4:00 P.M., with school over, she returns to campus again to play the role of the student—doing her homework for the following day. At 7:00 P.M. she plays the role of the leader as she acts as chairman of a sorority committee making plans for Spring Weekend. At 8:00 P.M. her date comes to call and she plays that role. Over the weekend she acts differently when going

to church than when going to a basketball game. She behaves differently as Student Council delegate than as big sister when she returns to her family to visit. "All the world's a stage!"

Many terms are used to identify the use of dramatics in a child's life. A definition of each of these terms is necessary if the material of this chapter is to be clearly understood.

1. *Dramatic play.* This term is used in referring to the spontaneous play of children. Many theories have been advanced regarding its meanings and functions. Some educators believe this to be a recapitulation of the experience of the race. Some in-

FIGURE 6-2 Four year olds "feel" a Sousa march in dramatic play.

terpret children's dramatic play as a rehearsal for the future role of the individual. Therapists and psychologists see it as a channel for growth in individual and social areas. Others see it as a means of emotional outlet—or a means by which the child works out his problems. All agree that playing out a situation is the most natural way a child learns to live in the world around him and that permitting a child to play freely in a setting of security and acceptance is a sound way to enable him to deal satisfactorily and healthfully with the problems he faces in life. It aids in his emotional development and his social adjustment; it is essential to normal growth. Through dramatic play the child develops an empathy for others in his world.

A good kindergarten and primary grade program makes provision for dramatic play as a technique by which children learn. Proper conditions are set for its development by providing dolls, pounding games, homemaking corners, large dollhouses, small dollhouses, a costume box, water and soap, replicas of life tools such as ironing boards, toy trucks, stoves, simple musical instruments, etc., and an out-of-doors play area. A part of the school day in all primary grades should be set aside for free dramatic play (Fig. 6–2). In the middle school years, dramatic play and other forms of dramatics may easily be incorporated into the curriculum in many ways as the following chapters demonstrate.

Hartley, Frank, and Goldenson[2] state that dramatic play serves many functions. Through this activity the child is given the opportunity to (1) imitate adults, (2) play out real-life roles in an intense way, (3) reflect relationships and experiences, (4) express pressing needs, (5) release unacceptable impulses, (6) reverse roles usually taken, (7) mirror growth, and (8) work out problems and experiences with solutions.

From the above description of dramatic play, we can conclude that it is one of the most natural ways of creative expression

2. Ruth Hartley, Lawrence Frank, and Robert Goldenson, *Understanding Children's Play* (New York: Columbia University Press, 1964).

which a young child has. In fact, dramatic play is proof positive that all children are born creative for no one "teaches" a child how to dramatically play these roles—from the age of two or three he just does it. Dramatic play is a spontaneous, natural way for children to develop their creative powers.

In many schools dramatic play is not provided for in the curriculum above the kindergarten or first grade. A common belief that as children mature this "baby stuff" should be put away is indeed unfortunate. Dramatic play goes on in life and should be a part of the entire school program. A group of boys will play cops and robbers, Robin Hood, or King of the Castle just as ardently at the age of eleven as they played milkman at the age of four.

Dramatic play may be legitimately sustained in the elementary school program through its use as role playing.

2. *Free play.* This term generally means the same as dramatic play. School programs allow children time for free play which children use to engage in dramatic play.

3. *Role playing.* This term has two general meanings. First it means acting out of the child of the sex role he will play in life. Studies in the play of children indicate that even at the nursery school age, there are sex differences in the play of three and four year olds, as children identify with adults in their society. Girls tend to be "mothers"; they cook food, play with dolls, clean the house, have tea parties, and dress up. Boys play they are fathers, boat captains, baseball stars, garagemen, etc. This role identification helps the child to play his proper role in society. If it is used excessively—that is, if boys are not allowed to cook, play with dolls, etc., and girls are not allowed to be boat captains, less understanding of the opposite sex role is developed and some of the ability to empathize is lost. Allowing children to engage in divergent roles in their play helps to develop their creativity. Creative boys tend to seem more "feminine" than others because they enjoy some of the activities of the girls and vice versa. They are more open to life experiences and can draw on more experiences from which to create.

5. *Dramatics or dramatization.* These terms apply to the acting out of a play—generally, but not always, written as a script and read or recited. Dramatics can be an excellent tool for the development of creativity, especially when the script is an original one written by the children. Dramatics may take many forms: puppet shows, shadow plays, pantomime, radio and television plays, choral speaking, book reports, etc. (Fig. 6–3). Dramatiza-

FIGURE 6–3   *A dramatization by twelve year olds of* The Wizard of Oz.

tions are generally planned to present before an audience. They may be impromptu and read off the cuff, or they may be a highly polished performance with scenery and costumes. Charades, as played by Mr. Randall's class, is a simple type of dramatization.

Situations for Dramatic Play in the Primary Grades

Much of the dramatic play in the primary grades will be natural. In the classroom children should be granted free time and the necessary environment to act out situations important to them. Many of these will be done to music. On the playground this is also true: equipment should be available that makes possible a great deal of dramatic play. Simple but unusual things can keep children highly motivated and give them opportunity to identify with a variety of roles. An old automobile, stripped of all projections which may cause harm, affords endless opportunities for children to pretend they are Daddy, the schoolbus driver, a taxi driver, an airplane pilot. A large drain pipe firmly anchored so it will not roll can be a tunnel, a bridge, a hiding place. Every playground should have a gate on which children can swing. An old piece of railroad track provides practice in balancing. Slices of a tree imbedded in the ground will serve as stepping stones, islands, and part of a marine obstacle course. An old bathtub partly sunk into the ground can provide a legitimate place for water play, for sailing boats, for blowing bubbles. A large sand box is a must, for all kinds of imaginative play can take place on it. A tire swing or two gives a safe outlet for twisting and twirling and playing the circus acrobat. There should be a flat, surfaced area for games like hopscotch and for driving tricycles and trucks. A pair of stairs built up to a fenced-in platform can be a tree house, a theater balcony, or a hill to climb. A small house or shed can become the hideout for cowboys, a club room, or a home.

All the usual commercially available playground equipment can contribute to dramatic play both in- and out-of-doors. Play equipment, like toys, will be limited in its use when it is too detailed. A toy bus painted to look like one is generally only a toy bus, but a block of wood with wheels can become a bus, a moving van, a truck, an automobile, an army transport, a tractor trailer, or a house trailer. The imagination of the child supplies the details, and he will adapt it to his needs.

The first requisite to encouraging dramatic play is in setting the proper conditions through environmental equipment and climate both in and out of school. It is also the first requisite for a good music program. Essential to all music is rhythm, but a child cannot identify the aspects of formal musical training without repeated experiences with the rhythm of life. The rhythm of the seesaw provides the music teacher the opportunity to draw from a common experience which the children can use to understand the dotted half note. The swing or the tire spring provides a feeling and the tempo for understanding the 1–2–3 beat of a waltz. A swinging gate involves the child in the 2/2 time measure; playing hopscotch involves the child in the rhythm of dotted quarter, half, and whole notes. Climbing the slide may be accomplished with 6/8 time followed by a rest.

Observing children at any age on a playground can provide a clever teacher with the meaningful experiences needed to effectively teach the rudiments of music.

"I saw you running today, Bill," she says. "Show me how you ran," and he does, and she has the children clap the rhythms.

"You were playing hopscotch, Maria," she says. "Show us how you did it," and the children clap the rhythm as Maria jumps and rests. It is but a step to transpose the rhythms to notes on a staff.

"Let's find some running music for tomorrow," she says. Or, "Can we make up a song to go with Maria's rhythm?" They do.

Hop Scotch
One and two
And three and four,
Jump and jump
And jump some more.
Throw a penny
On the floor
Turn around
On number four.
Jump and jump
Until you're sore
Take a rest
And count your score.

In more sophisticated dramatizations, music can play an even more important part. Using dramatization to develop music concepts and experiences may vary from simple experiences to complex experiences, and therefore be used with any age level at any stage of their growth. Children may move from a very simple activity such as selecting recordings or tapes to provide musical backgrounds for their plays to any or all of the following experiences:

(1) Selecting the music which goes with each character in a play. (2) Composing original scripts using music which goes with each character in a play and constructing an operetta effect by playing each character's theme each time he appears in the play (similar to the recordings of "Peter and the Wolf"). (See page 211.) (3) Composing original music for each character in a play. (4) Composing original scripts and plays. In the upper grades and high school, this can mean the production of operettas and short operas or musicals.

Situations Which Promote Motivation for Musical Experiences in the Primary Grades

1. Use playground or schoolroom equipment to develop a specific sense of rhythm.
2. Be an animal you saw on the way to school or on our science trip. What music fits the walking rhythm of your animal?
3. Imitate the postman, the doctor, an airline pilot. What music fits their movements?
4. Play at shopping at the supermarket. Find music to accompany your actions.

5.   Dramatize the bus trip to school. What sounds are like bus music?

6.   Play games which require dramatic interpretation such as "Go In and Out the Windows" or "John Brown's Baby," etc.

7.   Use action songs and dances to develop dramatic expression such as the "Hokey Pokey," "The Bunny Hop," "Itsy-Bitsy Spider."

8.   Dramatize light things: air, marshmallows, Kleenex, feathers, dust, dandelion seeds, etc. Find suitable music to accompany your dramatizations.

9.   Dramatize heavy things: bulldozers, iron, mud, stones, etc. Find suitable music.

10.   Dramatize moving things: trains, buses, cars, wheelbarrows, lawnmowers. Find "moving" music.

11.   Dramatize quiet things: a statue, a library, a rabbit. Find "quiet" music.

12.   Dramatize fast things: a snake, a race car, a train, a waterfall, a plane. Find "fast" music.

13.   Dramatize slow things: a turtle, an alligator, an old man, a worm. Find "slow" music.

14.   Dramatize noisy things: an eggbeater, a motorboat, an electric saw. Find "noisy" music.

15.   Play *statues* where one child twirls another, and then releases him. The twirled child "freezes" into the position in which he falls and all the children guess what he looks like. Create music which stops at the freeze point.

16.   Play primary charades: At the beginning of Chapter I is an illustration of the use of charades in the middle grades to help develop and solve a problem with music. Such an activity need not be restricted to middle graders. Miss Nash, after a unit on community helpers and people of the world, asked her primary children to choose and pantomime one type of helper or individual they had studied. From the twenty dramatizations they had studied, she selected five, and the children were to write music about each one, using a marimba to pick out the tune. Following is the song created for Ronald, who was a pirate (Fig. 6–4).

17.   Dramatize stories such as "The Little Rabbit Who Wanted Red Wings." Find music to accompany the dramatization.

18.   Dramatize poems and nursery rhymes such as "Jack Be Nimble," "Simple Simon," and "The Elf and the Doormouse," with music accompaniment.

19.   Take a painting someone in the class has made and act out a story that goes with it. Find music to go with it.

Ronald's Song

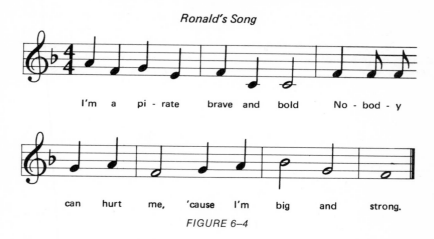

I'm a pi - rate brave and bold No - bod - y

can hurt me, 'cause I'm big and strong.

FIGURE 6–4

20. Do the same with an interesting magazine cover or advertisement or a famous painting.

21. Dramatize the great current events of the day: the launching of a rocket, the flight of an astronaut, the launching of a ship. Find or create music to accompany your dramatization.

22. Take the children to school assemblies, which are within their scope of understanding, especially musical presentations.

23. Use musical shadow plays, puppetry, magnetic puppet plays, and other forms of dramatization as variations to your programs.

24. Put fingerplays to music for quiet dramatizations—especially ones the children have created.

25. Create musical plays.

26. Dramatize the sounds of the various instruments of the orchestra.

Developing Creativity Through Dramatics and Music in the Intermediate Grades

If children have had their dramatic abilities stifled and are awkward or embarrassed in expressing themselves through bodily movement before class, the teacher may regenerate this creative ability by beginning in a simple way to set the proper social climate to free children to explore the creative use of their bodies. Mrs. McCarthy had such a group. Each day she spent a little time on dramatics until the proper free atmosphere was established.

On the first day of her work with the children she gave each a slip of paper on which she had written a direction. Each child acted out this direction and the class guessed what it was. Some of the slips of paper read as follows:

Be an Indian stalking a deer.
Pretend you are a cowboy setting up camp.
Act like the nurse to a wounded soldier.
Be Dr. Marcus Welby.
Imitate a woman shopping at the bargain basement.
Pretend you are a cow chewing her cud.

No evaluation was given at the end of the dramatizations because Mrs. McCarthy wanted the children to be completely comfortable with themselves.

The next day she asked them to play by groups a character suggested by a piece of music. She prepared a Sousa march for one group that decided to be soldiers; the "Dance of the Sugarplum Fairies" was played for one group that became elves and fairies; "Night on Bald Mountain" produced a witch, a devil, a gorilla, and a ghost.

On each succeeding day they were to initiate a favorite character from literature or one from their acquaintance. For those who could not think of a character, Mrs. McCarthy had prepared names on slips of paper in a box on her desk, and the children could choose one of these slips if they liked. The next day there were excellent interpretations of Sherlock Holmes, Davy Crockett, Daniel Boone, Amelia Earhart, Dr. Kildare, Lucille Ball, Frankenstein, Alan Shepard, Sammy Davis, David Cassidy, the First Lady, Florence Nightingale, Heidi, and others. Again musical selections were played and matched with the characters.

On the following day Mrs. McCarthy began to work on the skills of dramatization by having the children choose slips of paper which called for unique interpretations and special actions to portray character. She prepared slips from which the children chose; asked them to observe such a situation or such a character at home or on the streets and then to dramatize it the next day. Some of these slips read as follows:

Be an old man.
Be a shy boy.

Imitate a cat catching a mouse.
Imitate a cat lapping up milk.
Cry like a little baby.
Sit down like an old lady.
Run like a four year old.
Walk like a marine.

After the dramatizations the children were encouraged to evaluate each interpretation.

After a few periods of this work, Mrs. McCarthy held a discussion with the children and asked them how many expected to go to town with their parents over the weekend. Several planned to do so. She asked them to watch people on the street and a particular person or scene that appealed to them, and to be prepared to dramatize it on Monday morning in pantomime so the rest of the class might guess what each saw. One author was present in Mrs. McCarthy's class on that Monday morning and spent a delightful half-hour watching the children act out their skits. Five girls dramatized a mother taking a group picture at a Sunday family picnic. One was a little child who wouldn't stand still, and of course the inevitable happened when he turned his head just as the mother clicked the shutter.

Four boys showed their powers of observation when they presented their scene. They stood in various slouching positions, leaning against the doorway, hands in pockets, bored expressions, listless actions. One tossed a coin, another twirled a watch, one scratched the ground with his toe. Suddenly they all became electrified. All eyes turned to one direction, bodies tensed, hats were shoved back on their heads, eyes popped. All eyes and heads turned to the left and slowly swept to the right. Each boy stopped at least once in this process and let his eyes fall from eye level to the floor and up again. When all eyes and heads were finally as far to the right as possible all boys joined in one unanimous "wolf" whistle. They had observed a group of sailors loitering on a street corner when a pretty girl passed by.

Other dramatizations were equally imaginative and challenging. One girl imitated a boy scout helping an old lady across the street; one group imitated a Sunday school teacher trying to quiet her brood.

We visited Mrs. McCarthy's room many times after that. She added voices to the dramatizations as her next step, and then music. The creative dramatizations these children were producing were superior in every way. Many of the children were writing their own plays and musicals. Several of the suggestions on the following pages were ideas we saw being employed in Mrs. McCarthy's room.

One day a lively discussion was in progress. The children had been assigned as homework to watch Marcelle Marceau, the French pantomimist, on television. They were delighted with what they had seen and many times during the discussion a child would leap to his feet and imitate the great artist with no inhibitions. Mrs. McCarthy had led this group from a shy, inhibited, self-conscious one to the place where they could use their own bodies, uninhibited and free, to communicate creatively.

Open-ended stories provide excellent situations for creative dramatizations. The teacher reads the beginning of a story and the children are divided in groups—each group dramatizes a possible ending.

The children are encouraged to use music to accompany their dramatizations.

One day Mrs. McCarthy told the children that instead of dramatizing the ending they must do it with music, either sung or played. The story on that particular day was about Freddie, a little boy who wanted to go to the circus but had no money. The children in the group we observed got up and presented the following. Can you guess the ending of the story?

1. They made a song which went like this:
    I need a job
    I want a job
    I need to make some dough
    I need a job
    To get a job
    To the agency I'll go!
2. They played a portion of "I've Been Working on the Railroad" from a recording.
3. They hummed a portion of the "Peanuts" song.
4. They played a portion of "Old Man River."
5. They played a recording of a calliope.

The children guessed immediately that Freddie went to the employment agency to get a job; he first got one on the railroad, then selling peanuts, and then hauling cotton, and earned enough to go to the circus.

Actual historical scenes or events in other countries can be dramatized to help children feel the event more fully. Often the entire class can take part in such dramatizations with no audience to watch because the emphasis is on participation and involvement to develop creativity and empathy. One group dramatized a Mexican Christmas, a piñata party, and a Mexican fiesta. Appropriate music added greatly to the dramatization. Every child played his part in keeping with the situation. Another group dramatized a medieval fair.

Other events lend themselves to total group dramatization. Some are: a medieval tournament, a visit to the carnival, the election of a president, a day in Plymouth, a trip to New York, an evening around a campfire, the meeting of an Indian council, a day at Fort Niagara, etc. Music to accompany all activities enriches the dramas.

Situations Which Set Conditions for Creative Development in the Intermediate Grades

1. Imitate instances from life around you such as:
    A pitcher warming up to throw a ball.
    A football player delivering a forward pass.
    A girl applying makeup.
    Father shaving.
    Little brother throwing a tantrum.
    Older sister setting her hair.
    A man constructing a bookcase.
Select or create appropriate music to accompany your dramatizations.
2. Play some "dramatic" games such as charades or statues.
3. Make up stories and act them out to music.
4. Dramatize favorite stories, poems, and songs.
5. Play "Follow the Leader" where each child takes a turn at dramatizing and the rest follow. This idea may be built around themes such as a trip to the zoo, or a circus may be the theme.) Each child can sing or hum an appropriate tune to portray his character, and all children can then imitate both the action and the tune.
6. Dramatize the relative note values which children have chanted or walked and/or qualities of an inanimate object: a musical note, a G clef, a rest, a dotted half note.
7. Pretend you are a caveman with little or no verbal communication and ask groups in the classroom to show how a caveman might have communicated his need for song and rhythm.
8. Collect colloquialisms in music and dramatize them, such as:

You look jazzy.
He's a swinger.
It's a rock group.
He's got the beat.
She's horning in on my territory.
The strings of my heart.
Stop harping on it.

LITERATURE AND MUSIC

How can literature be used effectively to promote the goals of the music program in the elementary school? It always has been used for such purposes in the past. Unfortunately, it has rarely been used *conscientiously* to develop a knowledge or appreciation of music and rarely has it been subject to close scrutiny for the purpose of using music and literature harmoniously to develop creativity in students.

Musical stories built from good pieces of literature have long presented music to children in an interesting form. Examples of such classics are Humperdink's "Hansel and Gretel" and recordings of Grieg's "Peer Gynt Suite."

Children's stories have been set to music and made into films often with excellent results, such as *Alice in Wonderland, Mary Poppins, Dr. Doolittle, The Wizard of Oz,* and *Babes in Toyland.*

The making of cartoons from children's films has become an unsurpassed art, especially as promoted by the late Walt Disney. Music from these productions has run the gamut from poor to excellent, but has made a definite contribution to the American way of life.

Teachers can use music to help set the mood for great pieces of literature. It is often fun to play a background piece of music on the record player while reading a story to the children.

Perhaps music can be most appreciated by children when they make it work for them: helping to write and express the mood for their own stories.

One author recounts an interesting experience in a fourth grade where children used music to enhance their own study of contemporary literature. He read the poem *John J. Plenty and Fiddler Dan* by John Ciardi. The children were reminded of the manner in which movies helped to create a mood through music. Smith suggested that they record the sound track by each reading a segment of the poem into the microphone but that they also add music to create the proper mood.

John J. Plenty and Fiddler Dan is a modern version of the fable *The Grasshopper and the Ant.* For the opening scene the children chose the music of Beethoven's *Pastoral.* When the fiddler, Dan, appeared in the story, they faded the music by turning down the volume on the record player and bringing up the volume on another record player with a recording of Heifitz playing the violin. For the coming of winter, they introduced the storm with "The Flight of the Bumblebee," increasing the volume and then fading it back to the violin music when John J. Plenty came out of his ant house to find Fiddler Dan still alive. Each child then drew a picture of his portion of the story with magic chalk (chalk which shows color under a black light, but is white under normal room light), and pasted them in sequence on a long roll of mural paper (Fig. 6–5). In the darkened room, two children rolled the movie through towel-box theater and each picture burst into color as the magic light was turned on. All the while, the music background provided the proper "soundtrack" to the film.

Later, Smith recounts another creative use of this technique in making of a magic talking book, *The Wiggley Woo,* in which music played a very important part in providing the background for a completely original story (Fig. 6–6).

The Wiggley Woo: A Magic Talking Book

"*Today,*" said Miss Ellis, "*Let's make a magic talking book!*"
"*Magic? How magic?*"
"*How can a book talk?*"
"*Is the talking part of the magic?*"
"*Oh, let's!*"

I glanced down at the sheet of paper in my hand on which Miss Ellis had jotted her objectives. They read as follows:

As a result of this experience the children will:

1. Have the opportunity to share their oral vocabulary which will be used to develop a creative writing and a reading lesson.
2. Become aware of rhyming words and the rhythm and rhyme needed to create poetry.

FIGURE 6–5   *A magic scroll movie:* John J. Plenty and Fiddler Dan.

3. Create a rhyming poem using their spoken vocabulary.
4. Create a choral poem using their own vocabulary.
5. Express themselves by use of a new media: magic crayons and magic chalk.
6. Read familiar words in context.
7. Have an experience of organizing materials in a sequence.
8. Create a magic talking book (experiences in reading, oral expression, art, music appreciation, listening, and creative writing).
9. Create some appropriate music as a background for the experience.

What a delightful way to begin—all the children were motivated at once! I looked up to Miss Ellis.

"We will have to wait and see!" she said. "First, I'd like to do some warming up things to see how good you are. Let's make our book a poem—a fun poem. Is that all right with everybody?"

A unanimous "Yes" resounded to her question.

"Well," continued Miss Ellis, "To have a poem we generally, not always, but generally we have two things— rhythm and rhyme. Does anyone know what rhyming *is?" She lettered the words on the chalkboard.*

Charlie did. "It is putting two words together that sound alike at the end," he explained.

"Like what?" Miss Ellis probed.

"Ball and tall."

"Good," she said, "Let's try some more—what rhymes with beat?"

"Seat!"

"Man?"

"Pan!"

"Good—now just let's look a minute at these cards. See if you can tell me words that rhyme with the word I have printed on the top."

Miss Ellis then held up a card with the word BOO printed on it. "What rhymes with Woo?"

"Shoe."

"Glue."

"Blue."

"Moo."

"Zoo."

Miss Ellis printed the words. "Now look at this card," she said. The word was CROP and the children added stop, flop, drop, plop, cop, hop, and mop.

The next card had the word CAKE on the top. The children added make, fake, bake, lake, pancake, take, and rake.

Other cards were filled out in the same manner, and set along the chalkboard.

"Now let's talk about this other word," said Miss Ellis— "this word rhythm. Does anyone know what it means?"

Marie thought it was a dance.

"It is a dance—Marie is right, but it is even more. When we move in movements over and over or do the same thing over and over, we say we have rhythm. Joe, could you dance for us?"

After other demonstrations Miss Ellis said, "In rhyming poetry and in poetry that doesn't rhyme we have rhythm— words have rhythm.

"In our book we will need to use both rhythm and rhyme, and I know now that you will do it well."

"I have here a word that I would like you to figure out," said Miss Ellis holding up a strip of paper. "Raise your hand if you can tell me what it is—Jerry?"

"Wiggley Woo."

"Right," said Miss Ellis. "Wiggley Woo. Have any of you ever seen a Wiggley Woo?"

The children all laughed, exclaimed, and showed amazement in their answers.

"Well," said Miss Ellis, "I have never seen a Wiggley Woo either. A Wiggley Woo can look anyway you want him to, he can do *anything you want him to, he can* say *anything you want him to and can* be *anything you want him to.* Would it be fun to write our poem book about a Wiggley Woo?"

"Yes."

"Let's."

"O.K. Let's look at this card. Who can read it?"

On a series of long, heavy strips of paper Miss Ellis had printed words. The one on the top of the pile which she held up said,

"Have you ever heard of a Wiggley Woo?"

Sherry read it.

"Good," said Miss Ellis, "Now look at this card." It read, "He looks like a ——— ——— ——— ——— ——— ———."

"Now what we can do to make a rhyming poem," said Miss Ellis, "is to get the same rhythm in the second line as the first. Let's clap the first line while we read it together. Now let's clap the second line the way it must be. You can see how many sounds we must make to give it the same rhythm."

After the children had experimented with this, Miss Ellis said, "Now what must we also do to make the second line rhyme with the first?"

"Put a word on the end that sounds like Woo," said Casey.

"Right," said Miss Ellis, "And here we have a whole card full of words that rhyme with Woo. Who can choose one and put it at the end of a sentence that will have the same rhythm as line 1?"

There were deep frowns and "grinding wheels." Finally Bonnie said, "How about . . . He looks like a thing that left the zoo!"

The children were delighted with Bonnie's rhyme. They clapped the rhythm to be sure it fit.

Miss Ellis continued showing two cards at a time so the children could rhyme the second card with the first. They checked each of the companion lines for rhythm and rhyme. Miss Ellis had made enough lead lines so every child in the class would later have a line to work with. This is what resulted:

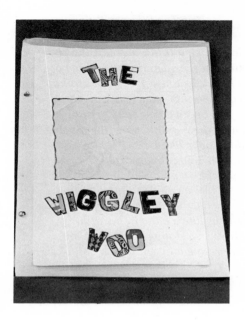

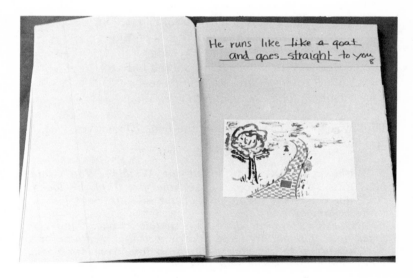

FIGURE 6–6   The Wiggley Woo: A magic talking book.

The Wiggley Woo

Have you ever heard of a Wiggley Woo?
He looks like a thing that left the zoo.
He lives in the swamp on the edge of the crop,
And he walks like a frog about to hop.
He eats peanuts, popcorn, and cake
And gets every day a belly ache.
He talks through his nose like an old tin horn
And he looks like he wished he wasn't born.
He smells like cabbage and perfume, too.
He runs like a goat and goes straight to you.
He acts like a cow with big, flat feet.
He cries like no one you'll ever meet.
He sleeps like a baby in his crib,
He drinks so sloppy he needs a bib.
He plays like a kitten with a ball of string.
He jumps like a lion through a circus ring.
He goes into town to have some fun.
He buys Cracker Jacks and a water gun.
He's funny, even funnier than you or me
And we find him hiding behind every tree.
He waddles like a duck on a rainy day,
He works like a horse on the first of May.
He weighs most a ton and is sloppy fat.
He holds his money in his old felt hat.
We'll try to get him back in the zoo,
Our big, old, funny, old Wiggley Woo.

Thus was the text provided for the book. Objectives 1, 2, and 3 met! Motivation ran high!

"With such description about the Wiggley Woo," said Miss Ellis, "I am anxious to see how you think he looks. And now comes the magic part of our talking book! This is what we are going to do!"

Miss Ellis then introduced the magic crayons and the black light. The children had experienced this media before.

"I am going to ask you to choose a line from our poem story. Then take a sheet of this paper and go over to the table where I have hung the magic light and draw a picture that will go with your line. If you use the magic crayons that are there the colors will disappear when you take the picture away from the magic light. Number your paper in the corner the same as the line I give you—because this is where the magic comes in. I shall not be able to tell what picture goes with what line if you don't number them. Without the light I will see only a white sheet of paper."

The children enjoyed using the glowing colors under the magic light. Miss Ellis had two of the lights hung over a large table so there was plenty of working area for many children.

As soon as a child finished his picture, Miss Ellis gave him a large piece of colored construction paper on which he mounted his picture and the line of poetry that went with it. Three children who finished early made a cover for the book with large letters "The Wiggley Woo."

As the pages of the book were finished one child was assigned to put them in the proper order. Then Miss Ellis helped put them together with two large paper fasteners.

Soon all the pages were in the book. What excitement prevailed in the classroom as the children placed one of the magic lights before the book and turned the pages so they could see each other's work! Such weird, fascinating, individual interpretations of the infamous Wiggley Woo! When it was over the children applauded—delighted and proud of their own creative product.

"It is beautiful—and such fun!" said Miss Ellis. "But I have something else in mind. Does anyone remember what I said we were going to make at the beginning of our project? Think hard!"

Hands were quick to go up.

"You said we were going to write a magic talking book," said Marcia.

"Yes," agreed Miss Ellis, "and we did make a poem book, and we did make a magic book, but we did not make a talking book. Shall we make it a talking book?"

"Yes!"

"Let's."

"All right. Now, how many of you can read the line of the poem on your page. Let's go through the book again and have each person read his line of the poem. If you need help, one of us will help you. Let's go." She then turned the pages again and each child practiced reading his line while other children prompted. (This gave Miss Ellis an excellent opportunity to point out similar endings, like consonant sounds and consonant blends.)

After each child had read his line Miss Ellis showed the children a cassette tape recorder which she had brought to class.

"We could make our book more interesting if we made

FIGURE 6–7   Charles's rhythm.

some music to play in the background while we read our lines," said Miss Ellis. "I have here some musical instruments which I thought might give you some ideas." At this point she took from a box a marimba, two metallophones, some rhythm instruments, and some drums. "Now," she continued, "what rhythm do you think of when you think of the Wiggley Woo?"

"I see him clomping along through the swamp," said Charles.

"Can you show us on one of these instruments?" asked Miss Ellis.

Charles selected a drum and made four accented beats like a huge animal lumbering along (Fig. 6–7).

"Good—that is a good base rhythm," said Miss Ellis. "Now does anyone want to come and experiment with these instruments until we have a rhythm that goes well with Charles's?"

Several children did until another was chosen as blending well with the first—a little tune on the metallophone (Fig. 6–8).

Still another tune was designed with bells to go with the first two (Fig. 6–9).

When the children were satisfied with the little tune they had created, some played the tune in the background while one child read his line of the poem into the microphone and then passed it along to the next person until everyone had read his line.

After it was completed, the tape recorder was placed behind the book. As the pages were turned the magic light made each picture glow and the children's music supplied

FIGURE 6–8   Metallophone tune.

FIGURE 6–9   *Bell tune.*

a background for each voice as the words on the page were read. It truly was a musical magic talking book!

Forms of music may be taught through the use of literature. Miss Black used *The Emperor's New Clothes* to introduce children to the opera.

The Making of an Opera

Miss Black and Mrs. Burns, the music teacher, collaborated on the following project which proved to be an exciting experience in creating and interpreting.

Some of the objectives copied from Miss Black's notebook read as follows:

As a result of this project, the children will:

1.   Understand the concept of the opera and how it differs from musical plays and dramatizations. This will be evaluated by the children's ability to recognize operatic music when played on records and to produce a small opera of their own with appropriate music style.

2.   Translate a favorite piece of literature into musical expression as evidenced by a final production.

3.   Create operatic music to be used in dramatizing a favorite story.

4.   Learn how to stage a production of this nature, and learn the skills required. These will be: painting scenery, making costumes, creating props, listening to music, writing scripts, speaking and singing effectively, making prints for posters and programs, and doing research. Evauation will lie in the final production.

One of the children brought the book *The Emperor's New Clothes* from the library and gave a report on it to the class. The children selected it as one of the stories to read together. So, Miss Black read it one day. The enthusiasm and interest of the children led them to select it as a proper vehicle for fulfilling the objectives of their project.

One day following the reading of the story, Miss Black and Mrs. Burns held a discussion. They encouraged the children to list the characters of the story. Next to each character the children then listed characteristics which described his personality. After the weavers, for instance, the children suggested crafty, busy, fussy, energetic, sly, and tricky. After the character of the king, they listed regal, royal, majestic, proud, bossy, stupid, and dressy. After the character of the little boy they listed the characteristics of: innocent, honest, and simple. They described the prime minister as being dishonest, crafty, sly, smug, mean, disloyal, and foxy.

After every actor had been so described, the children were encouraged to go to the piano and to create a theme for each person, trying to invent a musical pattern that would show the character of each.

The weavers needed busy music so the following notes were played to indicate the weavers (Fig. 6–10).

These words were added:

> *Busy, busy, busy*
> *are the weavers of the thread*
> *Hurry, Hurry, Hurry*
> *or the King will chop your head.*

The theme created for the king (stately, royal, proud music) was as follows (Fig. 6–11).

The Weavers' Tune

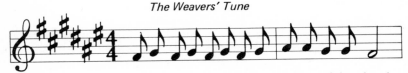

Bu- sy, bu- sy, bu- sy are the weav-ers of the thread

Hur-ry, hur-ry, hur-ry or the King will chop your head.

FIGURE 6–10   "The Weavers' Tune." (The children chose to use the black keys for these tunes.)

Make way, Make way, The King has come to-day. He

wears Roy-al Red and a crown up-on his head.

FIGURE 6–11

Words created to accompany his theme were:

> *Make way*
> *Make way*
> *The king has come today!*
> *He wears*
> *Royal red*
> *And a crown upon his head!*

For the innocent, honest, simple little boy, this theme was invented (Fig. 6–12):

And these words were added:

> *I am a little farmer boy*
> *I only tell you what I see*
> *I never never tell a lie*
> *I'm just as honest as can be.*

In addition to writing themes for the main characters, some music was created for some of the events such as the parade in the streets and the final show-down scene.

The story was rewritten by one committee so that it could be staged in three scenes: the king's reception room, the weaver's room, and on the street before the palace. Simple costumes were made (mostly from crepe paper). Some good lighting effects were worked out and the "opera" was presented.

As each character was introduced in Act I, the theme was played and the character sang his words. From that time on, the theme for each character was played every time that character

FIGURE 6–12

appeared—sometimes as a background to his chanted words. Parts of the narration were sung rather than spoken. The teachers and children worked hard at the end of the opera to create a song in which all the themes were blended.

Included in the production were vocal solos, ensembles, recitations (vocal declamations), and choruses as well as orchestral accompaniments from records.

During the creation of their opera the children listened to an opera, discovering that it was sung throughout. Some saw segments of an opera presented on television. The music teacher helped develop the concept that a comic opera sometimes had dialogue.

Music may be put to many other uses to enhance literature, and literature may be put to many uses to enhance music. In addition to teaching music for music's sake, the same might be said about literature for literature's sake, drama for drama's sake, and dance for dance's sake. Each is an art in itself but each is a tool to be used to enhance the other, or to serve the other. Children will make the creative arts a real part of their lives only when they can appreciate each as an art and use each as a tool.

MUSIC AND ART

Just as music can be used to develop dance, dramatics, literature, and movement, so can it become the inspiration for many art lessons and for the development of art appreciation.

We have already seen how teachers have used art to develop creativity in music, as well as how music has been used to develop creativity through art. Following are suggestions supplied by many classroom and music teachers for integrating art and music in the daily program with the intent of helping each child to become better able to express his creative drives.

Suggestions for Developing Creativity Through Art and Music

1.   Miss Morris often had her children paint to music, using a variety of media: finger paint, water colors, tempera paint, clay, crayon, and chalk (Fig. 6–13).

2.   Mr. Thompson brought samples of great paintings into his classroom and asked the children to select a recording suggested by the painting. The painting was hung for a few days in a frame in the front of the room. During study time the music was played.

3.   Miss Marsh often had the children interpret a painting with props, music, and dancing.

4.   Miss Ashley, an art teacher, chose music for different media. Mancini's *Elephant Walk* recording was played when the children were introduced to clay, *Dance of the Tumblers* was played when they were introduced to water color, Enesco's *Rumanian Rhapsody* was played while the children worked in tempera paint.

5.   Mr. Tosh had the children collect pictures for a bulletin-

FIGURE 6–13   A "dribble" painting made by a six year old while listening to "The Dance of the Sugar Plum Fairies." The dribbles are red, white, and yellow on a deep blue background.

board display which reminded them of the sound of a violin, the boom of a drum, the wailing of the saxophone, and a piano playing. This led to an interesting study of modern art.

6.   For an assembly program, Mr. Phelps had his children reproduce famous, favorite paintings in pantomime playing appropriate music for each scene.

7.   Mr. Smith played honky-tonk music on a record player and had the children paint on clear 16 mm film at the same time. Then the film was run on the projector with the music playing. The dancing colors across the screen delighted the children into making other sequences with different kinds of music such as a waltz, march, samba, and rock and roll.

8.   Children enjoy dramatizing many pieces of music such as "Frosty the Snowman" and "Rudolph the Red Nosed Reindeer" at Christmas time. Art may be incorporated into these dramatizations when they take on the form of puppet shows, shadow plays, or flannelboard stories.

9.   Children enjoy telling each other the lives of the composers through flannelboard stories, puppet plays, and shadow plays.

10.   Children can create a "mini ballet" by taking a piece of music such as "The Firefly," interpreting it through movement, and making simple scenery and costumes for the finished production.

SUMMARY

Throughout the ages, music, dance, literature, drama, and art have provided man with a creative means of communication and a positive outlet for his feelings. The chants and rhythms of the ancient tribes, the sign languages of the American Indian, the ballads of the minstrels, the wagon plays of the medieval church —all were creative forms of teaching long before the average man became literate.

Since literacy has spread among the masses of people, knowledge and skill have developed and have been recorded in the areas of music, dance, drama, literature, and art; and each of these areas of primitive communication has risen to the status of an art in itself. As an art each has been relegated to a place of honor in the elementary school curriculum where the science and skill of each is taught as part of the general education of all citizens.

Recent studies and writings in the area of creativity indicate that the creative development of each child would be greatly enhanced if, in addition to the teaching of the knowledge and skill necessary for literacy in each of these areas, they were restored in the school curiculum to a place comparable to their place in the history of mankind: that of providing each child with a creative means of communication and a creative outlet for his emotional reactions to his environment.

TO THE COLLEGE STUDENT AND THE TEACHING TEAM

1.   Puppets often provide a projective technique for children. Why will some children shy away from actual play-acting before a group, but enter fully into dramatics through the use of puppets? Could music be used in a similar manner?
2.   Think of all the projective techniques you can use in a classroom that will help children gain emotional release through the use of dramatics and music.
3.   Ask some children to dramatize noises such as the wail of a

siren, the scratch of chalk on the chalkboard, the sound of a felt pen squeaking, a lawn mower, a snowflake. Ask some adults to do this first, then try the children. Which group was more original, more creative? Less inhibited? Explain any differences you observe.

4. The following situation helps a teacher observe how well her children understand the various phases of music. In this instance, the dramatization was built around instruments of the orchestra. It could be built around a staff of notes, a meeting of composers, a conference of sounds. The basic rules are the same and the activity serves as a culminating unit for a particular phase of study.

A few people, usually three or four, are asked to leave the room. The remainder of the group decides (or is assigned) a *group* situation (in this case, the situation is the assembling of a symphony orchestra for a Van Cliburn concert). The situation is discussed and each person assigns himself a part by pantomiming that part. In this case children would decide which instrument they would be and would determine how to dramatize that particular instrument. The dramatization need not be the motions used in playing the instrument: The children may wish to dramatize the sound of the instrument, or its shape, or what it means to them. The room is then arranged to represent the required scene (a symphony orchestra setting with something out front to represent a director's podium and Mr. Cliburn's piano). The play begins in pantomime with each character doing his part. Music may be added for background effect provided the music does not give the scene away too obviously. One by one the people who have left the room are brought in. The "players" in the room react to them in as normal a manner as possible, and in such a way that after some observation, each person should be able to begin to play his own role in the group drama.

For instance, in the orchestra situation above, the children decided that the orchestra would be "warming up" when the pantomime began. Consequently, the first violinist was up front and each child was acting out his instrument in queer ways, bringing the instrument in tune. The podium and the stool at the piano (a large box) was empty.

When the first child was brought in, the concert master rapped his baton, all instruments became quiet, and the concert master ushered the guest conductor to the podium up front. A few people, playing the audience, rose and clapped vigorously. In only a few seconds, the child interpreted the situation and tested his guess by rapping the imaginary podium with an imaginary baton. The orchestra immediately responded. Soon the "conductor" began the concert and Person 2 was brought in. He watched for a while, and because he could not guess his role the concert master escorted him to the piano, the "audience" gave him a standing ovation, and Mr. Cliburn caught on.

Dramatizations of this nature involve every child. Even the teacher plays a part. The teacher can tell a great deal about the learnings of the children: how well they know the instruments of a symphony orchestra, the unique qualities of each instrument, the ethics of the concert, the role of each person at a concert, etc. Needless to say, the children who created the dramatization above had attended a symphony concert as a group.

5. If you have never tried, paint to music choosing a fluid medium which you enjoy.

SELECTED BIBLIOGRAPHY

Allstrom, Elizabeth. *Let's Play a Story*. New York: The Friendship Press, 1957.

Andrews, Gladys. *Creative Rhythmic Movement for Children*. Englewood Cliffs, N.J.: Prentice-Hall, 1954.

Arbuthnot, May Hill, and Zena Sutherland. *Children and Books*, rev. ed. Glenview, Ill.: Scott, Foresman, 1972.

Arnstein, Flora J. *Poetry in the Elementary Classroom*. New York: Appleton-Century-Crofts, 1962.

Association for Childhood Education International. *Creative Dramatics*. Washington, D.C.: Association for Childhood Education International, 1961.

Cole, Natalie. *Children's Art from Deep Down Inside*. New York: John Day, 1966.

Crossup, Richard. *Children and Dramatics*. New York: Charles Scribner's Sons, 1966.

Davis, Jed, and Mary Ann Watkins. *Children's Theater*. New York: Harper & Row, 1964.

Doyle, Brian (Ed.) *The Who's Who of Children's Literature*. New York: Schoeken Books, 1968.

Duff, Annis. *Bequest of Wings*. New York: Viking Press, 1963.

————. *Longer Flight*. New York: Viking Press, 1956.

Fenner, Phyllis. *The Proof of the Pudding*. New York: John Day, 1957.

Fitzgerald, Burdette. *World Tales for Creative Dramatics and Storytelling*. Englewood Cliffs, N.J.: Prentice-Hall, 1962.

Gaitskell, Charles D. *Children and Their Art*, 2nd ed. New York: Harcourt, Brace, Jovanovich, 1972.

Hartley, Ruth, Lawrence Frank, and Robert Goldenson. *Understanding Children's Play*. New York: Columbia University Press, 1964.

Hurwitz, Al (Ed.) *Programs of Promise: Art in the Schools*. New York: Harcourt, Brace, Jovanovich, 1972.

Jefferson, Blanche. *Teaching Art to Children*. Boston: Allyn and Bacon, 1959.

Kase, Robert. *Stories for Creative Acting*. New York: Samuel French, 1961.

Kerman, Gertrude. *Plays and Creative Ways with Children*. Irving-on-the-Hudson, N.Y.: Harvey House, 1961.

Lowenfeld, Viktor, and Lambert W. Brittain. *Creative and Mental Growth*. London: Collier-MacMillan, 1970.

Marsh, Mary Val. *Explore and Discover Music*. Riverside, N.J.: Macmillan, 1970.

McCaslin, Nellie. *Creative Dramatics in the Classroom*. New York: David McKay, 1968.

Myers, Emma. *The Whys and Hows of Hand Writing*. Columbus, Ohio: Zaner-Bloser, 1963.

Pierson, Howard. "Pupils, Teachers and Creative Dramatics." In James C. MacCampbell (Ed.), *Readings in the Language Arts in the Elementary School*. Boston: D. C. Heath, 1964, pp. 151–160.

Rasmussen, Carrie. *Let's Say Poetry Together and Have Fun*. Minneapolis: Burgess, 1962.

Sawyer, Ruth. *The Way of the Story Teller*, rev. ed. New York: Viking Press, 1962.

Siks, Geraldine Brain. *Children's Literature for Dramatization*. New York: Harper & Row, 1964.

————. *Children's Theater and Creative Dramatics: Principles and Practices*. Seattle: University of Washington Press, 1961.

————. *Creative Dramatics*. New York: Harper & Row, 1960.

Taylor, Loren E. *Story-Telling and Dramatization*. Minneapolis: Burgess, 1965.

Smith, James A. *Creative Teaching of the Language Arts in the Elementary School*, 2nd ed. Boston: Allyn and Bacon, 1973.

CHAPTER VII

Music Through Curriculum
Areas: The Language Arts

Music is well said to be the speech of Angels.

THOMAS CARLYLE[1]

INTRODUCTION

Modern conceptions of the development of creativity do not limit
it to the creative arts. Creativity can be developed in children in
all curriculum areas. Perhaps the area most suited to its development is the language arts. This chapter is designed to help the
teacher understand how the language arts curriculum can develop the creative powers in children. It also attempts to show
that music, more than being a subject in the elementary school
curriculum, is a tool to help teach all curriculum areas, especially the language arts. Without language there could be no
songs—music itself is a language! The music of the human
voice helps to communicate; the words of the human mind help
to give music meaning. With music and language so tightly fused
normally, it is easy to see how they can be taught together.

If music is to become a part of the everyday life of each individual, it must be put to use for reasons other than enjoyment
and esthetics. Children will need to know how to use it to contribute to meeting their needs at all times. Teachers must be
aware of the possibilities of using music as both a product and a
tool. This can best be done by integrating music frequently with

1. Thomas Carlyle, "The Opera," in *Sir Walter Scott, London and Westminster Review*, no. 12 (1838).

the total curriculum and using it to teach all areas of the curriculum: social studies, language arts, reading, and even mathematics. Children have too long been exposed to music in isolated periods once or twice a week. They need to be exposed to it each day—to develop creativity through the use of it whenever possible.

Goethe said, "A man should hear a little music, read a little poetry, and see a fine picture every day of his life, in order that worldly cares may not obliterate the sense of the beautiful which God has implanted in the human soul." Goethe was wise: Until music becomes a functional and esthetic part of each child's life every day of his life, the goals for teaching music as stated in this volume will not be met, and the entire music program may as well be shelved. The study of music is not a frill but the study of man himself and is essential to improve the quality of life for every human being.

MUSIC AND THE LANGUAGE ARTS

Next to the creative arts, the language arts appear to be the most natural form of expression for creativity in the elementary school program. Children enjoy writing poems, stories, and plays. Even before they can write, they enjoy verbalizing and carry out impromptu conversations in dramatic play, role playing, shadow plays, puppetry, and marionettes. The language arts are commonly referred to as the communication arts. Music is also a form of communication art. There should be many opportunities to integrate the two areas to improve the effectiveness of communication.

Part of the task of developing the esthetic aspects of music is to help the child verbalize his reactions to musical creatiòns. It has often been said that one test of creativity is the ability of a person to use metaphor. In this analogy, music and language become closely allied in expressing a reaction, feeling, or a certain sensitivity to a common musical experience.

The Sequence of Language Development

Language develops in a logical sequence. First a child must *experience*. Most of his experiencing in the early years of his life is through listening and through the other senses such as smell, taste, touch, and sight. After a year or so of listening the infant selects from the sounds he hears in his environment those which have meaning for him and attempts to reproduce them. Speech—oral expression—is born. After a period of time when he develops physically to the stage where his tongue, teeth, jaws, and voice apparatus make refined speech possible, he communicates on the oral level fluently. Parallel to this development is the ability to conceptualize and symbolize; soon he can recognize in symbols (print) those words which he is able to verbalize (speech).

Repeated sight of the visual image of letters and words makes possible the ability to write. Spelling, handwriting forms, capitalization, punctuation, and word usage are refinements of the handwriting act. The school develops these skills in children (because they are arbitrary standard forms accepted by the culture) in order that handwriting and reading can be more effective among peoples.

The progression of the development of handwriting skills has been shown simply on the chart in Figure 7–1. As a child progresses from the top to the bottom of this chart, a high level of intelligence is called into play. The slow learning or retarded child learns best through the use of those skills developed at the top of the chart. His ability to conceptualize and his ability to use symbols is weak; consequently he may never read or spell well.

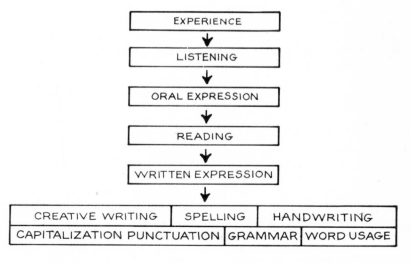

FIGURE 7–1   The progression of the development of language skills.

Most of his instruction, to be effective, must appeal to his senses and will take place at the listening–oral expression level. Bright children, on the other hand, are capable of using symbols and of dealing with concepts and symbols readily and can be taught to read, write, spell, and use language forms effectively.

The development of music ability runs parallel to the development of communication skills. It has been pointed out that infants hum tunes before they learn to speak. A little baby, placed in a bouncing chair in a room where there is a playing radio or television set, will bounce or react in some other manner to the music he hears. Obviously he is in the listening stage of communication development.

His creation of small tunes is the oral expression stage of music development, corresponding to the oral expression stage of speech only much more creative in that he does not reproduce exactly but composes fragments of sounds he has heard and already demonstrates his ability to put these fragments together into new sounds. What a shame it is that this creativeness goes undeveloped and is suppressed by teaching the child only familiar *known* tunes such as nursery rhymes and other childhood melodies. That he should build a repertoire of familiar melodies is probably necessary but not at the expense of his creative powers.

While the child is developing his conceptual ability and his ability to use symbols for use in learning to read and write, he is also developing the readiness to read and write the symbols for music. There is a music readiness period in the child's life as important as the reading readiness period of his development. He will be able to read notes, understand key signatures, and recognize all the symbolism of music only after he has an experience to which to attach it. The reading of music should never precede the experience for which the symbol stands.

Because the normal physical development of children mandates respect for certain stages of ability in children in order for them to be able to learn, the language arts and music are closely related. Earlier, Miss Hill paid respect to the normal development of the child in her lesson with the flashlights, by considering the current stage of development of the children (their age) and by planning her lesson so that the children are provided with a unique experience, during which they listen, then verbalize, then go on to see their verbalizations in written symbols (reading), and finally use the symbols in their own work (writing). This strategy was employed in the creation of the opera by Miss Black on page 211 and where she began with direct experience with words and music which were then transposed into symbols.

FIGURE 7–2   The first step in musical communication is listening.

A MUSIC-LANGUAGE EXPERIENCE

In the *Creative Teaching of the Language Arts* (Book IV of this series) other instances are given in which music and the language arts are integrated to provide the children with a creative experience. A few such experiences are reported here.[2]

Miss Norris had her sixth grade explore various possible combinations of words and music. At the Thanksgiving program the children dressed as Pilgrims and half the class recited "The Landing of the Pilgrim Fathers" by Joaquin Miller, while the other half sang and hummed "The Doxology" as a background. For other programs Miss Norris' group found the following combinations very beautiful:

Voice	*Music*
The 23rd Psalm	Singing and humming "Battle Hymn of the Republic"
"Snowbound" by Whittier	"Jingle Bells" played and sung softly
"Have You Ever Heard the Wind?" by Stevenson	An Arabesque by Debussy

2. James A. Smith, *Creative Teaching of the Language Arts in the Elementary School,* 2nd ed. (Boston: Allyn and Bacon, 1973).

Miss Norris also encouraged her children to find their own combinations.

Sharon, age 7, selected "April in Portugal" to be played as a background to the reading of her poem:

Snow

The snow falls down to the ground
Until it covers the town
It is so soft and white
And sparkles in the morning light.

Raymond, age 9, had a group of boys hum "Home on the Range" while he read:

Cowboys

I wish I were a cowboy
Riding on my horse
Slowly over the plains.

The lowing of the cattle,
The singing of the cowboys,
The feel of summer rains,

The baking sun,
The cooling breeze,
The campfire in the night,

The moon's bright light,
The friendly dog;
The feeling all is right.

Some illustrations that teachers have used to successfully develop creative thinking through the use of music and the language arts follow.

1. Play music and encourage children to describe what it says to them.

2. Encourage children to put words to popular music or music created by them.

3. Play a line of a piece of music on the piano (or a record player) and allow the class to make up words to go with it; then play the next line, etc., until they have written their own lyrics to the music.

4. Try the above in reverse. Select a theme such as "Elephants." Ask a child to tell you something about elephants. After he does, create a line of music to reflect his thinking. Then ask another

child to tell something about elephants, and so on, until a poem-song has been worked out which the entire class may say together.

> *The elephant walks heavy*
> *(heavy music)*
> *The elephant is big*
> *(loud, voluminous music)*
> *The elephant can dance*
> *(light, airy music)*
> *He'll dance us a jig*
> *(jig music)*

5. Help children to blend music and words through creative experimentation.

Miss Jarvey, a third-grade teacher, played three or four pieces of music on a record player. She then asked the class to select the one composition they considered to be the most beautiful. In this instance the children chose "Blue Star." Miss Jarvey asked each child to think what was the most beautiful thing in the world to him. When each child said he had an idea, Miss Jarvey had the children sit in a circle. In the center of the circle she placed a tape recorder and a record player. She then played "Blue Star" and recorded the opening theme on the tape recorder. Then she handed the microphone to the first child, who said, "The most beautiful thing in the world is my mother." While the child was speaking, Miss Jarvey turned down the volume of the record player. As soon as he finished, she increased the volume and passed the microphone on to the next child. When he spoke, she again decreased the volume and so on around the circle until each child had recorded his idea. In the playback she got, first of all, beautiful music, which softened when a childish voice spoke. "The most beautiful thing in the world is my mother," then swelled forth and softened again as another childish voice said, "The most beautiful thing in the world are the stars twinkling in the sky at night," and so on. This created a very effective tone poem.

Variations of the idea may be employed on all grade levels using different themes such as:

The saddest thing in the world
The loudest thing in the world
The softest thing in the world
The ugliest thing in the world

6. On some holidays tape special recordings. On Halloween, for instance, the children may create a tape on "The spookiest

thing in the world" spoken with *Danse Macabre* or *A Night on Bald Mountain.* Lincoln's Birthday can bring about the question, "What is the noblest (or most patriotic or finest) thing in the world?" recorded against military music, or "America, the Beautiful."

7. Create a mood for creative writing by playing different kinds of background music at different times while the children write.

8. Write ficticious stories about music topics such as "My Life as a Violin String," "Boom, the Drum," "Pete the Piccolo," "The Day the Flute Was Hero," and "How It Feels to Be Music."

9. Create music to show abstract symbols such as a comma, a period, a dash. Create some stories and read them but "play" the punctuation using rhythm instruments.

10. Create music bulletin boards of pictures, cartoons, and articles which appear in the local daily paper.

11. Dramatize favorite musical selections such as *Sweet Betsy from Pike, Old MacDonald Had a Farm, Yankee Doodle,* etc.

12. Create music or find appropriate music as backgrounds for radio, television, or dramatic skits.

13. Encourage children to write jingles and put them to music. Adapt this to having them write TV commercials with jingle accompaniment.

14. Take children to programs of readings where music helps supply the mood—or listen to radio programs or TV programs for the purpose of observing specifically the part that music plays in communicating the message of the program.

15. Have the children listen to music and select that which suggests various prepositions such as: up, around, into, down, by. Jerry felt "The Flight of the Bumblebee" suggested the preposition "around" and Sarah chose "The Elephant Walk" as "down" music.

16. Encourage the children to listen to music and select pieces which provide a suitable background for their own poems or prose writing as noted above.

17. Divide the class into five groups. In a bag for each group place five musical facts or objects which the children know. For instance, one sack might contain five notes. Another may contain a card with each of these symbols: a G clef, a staff, a bar, a double bar, and a note. Another might contain a harmonica, a flutophone, a bell, a triangle, and a shaker. Another might contain five songs. Each group is to do something with all the objects in the bag, and put on a skit or performance for the remainder of the class.

18. Teachers can often obtain unusual and beautiful answers

to certain questions which are appropriate to set to music and serve the purpose of demonstrating to children how music can establish moods similar to the activity suggested above. To the question, "What is sadness?" a teacher received these answers from her seven year olds:

Sadness is not going on a picnic because it rained.
Death is sadness.
Seeing my mother crying is sadness.
Losing my allowance is a sad thing.
Getting hurt when I fall off my bicycle is sadness.

One middle school group of children wrote the following poem after listing the sad things from their experiences.

What Is Sad?

Sad is a dying dog,
A mother's tears,
A stomachache.

Sad is losing a friend,
Breaking a toy,
Squashing a cake.

Sad is missing a party,
Not having been invited.
A pain you had.

Losing your picnic lunch.
Getting the measles.
These are sad!

The children decided then to read the poem as a choral piece and tape it. They chose the music "Liebestraum" to play as a musical background. This inspired many individual children in the group to write poems or short pieces of prose on such topics as "What is happy?" "What is quiet?" "What is exciting?" "What is funny?" Each child selected appropriate music to go with his writing.

The teacher then used this experience to show how the music was written so it was played joyfully, slowly, sadly, quietly, or happily. Key signatures were introduced. The class eventually used some of the children's writings to create a melody and learned how to write music on paper.

19. *Rhyming.* The teacher says, "Afraid, afraid, who's afraid?" and any child who can think of a rhyming word says it, as when Mary said in response to the above, "The maid, the maid!" The

answers can be sensible or nonsensical, whichever the class agrees they should be. Almost any sentence can be answered by a rhyming one such as: "Great, great, what is great?" "High, high, what is high?" "Down, down, what is down?" "Airy, airy, what is airy?"

This idea can further be developed by the teacher who might have a question box on her desk which she uses to phrase rhyming questions. The teacher asks, "Why is a rabbit's nose so twitchy?" and the children will invariably respond, "Maybe it's because it's itchy!"

Rhymes often suggest musical lines—the teacher may sing a jingle such as "Joy, joy, what is joy?" to an original tune or with a familiar tune such as "One, Two, Three, A-Larry" leaving the end of the phrase suspended and pointing to a child who sings in response, finishing the musical phrase.

20. Here is how one teacher used "Hickory Dickory Dock" to develop a good feeling for note value through the use of choral speaking.

Miss Nellis asked if anyone had ever seen a grandfather's clock. Teddy had, so she asked how the pendulum worked. Teddy clenched his fist and swung it through the air at arm's length like a pendulum. The children talked about the grandfather's clock, and the teacher showed a picture of one for those who had never seen one. Then Miss Nellis developed her theme as follows.

She asked the children to say the nursery rhyme in time to Teddy's swinging fist.

"What does the grandfather's clock say?" Miss Nellis then asked. "Tick Tock, Tick Tock," Teddy volunteered. "Well, let's put the tick tock into our poem," said Miss Nellis. "How will it be if this half of the class says, 'Tick tock,' while Teddy swings the pendulum and this half will say the poem. Watch me for the signal, and we'll have the tick tock begin first."

After this was done Miss Nellis asked if the children had ever heard of any other kind of clock.

"My wrist watch," Martha said.

"Listen to it and tell what it says," said Miss Nellis.

"It says tick tick-tick tick," said Martha.

"Let's put Martha's watch into our poem," said Miss Nellis. "This time these two groups will be the wrist watch, these two will be the ticking, and these two will be the poem. Watch Teddy and we will let the "tick-tick-tick-tick" go first, then the "tick tock" and then the poem. It went according to this pattern.

Group 1		*Group 2*		*Group 3*	
1	2	1	2	*1*	*2*
tick tick tick tick		*tick tock*		*Hickory Dickory Dock*	
tick tick tick tick		*tick tock*		*The mouse ran up the clock*	
tick tick tick tick		*tick tock*		*The clock struck one*	
tick tick tick tick		*tick tock*		*Down he run*	
tick tick tick tick		*tick tock*		*Hickory Dickory Dock*	

The children were delighted with the result. Miss Nellis asked for other ways they could do it. Sally suggested they all shout, "tick tock" at the end. The children were pleased at this, and Miss Nellis taped the results so the children could hear for themselves how nicely it went together.

When this same technique was used in a sixth grade, a group of boys added the sound of Big Ben as they imagined it. They were studying Great Britain, and Big Ben had been a fascinating part of their work. They sang, "bong bong" in deep chants of the group. Others clicked their tongues. One boy wanted to try to end the chant with "cuck-oo" for the cuckoo clock. All these creative ways of saying this rhyme stimulated the imaginations of the children.

It was but a step to demonstrating the speaking parts by note value such as:

Part singing was another easy step followed by working out all the beats to many choral poems and representing them on the chalkboard by notes and rests. It was but another step to the reading of note value in each bar of music.

THE LANGUAGE CONTENT OF MUSIC

Much of the content of music is at the finger tips of the teacher in the form of materials written by the children. This material is meaningful and relevant to them and can often be used for teaching music facts or for composing music. Children write about everything, as the following material indicates.

In many elementary schools a great deal of emphasis is currently being placed on creative writing. The illustrations of children's writing below demonstrate in another way the inherent ability and need of children to express themselves through harmony and rhythm. Writing for children by children is a sure-fire way to make music a personal thing for each child.

Mrs. Carter's children wrote about nature. The words of these children practically suggest the type of music to be sung as accompaniment.

In April's Sweet Month

In April's sweet month,
When leaves begin to spring,
Little lambs skip like fairies,
And birds build and sing.

LINDA, *Grade 3*

Little Wind

Little wind, blow on the hill top;
Little wind, blow down the plain;
Little wind, blow up the sunshine;
Little wind, blow off the rain.

LINDA, *Grade 3*

Nature

Nature is forest,
Forest has trees.
Trees grow tall,
Some small.
Trees have big leaves
And branches,
That stretch from here to there.
Trees are beautiful,
Aren't they?

Nature is wildlife,
Such as bear and deer.
Birds and bees in the flowers and trees,
Fish in the water,
Rabbits in the holes,
Woodpeckers pecking big holes.
Nature is beautiful,
Isn't it?

FIGURE 7–3   Puppets can be a great motivating force in teaching music appreciation and music facts.

That is nature.
Nature is beautiful,
Isn't it?

KENNETH, *Grade 6*

Mr. Farley made a collection of poems by his children with the coming of holidays. The class used these poems to create appropriate holiday music.

On Halloween Night

On Halloween night, what a fright!
The witches were stirring their brew
The black cats were purring while
The witches were stirring
And the goblins jumped up and yelled, "Boo!"

Thanksgiving

The Pilgrims sailed across the sea
Because they wanted to be free
To worship God in their own way.
Their first year was good
So they thought they should
Have a First Thanksgiving Day.

Our Christmas Tree

Our Christmas tree is small
But it makes us feel so gay—
We're waiting one and all
For that happy Christmas day.

Memorial Day

Oh, Tom, it's time for the parade!
So don't be late,
Memorial Day
Is for the great.
Now we honor the army, navy, and marines
Who fought in those bloody battle scenes.
May 30th is the date,
For those heroes strong and great.

DONALD, *Grade 6*

Mothers

Mothers are
  Very kind and sweet,
  Clean and neat,
  Helpful in all ways
Mothers are
  Wonderful, pretty, and nice,
  Sometimes afraid of mice
  Soft and delicate sometimes
Mothers are
  Always ready to help you,
  Maybe angry, too
  Nice to have around
Mothers are
  Always on the go,
  Never, never slow
  Thoughtful and considerate
Oh, what would we do without mothers?

BARBARA, *Grade 5*

Children like to write about the seasons. These poems can become the lyrics to little tunes picked out on marimbas, tuned glasses, the piano, the metallophone, flutophone, or autoharp.

FIGURE 7–4   Musical sounds are explored to create a taped background for Where the Wild Things Are.

Fall

Fall means a change of things.
Birds fly South and use their wings.
The chestnuts ripen on the trees.
We see the autumn-colored leaves.

MARCIA, *Grade 2*

Raindrops

I looked out the window today.
My eyes felt all shiny and gay.
Raindrops falling down
All over town
Splitter, splatter, plitter, platter
Just listen to them spatter.

GRADE 1

The Telephone

When you're at home,
You use the telephone.
You use it all the time
But when away, it costs a dime
When your parents say,
Get off that phone right away!
Because I must make a call,
To the town's City Hall.
And when teen-agers get a hold of it
They never shall let go of it
To get them off, you must strive and strive
In case that an emergency might arrive.

MILLICENT, *Grade 5*

Mr. Hilton had his children write myths to which he had them add musical sound effects. The results were fun for the children and developed good listening habits as well.

Why It Rains

Long, long ago, long before your grandmother or your great-grandmother was born, a beautiful lady reigned the heavens. No where was there a more lovely woman than she. She was called Lady Esther.

One day Lady Esther was walking in her garden. She saw a little box with curious markings all over it. Quietly she picked up the box, put it in her pocket and walked on.

When she got home she put the box on her dresser. Then she dressed for the sky banquet. She forgot the box for a minute. Suddenly she remembered it. She approached the box and touched it. Strangely, it seemed wet.

She opened it and much to her surprise, a funny little imp on springs jumped out. It made humorous noises. She laughed and laughed and laughed till tears came to her eyes. She cried and cried it was so funny. Every time she remembers it now she laughs and laughs till tears come to her eyes. They form our rain.

*It looks like rain now so I had better stop my story lest I
get wet.*

PETER, *Age 10*

When I Was Water

*Once upon a time I was in a creek. I was the famous
water. They called me spring water. I ran in a big pond. I
had fun pushing the fish round.*

*But when winter came I froze. Three men cut me up.
One sawed me. The other carried me. I was ordered by a
customer. They put me in an ice box. I melted minute by
minute. I ran through the bottom of the ice box, and on the
floor and out the door, back into the creek, and lived happy
since then.*

JOSEPH, *Grade 6*

SUMMARY

Music should be taught to give joy to life and to help man express his emotions. But it plays another important function in
his life style. It serves as a tool to help him solve problems, to
give vent to his feelings, and to help him learn. From the beginning of life, music is present in the development of children.
The development of communication skills and the development
of music skills run parallel and are closely interrelated. The
children's own music and writing can well serve as content for a
school music program. Both music and language can be utilized
to develop the creative communication ability of children.

TO THE COLLEGE STUDENT AND THE TEACHING TEAM

1. In light of the discussion in this chapter do you think that
   creative products in the elementary classroom can be graded
   with letter or number grades? Discuss this.
2. Take some of the poems your students write and encourage
   them to put them to music; or better yet, try putting some of
   your own to music.
3. After children write poems, encourage them to choose an
   appropriate recording to serve as a musical background
   while each reads his poem to the class.
4. Encourage the children to select music to serve as a background for a choral speaking exercise.

5. Take the vocabulary being studied by any particular group of children (spelling words, vocabulary chart words, etc.) and have the children find a rhythm instrument that denotes the character of each word. Example: *tickle* (a quick rapping on the triangle); *erase* (swishing of sand blocks); *regal* (pompous crash of a bar on the cymbals).

6. Collect picturesque speech from current magazines. Print it on cards or on the chalkboard and encourage other students in your classes, or the children with whom you work, to make up musical phrases from rhythm or musical instruments which sound like the picturesque speech or which will accompany it when read. Tape some of these.

7. A regular source of creative ideas for teaching the language arts and music is the *Sesame Street Magazine* published in October, December, February, and April (North Road, Poughkeepsie, New York 13601). Even if children cannot view this program the magazine is worthy of study.

8. Put a word or phrase on the chalkboard and have each member of the class write a musical metaphor or simile about it. Fold the papers and put them in a box. Then have everyone draw one out and read it to the rest of the class. How many *different* ideas were created? Group creativity is generally the more productive kind.

9. How acute is your listening? Have members of the class number from 1 to 10 on a piece of paper. Behind a screen, pluck or play a note or two on many rhythm or melody instruments. Can the class members identify the instrument? (Slip in a few notes from a music box for fun.)

10. Statements for discussion:
    a. Individual creativity is practically dying out in lieu of group creativity.
    b. The mass media have pretty much dictated the musical tastes of most of America.
    c. Marginal listening (listening to one thing while other sounds are present in the background) is not very effective and is detrimental to children's listening habits.
    d. Marginal listening is rarely an effective type of listening.
    e. There must be music readiness in children just as there is reading readiness. In fact, the requirements for reading ability and music ability are similar.

SELECTED BIBLIOGRAPHY

Anderson, Rhea, Lucille Minshall, and Iris Tracy Comfort. "How to Teach Better Listening." *N.E.A. Elementary Instructional Service Leaflet.* Washington, D.C.: National Education Association, 1962.

Applegate, Mauree. *Helping Children Write*. Evanston, Ill.: Row, Peterson, 1954.

Arnstein, Flora J. *Children Write Poetry: A Creative Approach*. New York: Dover Publications, 1967.

Bamman, Henry J., Mildred A. Dawson, and Robert J. Whitehead. *Oral Interpretation of Children's Literature*. Dubuque, Iowa: William C. Brown, 1964.

Bellack, Arno A., et al. *The Language of the Classroom*. New York: Teachers College Press, 1967.

Benward, Bruce. *Sightsinging Complete*. Dubuque, Iowa: William C. Brown, 1965.

Berkowitz, Sol, Gabriel Fontrier, and Leo Kraft. *A New Approach to Sight Singing*. New York: W. W. Norton, 1960.

Burns, Paul C., and Alberta L. Lowe. *The Language Arts in Childhood Education*. Chicago: Rand McNally, 1966.

Byrne, Margaret. *The Child Speaks*. New York: Harper, 1965.

Calder, Clarence R., Jr., and Eleanor M. Antan. *Techniques and Activities to Stimulate Verbal Learning*. New York: Macmillan, 1970.

Canfield, Robert. "How Useful Are Lessons for Listening?" *The Elementary School Journal*, vol. 62 (December, 1961), pp. 147–151.

Carroll, E. Reed (Ed.) *Learning of Language*. New York: Appleton-Century-Crofts, 1971.

Chambers, Dewey W. *Children's Literature in the Curriculum*. Chicago: Rand McNally, 1971.

Cullinan, Bernice E. *Literature for Children: Its Discipline and Content*. Dubuque, Iowa: William C. Brown, 1971.

Cullum, Albert. *Push Back the Desks*. New York: Citation Press, 1968.

Greene, Harry A., and Walter T. Petty. *Developing Language Skills in the Elementary Schools*, 4th ed. Boston: Allyn and Bacon, 1971.

Hermann, Edward J. *Supervising Music in the Elementary School*. Englewood Cliffs, N.J.: Prentice-Hall, 1965.

Lewis, Richard. *Journeys: Prose by Children of the English Speaking World*. New York: Simon and Schuster, 1969.

————. *Miracles*. New York: Simon and Schuster, 1966. (Poems by children of the English-speaking World.)

Luck, James. *Creative Music for the Classroom Teacher*. New York: Random House, Alfred A. Knopf, 1971.

Lundsteen, Sara W. "Language Arts in the Elementary School." In *Teaching for Creative Endeavor*, W. B. Michael (Ed.) Bloomington: Indiana University Press, 1968.

Powell, Brian. *English Through Poetry Writing.* Itasca, Ill.: F. E. Peacock, 1968.

Rasmussen, Carie. *Speech Methods in the Elementary School.* New York: Ronald Press, 1962.

Reasoner, Charles F. *Releasing Children to Literature.* New York: Dell, 1968.

Smith, Brooks E., Kenneth S. Goodman, and Robert Meredith. *Language and Thinking in the Elementary School,* Chapter IV, "Language in Communication," pp. 189–246. Boston: Allyn and Bacon, 1971.

Smith, James A. *Creative Teaching of the Language Arts in the Elementary School,* 2nd ed. Boston: Allyn and Bacon, 1973.

CHAPTER VIII

Music and the Social Studies

The objective of world peace is dependent to a very great extent upon an understanding of other cultures in addition to our own. Music is an integral part of all cultures and the hopes, fears, aspirations, and beliefs of various ethnic groups are often expressed through their folk music. Complete understanding of these peoples cannot be achieved unless all aspects of their cultures, including music, are included in the units of study taught in the schools.

—ROBERT L. GARRETSON[1]

INTRODUCTION

The authors recently visited a fourth-grade classroom where the children had been studying Indians. They had listed the names of the following tribes on the chalkboard: Chocktau, Chickawa, Cheekau, Sioux, Iroquois, Seneca, Mohawk, and Chu.

When one young fellow started to read the names, he exclaimed with a start, "Hey, you can't read those names like that —you have to sing them."

His discovery resulted in a delightful song composed of the names of the Indian tribes. Read the lines again and see what he meant. Add to them and create an Indian song of your own. This experience proved to be a remotivation to the unit and resulted in a culminating activity which included Indian songs and chants based on the authentic characteristics of each culture.

1. Robert L. Garretson, *Music in Childhood Education* (New York: Appleton-Century-Crofts, 1966), p. 4.

FIGURE 8–1   Music is an integral part of life.

MUSIC AND THE SOCIAL STUDIES

Educators use the terms *integration, correlation,* and *fusion* to refer to the combination of subject matter. Regardless of the name applied, it is important to use all our resources to help children better understand and develop a feeling for the particular subject being considered. This offers a great opportunity to all teachers to include a great deal of music in the curriculum. It is interesting to note students have sometimes been known to accept and enjoy music if it is included in the context of another subject matter area more readily than when it is confined to the music period. One college class, for example, readily accepted a variety of compositions from the classical and baroque periods in an art class but seemed unimpressed when introduced to similar compositions during the music class.

There have been many instances that show that students do enjoy seeing a relationship between subject areas. Perhaps the fact that someone other than the music teacher finds music worth the time adds interest to the experience.

It is more important to help children develop a feeling for the people of the world than for mere facts about them. How can this occur unless the music is included when learning about a country? Music is called a universal language, as it expresses the emotions and feelings about the people, but the people of each country express these feelings and emotions in a way peculiar to it. The instruments and the scale vary from one part of the world to another. Contrast, for example, the Queen's Own Band of London and the Gamelin (the oriental orchestra, made up of bells, gongs, flutes, drums, etc.) of Indonesia. They are completely different yet each is suited to its environment. Hearing each helps one feel better acquainted with the people it represents.

MUSIC AND HISTORY

Music and history are a natural combination. Picture the time of George Washington, with women in long dresses with many petticoats and men in velvets, brocades, and laces dancing the minuet to music played by stringed instruments and the delicate tones of the harpsichord. Now contrast this with mini-skirted girls and long-haired boys dancing to our modern bands of drums, saxophones, flutes, electric guitars, and brass instruments. Each period of history could be introduced with the music of the period. One class illustrated the difference by dancing the minuet as it was done in Washington's time and then as it would be done today. This led to a comparison that added excitement and interest to the area of study as well as a better understanding of each period.

Small children often study the community—first the school, the neighborhood, the town, the county, the state, and then the nation. How many times do we go beyond the postman and the fireman to include cultural groups in the community? How many church choirs are there in the community that could be tapped? Is there a community choir or orchestra? Are there dance groups? Do concert artists visit the area? What ethnic groups are dominant in the community? Did these people bring their songs and dances with them? Could we learn them? Do we know their songs? What about our own room? Could we learn a song our grandmother or grandfather sang?

Not all these ideas can or should be adapted to all situations, but perhaps out of these some could be used to help children better understand and develop a deeper feeling for people and for history. Sometimes the teacher will create the opportunity for including music in this way, if there is a hesitancy to sing or dance on the part of the children. Special teachers, parents, older students: all can be used as resource people to assist in the music approach to the curriculum. The topics where social studies and music provide intermotivation do not need to be related always to the past.

Without integrating music in the school curriculum it is very difficult to understand how a majority of the songs can be understood or appreciated. Ethnic music is what it is because of the peculiar situations in which it was born. The terrain and geography of the country or area are in it, the history of the people is in it, the clothing worn at the time it was written dictates its tempo to a great degree, the materials in the environment determine to some degree which instruments could be made to create the sounds. Children will understand the reasons for the differences in an Irish jig, a Bavarian folk dance, a Russian boat song, and a Spanish flamingo dance when they understand the country itself and the character of the people produced by that country.

A Unit on Pollution

Following is an account of a unit on pollution which was carried out by a fourth grade. It is an excellent example, showing how social studies lessons provided the context for music experiences over a period of time, and how music in turn was used to enrich the social studies curriculum.

In this particular fourth grade, the topic of pollution first came before the class in an article about litter in the weekly newspaper. A discussion about the article brought about an awareness of the seriousness of it. The children soon brought in clippings, pictures, and cartoons from the local newspapers and current periodicals. A lively interest in all pollution in general resulted, and a concern over the dangerous effects on our health and our future lives.

The children divided the main topic into three categories: air, earth, and water pollution, and read widely to identify the causes, effects, and some of the remedial measures now being developed and used to combat the deadly and far-reaching effects of pollution. The children became alerted to their own local problems caused by a fast growing population, the tremendous increase in cars and trucks on the highways, increased industrial production with its waste disposal problems, and the deplorable condition of their own once beautiful lake.

A group of boys made a very beautiful and effective bulletin board bearing the caption POLLUTION IS EVERYWHERE! The children learned the meaning and spelling of many new words. Science was studied in many ways: causes of pollution, the normal life in water, purification processes, waste disposal systems, sewage disposal, nonpolluting exhaust systems, values of top soil, types of soil, pollen counts, air pollution measurement, atomic-generated electricity versus coal-made electricity, comparisons of various pollution producing industries, etc.

Geography was studied in discussions of local topography and a study of various topological maps, in soil erosion and conservation, in determining causes for river pollution and in studying water flow and the formation of valleys, islands, and deltas. The greatest pollution areas of the country were located. Even pollution in outer space was investigated.

A study of history was necessary to learn the reasons for the beginnings of the problems and what had been done about them down through the years.

Mathematics was studied in many ways: in taking pollution counts and pollen counts, in measuring distances to determine the widespread effect of pollution caused by one city, in measuring the depth of water, in measuring heights of air, and longitude and latitude.

Art was used constantly in this project and the art teacher became an important member of the teaching team. Pollution booklets were made with covers done in print processes, a mural was made from junk collected on an after-school junk drive, bulletin boards were made throughout the school, various types of printing were taught, and costumes were made for the final play and the videotape.

The teachers introduced the children to modern "electric" sounds and new musical sounds which might well serve as background music to pollution reports and for the final play. Songs about pollution were found and sung. As part of the history aspect of the unit, children collected songs from the past that they felt told the pollution story of then and now. Some children wrote parodies that accentuated the pollution problem. Such songs as "America the Beautiful," "God Bless America," and Kilmer's "Trees," were especially good for this satire. One parody on "America the Beautiful" appears on page 246.

Oh miserable are the foggy skies,
Rotting the fields of grain.
Lost is the mountains majesty
In smog above the plains
America, America
How did this come to be?
Sewage, litter, filth, and waste
From sea to shining sea.

One parody on "Trees" was submitted by an older boy who came to help with the scenery:

I think my child shall never see
An elm, that stately handsome tree
An elm where you can hang a swing
An elm whose shade can make you sing.
An elm that looks to God all day
And raises leafy arms to pray.
An elm who may in summer wear
Elm beetles running in its hair.
Elms which die from beetles there
And neglect by man—and lack of care
Poems are made by fools like me,
Fools who exterminate the elm tree.

At the close of the unit the children decided with their teachers to share their findings and their work and to alert the rest of the school to the dangers of the problem, by creating a play which told about the past, present, and future of pollution. The three-act play which resulted was completely original. The children worked in groups to write skits, make costumes and scenery, and to compose or adapt music selections to the text. Four original songs resulted. The music teacher was called in to serve in a consulting capacity to work out the melodies. The songs were used between acts to tie the skits together and for the finale. The final production was so effective that the school's audiovisual department made a videotape of it, and it was shown over a local television station. Pictures and an article also appeared in a local newspaper.

Following are the words to the songs created by the children.

Pollution

Dirty clouds floating by,
from the factory up so high,
If you're polluted stay away,
Show the sun and let it stay.

The waters turn a slimy green,
The fish no longer fill the stream.
Fishing's just a long lost dream,
The rivers look like shaving cream.

Don't throw that garbage all around,
Please keep pollution off the ground,
We want to keep our cities clean,
Also our rivers, lakes, and streams.

Pollution Limericks

There once was a man from Lulution,
Who started the theme of pollution.
He lighted a fire,
And threw in a tire,
That selfish old man from Lulution.

There once was a city named Bog,
Which was always full of smog.
The air was so thick,
It made everyone sick,
That smoggy old city named Bog.

There once was a city named Perth,
That started this nonsense on Earth
They put waste in the water,
And smoke in the sky,
And now we're stuck with it, you and I.

There was an old man named Ritter,
Who threw around lots of litter,
He made such a mess,
He made people protest,
The thoughtless man named Ritter.

A young hippie who sang a sad song,
Knew the way that he lived was so wrong.
When he changed his old ways,
He found that it pays,
Good luck and good friends came along.

There once was a fellow named Sandy
Who always ate lots of candy.
He threw scraps all around,
Till he covered the ground
As a litterbug he was a dandy!

Pollution

What have you got to say for yourselves?
What have you got to show?
The world's turning into a giant dump
And you should feel pretty low.

The garbage that's scattered all over the world
The trash that's always knee deep
The litter that's in the lakes
Some nights I can't even sleep.

If everyone in the whole wide world
Took a rake, a shovel, and a mop,
A pail of water, some soap and all,
We'd clean the world of its slop.

Maybe it's not that easy,
It takes plenty of elbow grease;
So all together let's pitch right in,
Pollution, we hope, will decrease.

Litter Song (The grand finale)

(Sung to the tune of
"If Everyone Lighted Just One Little Candle.")

If everyone dropped just one little paper
What a mess our land would be!
If everyone made just one bit of litter,
Soon a mountain you would see.
It's everyone's responsibility to keep America litter free.
If everyone threw just one little paper,
What a sight our world would be!

If everyone picked up just one little paper,
What a great help it would be!
If everyone joined in the fight against litter,
A much cleaner world you'd see.
It's everyone's responsibility to keep America litter free.
If everyone cleaned just one little corner,
What a bright world this would be!

The illustrations of the trip to the farm and the Halloween story in Chapter III are two illustrations of the manner in which social studies may be used as content for the teaching of music in the primary grades.

In both these illustrations, children are using music to help them communicate. The teachers are helping them discover that music is essential to living and that life is enriched through its use. At the same time children are learning to create and grow and develop toward using and enjoying music as we hope every adult will.

There have been many other illustrations throughout this book in which social studies serves as a content for music experiences. A few other experiences are told below, but they by no means exhaust the possibilities.

A Unit on Mexico

One group of children who studied Mexico experienced a great many interesting music activities as a result of their interest. Some are listed here to show how the immediate interests of the children can provide rich subject matter for musical experiences if the teacher capitalizes on them.

1.   The class learned to sing some Mexican songs (some in parts) such as "Buy My Tortillas," "Celito Lindo," "The Pearl," "The Samba," and "The Dove."

2.   They made up and learned some Mexican dances (e.g., The Hat Dance) to go with the songs.

3.   The class learned to sing some songs in Spanish: "Pala-pala," "The Samba."

4.   The class became interested in the origin and rhythm of Spanish music. As a result of this, they played many recordings of Spanish music.

5.   The class became interested in the opera *Carmen*. They read the children's version and played the music from *Carmen* on the record player. They planned and took a trip to see *Carmen* presented by a traveling opera company. They divided into committees and watched a performance of *Carmen* on television.

6.   They made an exhibit of musical instruments peculiar to the Spanish influence. They made some castanets from nut shells and they made tambourines from ice cream container tops and bells.

7.   They learned some ancient Aztec songs and created an Aztec dance in costume.

8.   They learned to conga and samba and listened to the music of Xavier Cugat.

9.   They learned to play some Mexican songs on the fluto-phone, and they wrote and set to music some songs on Mexico.

10.   They used Mexican music and dances in the program that they presented to the rest of the school in the manner of a fiesta.

FIGURE 8–2   A musical presentation of an original Charlie Brown story.

These rich musical experiences were possible only because the children had been skillfully introduced and guided into a whole new world of unknown experiences. No predetermined course of study could have produced such a variety and wealth of experiences with as much meaning to each child. These experiences greatly enrich the life of each child and the technique used in developing these experiences built positive values and attitudes about music.

To Holland Through Music

As a result of a study on Holland and Germany, Mr. Cooper introduced his fifth-year students in the middle school to the music of Humperdinck. All of them had read *Hansel and Gretel* as young children but their interest was completely renewed when they heard the music Humperdinck had written for the opera. After reading the story again and hearing the music, the children asked if they could present the opera.

Plans were made. On a large chart before the classroom the children made a summary of each scene and the action to take place. Committees of children then wrote the scenes. "Production numbers" were planned for the musical selections, especially "Brother Come and Dance with Me," which dictates the dance steps. The children made scenery and costumes. The music teacher was called in for a period of several days to teach the songs and to work with soloists for those numbers requiring special treatment. The shop teacher showed one committee how to make scenery flats. The home economics teacher helped with the simple costumes, and the art teacher helped with the scenery and advertising posters.

Excellent opportunities were afforded for the use of brainstorming techniques in planning the action during the musical numbers. One knotty problem which plagued the children was how to produce "The Children's Prayer" scene with the fourteen angels appearing. In a brainstorming session, several ideas were suggested. A combination of some resulted in a very effective number which demonstrated well the creative ability of fifth-year children. Hansel and Gretel are in the forest, and Hansel tells Gretel to go to sleep. The lights dim. A soft spotlight is on the two children. Hansel yawns and stretches as the music softly comes from the orchestra. Gretel, too, falls asleep. The words to the song begin and Hansel sits on his knees to sing them.

Behind the children is a cheesecloth curtain made by the children. Trees are on the edges of the stage. Their leaves extend across the top, but the center is plain blue. A light comes up on Gretel. Then, as the line "Fourteen angels watch do keep," is sung, two children, unseen by the audience, take their places behind the cheesecloth curtain. They are wearing cardboard wings covered with gold glitter and a gold piece of tinsel around their heads with a star on the forehead. As the line "Two my right hand guardeth" is sung the children snap on flashlights concealed in their folded hands yet tilted in such a way as to light the upper part of their bodies, giving the illusion that they are floating in air. As each line is sung, two more flashlights go on until all fourteen angels, standing at different levels on chairs, appear to float in the sky. The total effect was beautiful.

INTEGRATING THE CURRICULUM

This volume presents many other illustrations as to how the social studies may be used as the content for the music program. There are also many examples showing how social studies may be taught through the use of music.

Children learn best when material is related. Long ago research showed this statement to be a fact, and it has never been disproved. Yet, strange things happen in public schools when children become the victims of organizational plans. As a case in point, the authors visited a middle school classroom where children were grouped for instruction. This school claimed to have team teaching. Actually, there was very little team planning among the teachers. The one child whom we followed through the day was exposed to the following topics:

Stocks and Bonds (Mathematics)
Personification (English)
American Jazz (Music)
Drug Abuse (Health)
Volleyball (Physical Education)

Real planning would result in some correlation among the above areas. The great music and dances of Early Americans could have been taught in a true team teaching situation. Inasmuch as the social studies often provide the core for content studies, a real team learning situation might be induced if teachers would team to teach across subject matter areas rather than within them. Music could be a meaningful part of this particular child's day if he had studied the songs of the West in music periods to go along with his studies of the westward movement. He might have listened to some of the "Westward Ho" songs. How much more meaningful the day could have been if he had then danced some of the folk dances of the West in his physical education class, or learned some of the folk dances taken west by the early settlers. If the English teacher felt she had to teach personification at this time, what better way to go about it than to have children write creative stories in which they imagined they were horses pulling the wagons going west. Or, the untouched prairie, the cactus flowers, the mountains. Playing music such as "Casey Jones" might have been a motivation and imagining they were driving the spikes for the railroad joining the country or the first train to cross the country.

It is difficult to imagine adults without music as a part of their lives in many forms throughout every day. The schools should teach it this way.

SUMMARY

The social studies curriculum of the elementary school deals with those areas that show man's relationship to man: history, politics, anthropology, sociology, geography, and civics. Many scholars feel that music rightfully belongs in this area for much of man's relationship is communicated through music; in fact it has been called the only international language yet in existence. Surely music can be an aid in developing world understanding among nations. Music presents all races and creeds, all socio-economic levels, and all degrees of cultural sophistication with its best foot forward. Man, through his music, is seen as an intelligent human being and this is exhibited through his creative efforts.

TO THE COLLEGE STUDENT AND THE TEACHING TEAM

1. Observe carefully and draw the attention of your college classmates to really outstanding creative products of current interest in your environment. Notice especially creative television shows, cartoons, musicals, dramas, musical compositions, types of architecture, editorials, short stories, paintings, etc. Keep the bulletin board in your classroom full of examples of truly creative work.

2. Teachers can set conditions for developing creativity simply by the things they say. An example of this is shown in Manuel Barkan's *Through Art to Creativity* (Boston: Allyn and Bacon, 1960). Read it and observe carefully how creative teachers employ this skill.

3. Which songs can be taught with the units you teach at your grade level? Lists in Chapter 10 may be of help to you.

4. Examine your plan of classroom organization for the school day and consider these questions: At what times during the school day does my plan best allow for creative development through the use of music? At what times during my school day do I use music as a tool?

5. How can teaching by machines be creative?

6. Mrs. Wylie is a fifth-grade teacher. She believes children must know the facts presented in the social studies text. Her social studies periods consist of having the children open their books to the topic under study and then read to find answers to the questions she poses. Each day she gives a review test (written or oral) on the facts of the previous day's lesson. Mrs. Wylie's children know the names of all the states and their capitals, the population of each state, the major rivers and watersheds in the United States, the countries of South America, and a whole bookful of dates. What is good about Mrs. Wylie's system of teaching? What is poor about it?

7. Planning a unit of work is essential before teaching it. Some reasons are listed below:

    a.   Education is a selective process. The teacher must know what (from all the information available on each topic) is suitable for use with her group.

    b.   The teacher must have an awareness of the subject matter of the unit so she can guide children in finding it and can check the authenticity with which they report it.

    c.   The teacher must have goals and objectives in mind for herself and for individuals. This does not mean that the children will not also have objectives of their own; it does mean the teacher may have some objectives the children do not have.

    d.   The teacher must know the resources available in the school and in the community in order to fulfill her objectives.

    e.   The teacher must be able to organize a large body of material into workable form, including the appropriate music experiences.

    List some other reasons why planning ahead of time is necessary. Try planning a unit to teach to a classroom of children you have recently observed; or, better yet, if you plan to do your student teaching soon, plan a unit to teach to your own group. Search for all the music experiences which can be included in your unit.

8.   In a rural community, an intelligent but uneducated farmer came to school at the invitation of his fifth-grade son to attend the culminating activity of a unit that was a dramatization and exhibit on Alaska. In the exhibit was a great deal of music written by the children. He made this comment, "I don't see why Harry has to spend so much time in school foolin' around with music—he ain't ever goin' to be no musician—he's goin' to work on my farm. Seems to me you folks waste a lot of time and tax money lettin' kids fool around with all this music."

    How would you defend your program to this taxpayer? Does his comment indicate the need for an adult education program?

9.   If you could wave a magic wand and have the ideal social studies program you want in your school, what would it be? The ideal music program?

10.   Various psychologists have observed these traits in creative children: a willingness to take a calculated risk, an ability to sense and question the implicit, a capacity to be puzzled, an openness to the seemingly irrational in himself, considerable sensitivity and exuberance, and a greater acceptance of himself than is the norm. How do you regard the children in your class who possess these traits? Do you value them or consider them problems?

11. How could you have your students create a musical poem called "The City" without using musical instruments? "The Country?"

12. Make lists of the contemporary songs which reflect aspects of man's life on this earth: for example, some of the music from *West Side Story* to depict city life; the bicycle song from *Butch Cassidy and the Sundance Kid* ("Raindrops Keep Falling on My Head"); and "The Age of Aquarius" from *Hair*.

SELECTED BIBLIOGRAPHY

Chase, Linwood, and Martha Tyler John. *A Guide for the Elementary Social Studies Teacher*, 2nd ed. Boston: Allyn and Bacon, 1972.

Cléments, H. M., W. R. Fielder, and B. R. Tabachnick. *Social Study: Inquiry in Elementary Classrooms.* Indianapolis: Bobbs-Merrill, 1966.

Cutts, Norma E., and Nicholas Moseley. *Providing for Individual Differences in the Elementary School.* Englewood Cliffs, N.J.: Prentice-Hall, 1960.

Gardner, J. W. *Self-Renewal.* New York: Harper and Row, 1964.

Gillespie, Margaret C., and A. Gray Thompson. *Social Studies for Living in a Multi-Ethnic Society: A Unit Approach.* Columbus, Ohio: Charles E. Merrill, 1972.

Jarolimek, John. *Social Studies in Elementary Education*, 3rd ed. New York: Macmillan, 1967.

Merritt, Edith. *Working with Children in the Social Studies.* San Francisco: Wadsworth, 1961.

Michaelis, John. *Social Studies for Children in a Democracy*, 4th ed. Englewood Cliffs, N.J.: Prentice-Hall, 1968.

Miel, Alice. *Creativity in Teaching.* Belmont, Calif.: Wadsworth, 1961.

Smith, James A. *Creative Teaching of the Social Studies in the Elementary School.* Boston: Allyn and Bacon, 1968.

Torrance, E. Paul. *Education and the Creative Potential.* Englewood Cliffs, N.J.: Prentice-Hall, 1963.

————. *Guiding Creative Talent.* Englewood Cliffs, N.J.: Prentice-Hall, 1962.

————. *Role of Evaluation in Creative Thinking.* University of Minnesota, Bureau of Educational Research, 1964.

CHAPTER IX

Music with Math and Science

Music hath charms to soothe the savage breast, to soften rocks, or bend a knotted oak.

—WILLIAM CONGREVE[1]

INTRODUCTION

Educators sometimes view science and mathematics at opposite ends of the curriculum continuum from music. But music is created through the combination of the elements of music (melody, rhythm, and harmony) plus its expressive qualities. The study of both science and mathematics tends to help the individual better understand these basic elements.

Before you read this chapter, list all the ways you can think of to teach science through music. Mathematics?

MUSIC THROUGH MATHEMATICS

The relationship between music and mathematics is obvious when we, as teachers, begin to work with time signatures and music notation. Creative approaches to music imply a wide range of experiences that will be used to inspire learnings among children.

1. *The Mourning Bride.* Act 1, Scene 1.

In exploring the meaning of numbers, for instance, the concept of the octave may be included in developing the meaning of the number 8. In teaching the meaning of a musical scale a teacher can compare the scale to units that measure weight and distance with the intervals being a unit of measurement of music much as inches are units of measure of length or distance.

Garretson states, "Comprehension of the concept of the bottom number in the meter signature representing the type of beat note, is dependent upon the group's understanding of the actual names of the notes, their symbols and the mathematical relationship between them. Often this relationship, based upon fractions, does not become clear until the fourth grade."[2] He goes on to state that in teaching by analogy, the whole note may be compared to a dollar, the half note to a half dollar, and the quarter note to a quarter.

Miss Austin and Miss Farr, a music teacher and a classroom teacher, collaborated on fusing several music and mathematics lessons when Miss Austin was introducing fractions to her group. They felt the fractions used in writing time signatures would be of special significance to the children because of the many creative experiences they had been having with music. Up to this time they had created music and recorded it largely by color; now Miss Farr felt they were ready for time signatures.

Miss Farr had the children beat out rhythms and time with hands, voices, and homemade and commercial rhythm instruments. On one occasion she had used flashlights as a technique for showing the rhythms of various pieces of music on the walls of the room, much the same as Miss Hill did on page 78. The children had responded so well to the flashlights and had enjoyed them so much that the two teachers decided to use them again for the development of fraction concepts.

The two teachers listed their objectives as follows: As a result of this lesson, the children will learn:

1. The relationship of accent to the top number of the time signature fraction.
2. The basic beat of the music dictated by the time signature fraction.
3. The meaning of the lower number of the time signature.
4. The manner in which rhythmic patterns are notated in music.

2. P. L. Garretson, *Music for Elementary Teachers* (New York: Appleton-Century-Crofts, 1966), p. 187.

The "lesson" was really a whole afternoon of enjoyment and learning and proceded much in the same fashion as Miss Hill's lesson.

It was but a step to change the note patterns on the chalkboard to time signatures. In fact, when Miss Farr introduced the bars of music showing the time signatures for the selections played, the children volunteered the information below.

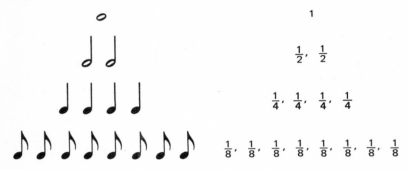

From this exercise the following facts about *math* became obvious and provided the teachers the opportunity to show that the *math* concept is not always a musical concept.

$$1 = 2/2, 4/4, 8/8$$

$$2/4 = 4/8 = 1/2$$

$$1/4 = 2/8$$

$$3/4 = 6/8$$

Also, the manner in which a fraction is written took on meaning such as ¾ means that there are 3 notes to a measure and a quarter-note gets one beat.

Miss Farr was careful to point out to the children that the situation with which they were working was a *specific* case and that all their learnings were not absolute. Note values are relative. For example, a quarter-note does not always receive one beat. The children looked through music books to find instances when this was demonstrated.

Exercises in constructing possible combinations for various measures gave the children some meaningful drill. Later, they enjoyed translating their written combinations into sound by using percussion instruments and/or clapping and stamping.

For instance, a bar in ¾ time may legitimately look like any of the following patterns.

$$\frac{3}{4} = \;\; \text{♩♩♩} \;|\; \text{♩♩♩} \;|\; \text{♩♩♫♩} \;|\; \text{♩.} \;|\; \text{♫♫♫♫} \;|$$

The mathematics of music may be dramatized in the use of musical terminology and the manner in which numbers help to "fix" musical truths in such phrases as scale, lines, spaces, octave, sharps, flats, accent, measure, beat, cut time, range, and many others.

MUSIC THROUGH SCIENCE

Since music exists because of sound, every child needs somewhere in his early years to experience sound in many experimental situations.

Science units in sound can help children enormously in understanding the function and potential of all musical instruments. An understanding of the instrument helps a child to play it with greater ease and with better care.

What makes sound? How do the pleasant as well as the irritating sounds of the world come to be? What makes a sound such as writing with a hard chalk on a chalkboard "get on our nerves" while the sound of wind chimes or a baby's laugh is "delightful"?

The origins of sound are, of course, a science—a science studied and learned by man even thousands of years ago. Although musical sounds were probably discovered by accident and random experimentation on the part of primitive man, he learned how to make various sounds and effects realitively soon in his history. Consequently each sound in music has a history worth exploring: Each instrument has a unique potential for historical exploration.

To fully appreciate musical instruments, orchestration, ensemble music, symphonies, jazz bands, rock groups, and the like the history of the origins of sounds should be a part of the elementary school social studies curriculum. The study of the sounds themselves and how they are used to produce various effects should be an integral part of the science curriculum.

Many schools do include such a unit on sound in the elementary school program. Some excerpts from one such course outline are given below to show the possibilities in correlating science and music to make a rich school experience.

In one middle school unit on sound, the following activities were integrated in a team teaching situation which included the science teacher, the music teacher, and the teacher for the language arts. Some of the beginning activities of this unit *could* be tried in the primary grades.

The children involved in these classes were motivated to study sound by listening to tapes made by the science teacher of sounds around the school which the children tried to identify. There was the sound of the snow blower outside, the scratching of chalk on the chalkboard, the ringing of the "passing" bell, the buzz of the pencil sharpener, the bouncing of a basketball in the gymnasium, the clatter of dishes in the cafeteria, the gurgling of milk from the milk machine, the spinning of the potter's wheel in the art room, and so on.

After these records were heard, children who had tape recorders available made some tapes of their own and brought them to class for others to hear. Thus an awareness and sensitivity to sound was developed. Children were also developing refined audio acuity.

The problems "What is sound" and "How is it made?" introduced many periods of research, discussion, and experimentation. With the understanding that air carries sound, the children explored vibrations and sound waves. They experimented with every kind of material possible in order to identify those materials which transmitted sound and those which did not. Lists were carefully kept, from which generalizations were made. For instance, can sound be transmitted by cloth? A necktie was stretched through a hole in a screen so students standing on each end of the necktie could not see each other. Each student then pulled the necktie taut and placed his ear to it while another student hit the necktie on one end with a metal mallet and then a wood mallet. Each student then recorded his reaction on a sheet of paper previously set up for this purpose.

The experiment was repeated with rope, string, a wooden dowel, a piece of 2″ x 4″, a metal bar, a hollow pipe, a ceramic tube, a cardboard tube, a solid piece of cardboard, a taut wire, a tube of plastic, and other materials.

From their lists the children determined which materials "carried" sound and which did not and then set about to find why through experimentation and research in books.

Next they experimented with sound vibrations. Rhythm instruments were explored to identify those sounds made by each.

Classification of the types of sounds by similar instruments began such as blowing sounds for woodwinds, plucking, picking, and strumming sounds for strings, and shaking and tapping sounds for percussions.

Volume and tone were explored and the new electric sounds and instruments introduced by means of recordings. Any child who played an instrument was encouraged to bring it to school and an exploration of the sound made by each was undertaken. Children experimented with new sounds and used these new sounds in musical stories and songs.

The music (sounds) of the ages was explored to show how tastes in sounds change, and children came to understand better the waltz era, the classics, the swing era, the jazz age, and rock and roll.

The construction of the instruments was studied so the sound created was better understood. Children received a great deal of pleasure from making their own sounds through the invention of new musical instruments.

The concept of the difference between a "sound" and a "musical tone" was also developed. The children learned that a tone is a sound of definite pitch and duration, produced by regular vibration in contrast to a noise sound, which is produced by irregular vibrations. It was also decided that percussion instruments of indefinite pitch might be an exception.

Another aspect of this science unit was the transmittance of sound: through communication media such as telephone, radio, transistor radio, television, and walkie-talkie. This unit on sound exemplifies the natural fusion of science and music. Similar units on music as it relates to color, to nature, to animal sounds, to electronics, and to a host of other topics provide ways of including it as an area of study within the science program. Several illustrations appear in this book showing activities used as part of science instruction.

In Chapter I, Miss Parker and her first-grade children experimented with high and low sounds in writing their story about the trip to the zoo. The percussion sounds were explored by Mr. Gaines in Chapter I. The fifth grade in Chapter II orchestrated sounds. In Chapter III Miss Hill experimented with sound, light, color, and movement (see p. 78). These children correlated this unit with science by studying the sources of light, including batteries as used in the flashlights.

One group enriched their entire unit on pollution by adding music to develop moods for their plays and songs. Other units which can be enriched with music would be units on the body,

FIGURE 9–1   *The science of sound and music.*

voice, hearing, other senses, mechanical aids (record players, tape recorders, etc.), mass communication, dance and movement, transportation, electricity, magnetism, and a host of others.

SUMMARY

Without the precision of mathematical concepts and scientific investigation there could be little music—especially recorded music. Science and mathematics can play an important part in the development of a good music program. Imaginative teachers can teach both by the use of music or can teach music through the use of mathematics and science.

TO THE COLLEGE STUDENT AND THE TEACHING TEAM

1. Mathematical concepts can be shown through dance steps. A simple problem such as multiplying by 2s can be used as a base for a gymnasium dance. While the class chants "2 times 1 is 2," one couple skips around the room. At the change of the chant to "2 times 2 is 4," they select another couple, and the four of them do a new step. These four in turn choose four more and so on until the entire class is in action. Other concepts may be utilized such as: Ten ones equals one ten.

2. Experiment with various objects to see what sounds can be produced: marbles, sandpaper, tin, bells, glass, etc. Compose these sounds into sound stories, musical compositions or background sound tracks for class-made, abstract moving pictures.

3. Write poems and songs related to science topics such as a study of birds, butterflies, insects, automobiles, electricity, space, animals, wind, matter and energy, and marine life.

4. Form a "Taste-a-Bite" Club. Write poems about how the tastes feel in your mouth and put them to music. Here is an example of one such experience written by a sixth-grade child.

> *The lemon made me*
> *Squint my eyes*
> *Pucker my mouth*
> *Shake my head*
> *A lemon is a useful fruit.*
> *I guess I'll eat an orange instead!*

5. Close your eyes and listen to all the sounds around you: sounds of nature, human voices, mechanical sounds.
6. Make a funnel out of a piece of paper and talk through it. Your voice is much louder because it all goes in one direction.
7. Hold a watch as far away from you as your arm will reach. Listen to it. Now put the watch on a wooden table, and listen. You can hear the watch much better on the table, and better with your ear closer. Sound can travel through certain materials better than it can travel through air. Also, the wood is acting as a resonator.
8. Put a nail hole in the bottoms of two small cans. Run a long string from the bottom of one can to the bottom of the other. Tie large knots on the inside of each can. Stretch the string tight, so that one child has a can to speak into and the other has a can to put to his ear. The child at the far end of the string will hear very well. The vibrations of the tin are carried along the string, causing the other tin to vibrate. The sound waves propagated by the vibrating can bottom are resonated by the other can and so are easily audible.
9. Some recordings deal with unusual sounds, many of which are now utilized in current musical compositions. Play some of these recordings for appreciative listening. Can you, or the children, identify how the sounds are made?
10. Have the children do reading research on the number systems of the ancient peoples and then challenge them to search for the relationships between these number systems and the music of the times.

SELECTED BIBLIOGRAPHY

Ashlock, Robert B., and Wayne L. Herman. *Current Research in Elementary School Mathematics.* New York: Macmillan, 1970.

Banks, J. Houston. *Learning and Teaching Arithmetic.* Boston: Allyn and Bacon, 1964.

Copeland, Richard W. *How Children Learn Mathematics.* New York: Macmillan, 1970.

————. *Mathematics and the Elementary Teacher,* 2nd ed. Philadelphia: W. B. Saunders, 1972.

Crescimbeni, Joseph. *Arithmetic Enrichment Activities for Elementary School Children.* West Nyack, N.Y.: Parker, 1965.

Crowder, Alex B., and Olive Boone Wheeler. *Elementary School Mathematics: Methods and Materials.* Dubuque, Iowa: William C. Brown, 1972.

Fehr, Howard F., and Thomas J. Hill. *Contemporary Mathematics for Elementary Teachers.* Boston: D. C. Heath, 1966.

Friedl, Alfred E. *Teaching Science to Children.* New York: Random House, 1972.

Good, Ronald G. *Readings in Elementary Science Education.* Dubuque, Iowa: William C. Brown, 1972.

Kramer, Klass. *Teaching Elementary School Mathematics.* Boston: Allyn and Bacon, 1970.

Lewis, June E., and Irene C. Potter. *The Teaching of Science in the Elementary School,* 2nd ed. Englewood Cliffs, N.J.: Prentice-Hall, 1970.

Marks, John L., Richard Prudy, and Lucien Kinney. *Teaching Elementary School Mathematics for Understanding,* 2nd ed. New York: McGraw-Hill, 1965.

McFarland, Dora, and Eunice M. Lewis. *Introduction to Modern Mathematics.* Boston: D. C. Heath, 1966.

Nelson, Leslie, and George Lorbeer. *Science Activities for Elementary Children,* 5th ed. Dubuque, Iowa: William C. Brown, 1972.

Piltz, Albert, and Robert Sund. *Creative Teaching of Science in the Elementary School.* Boston: Allyn and Bacon, 1974.

Rooze, Gene E., and Leona M. Foerster. *Teaching Elementary Social Studies: A New Perspective.* Columbus, Ohio: Charles E. Merrill, 1972.

Underhill, Robert G. *Teaching Elementary School Mathematics.* Columbus, Ohio: Charles E. Merrill, 1972.

Victor, Edward. *Science in the Elementary School.* New York: Macmillan, 1970.

Westcott, Alvin, and John Schluep. *Fun with Timothy Triangle.* Mankato, Minn.: Oddo, 1966.

————, and James A. Smith. *Creative Teaching of Mathematics in the Elementary School.* Boston: Allyn and Bacon, 1967.

CHAPTER X

Materials for Teaching Music

Music is the universal language of mankind—poetry their universal pastime and delight.

—HENRY WADSWORTH LONGFELLOW[1]

INTRODUCTION

Many times in this text the authors have indicated that any teacher can provide a rich music experience for children, even if she is not particularly gifted or talented. They suggest that she first of all survey her own skills, then those of her students, then the resources of the school and community to see what is available; then go ahead and use what is available to plan a meaningful music program. In this chapter the authors have attempted to list materials currently available for classroom use that will help the classroom teacher and the music teacher in developing such a program. The list is in no manner exhaustive but should be of help in the selection of materials which will lead to the fulfillment of the objectives for the teaching of music.

RESOURCES ARE EVERYWHERE

A glance back through the pages of this book will point out to the classroom teacher and the music teacher that the most exciting

1. Henry Wadsworth Longfellow, *Outre-Mer* (1833–34).

and best-received music lessons are not necessarily those in which expensive equipment and highly talented personnel are present.

Take, for instance, the exciting music lesson developed on pages 130–131 by the kindergarten teacher who created a song about the life story of the leaves simply by using the words of the children as they freely expressed themselves. Or take the lesson on page 78 in which Miss Hill developed the concept of rhythm and rhyme and moved from an actual experience with note value to symbolism with the notes. Little equipment was necessary for this lesson, except perhaps the flashlights, which Miss Hill asked the children to bring from home. A record player or piano suffice for developing most lessons. Notice how little extra equipment was needed for developing the pollution unit described in Chapter VIII.

The success of these lessons can only be measured in terms of the objectives set for the lessons. Basically, did the children learn what the teacher set out to teach, did they enjoy the experience, and did the completed lesson contribute to the fulfillment of the bigger objectives for the overall development of the music program as stated on pages 39–40?

In each case the answer is affirmative. As teachers in these situations or observers in them, the authors saw that music *facts* were learned by simple performance behavior (such as selecting notes to go with beats and placing them properly on a flannelboard) or filling out simple ditto work sheets, which showed an understanding of time signatures. We observed keen enjoyment in each lesson by studying the behavior in the children during and after each lesson. ("Let's read it again," "Can we do this tomorrow?" "I'm going to bring in a record I have from home.")

The success of these lessons also hinged on the wise use of materials available, yet a survey of these resources shows most of them to be obtainable in any school or community setting.

RESOURCES USED FOR MUSIC EXPERIENCES

First of all a record player is a must. This, of course, implies a wide selection of recordings. But these recordings do not all necessarily have to be part of a school library. Children can and will bring their records from home and share them. Many of the music adventures in this book were made possible because of the presence of a record player.

Running a close second to the record player is the need for a good cassette tape recorder and, if possible, a collection of tapes (see below).

Other resources in the school mentioned in this book are the voices of teachers who sing, the talent of teachers or school personnel who play musical instruments, the talent of students who play instruments or sing, the talent of parents and the talent of the community (town bands, church choirs, choral groups, dancing groups, ethnic groups, and marching bands). A nearby college can offer unlimited resources in both equipment and talent among students. Radio and television programs can be used effectively with a little care and planning. School and community libraries offer boundless resources for materials. Music is such an important part of American life that evidences of it are everywhere. We have become so accustomed to it that we do not always see the many applications or resources of it around us. One of the main jobs of a music or classroom teacher is to muster these resources so they may be incorporated into a total curriculum plan.

The Tape Recorder

Many schools have reel and cassette tape recorders available for classroom use. Some students have their own cassette recorders and enjoy using them in and out of the classroom. The cassettes have the limitation of having only one speed in contrast to the open tape recorder. However, they are portable and more usable for making recordings outside the classroom.

Tape recorders offer many opportunities for creative activities. With two tape recorders the possibilities are limitless. As an example, children can tape sounds at one speed, then, rerecording them at faster or slower speeds, they can combine natural sounds or create sound effects by changing the speed of a voice. Perhaps they will imitate a siren, play a glissando on an autoharp, or change the sound of a violin string being tuned by increasing the volume and the tempo. Students' ideas seem to go beyond adults' wildest imaginations.

One day a class made a list of soft sounds, loud sounds, high sounds, and low sounds. They imitated the countdown heard when a rocket is launched, the take off, the sounds of the local rifle range, snowmobiles, motorcycles, and the sound of a bass drum. Somehow they had a more difficult time listing soft sounds. They started with a whisper, added a lullaby, footsteps sneaking across a room, a small tinkling bell, and a kitten purring. Before they finished taping, some of the sounds were so altered they were not recognizable, but this was not the point. They had explored sound, chosen those they felt to be most effective for a given situation, and created a contemporary composition of their own. They also decided the composition sounded best when the volume was soft in the beginning, reached a climax gradually, and then disappeared into a soft pianissimo—but added one crash for a dramatic ending.

Tape recorders are excellent for recording sound effects for stories and dramatic activities such as those described in this book. Dragging a chain across a floor or shaking a piece of tin in front of a microphone to create a storm effect as several children blow into a microphone creates interest in sound. "Sounds of the season" is an excellent topic for creating tape stories and can be tied in with literature, science, and art.

Usually the quality of playing or singing tends to improve if a tape recorder is used frequently, listened to carefully, the recording discussed critically by students, and the material rerecorded after alterations have been made. This is a good way to find tempos suited to the situation, dynamic levels, and to discover the need for special effects.

Many communities have enthusiastic audio buffs who can provide information on the latest available equipment. Service becomes a most important item to consider in obtaining a tape recorder. It is also important to consider some battery-operated sets for easy mobility in any unusual situation in which you choose to record.

The Voice

Few schools today lack record players but music could be taught even if a record player were not available. Music existed long before Mr. Edison. People sang, played instruments, and danced. Folk music and concert music were enjoyed by many. Surely recorded music is a great asset and joy to our modern world, but we can still have music without it because children can sing if we will allow and encourage them. The teacher need not pass along the handicap of having a poor singing voice to the children. She can, instead, make a special effort to be sure the children discover the joy of singing with their own voices.

It would be a rare classroom where one could not find at least one child who could sing well. Sometimes, if the teacher cannot sing, an older student, a class leader, a fellow teacher, or a singing parent may substitute. The main goal is that children have an opportunity to use their singing voices and that they acquire a repertoire of songs.

Accompaniment Instruments

What should be used as an accompaniment? Since an accompaniment should function in creating a mood, establishing pitch, setting a tempo, and enhancing the song in every way, it is possible to use many kinds of accompaniments. Hand clapping and foot stamping were used by some people to establish the tempo and rhythm of some of their songs most effectively. Guitars, ukuleles, bells, percussion instruments, small organs, and the piano may all be used to create a musical accompaniment. The recordings included with various commercial song series and pop tunes often serve as valuable accompaniments. Listen to records of songs and notice the accompaniment. Some folk singers' recordings use an accompaniment very sparingly. Often a piano or melody instrument serves a most useful function when teaching a song just to give students and the teacher the courage to try: In such records then the melody and text should predominate. Many teachers prefer not to use an accompaniment when teaching a new song but add it to enhance the beauty and interest in the song at a later time.

The Ukulele. The ukulele is a relatively easy instrument to learn and provides an interesting accompaniment for young singers. Elementary school students are able to play and enjoy the baritone ukulele. Teachers and children tend to favor the baritone because of its rich sound.

Some teachers prefer the soprano ukulele because it is pitched higher and is small and therefore easier for children to hold. Even three and four year olds have enjoyed strumming the ukulele as some older child or teacher held the strings down for the appropriate chords.

The Autoharp. The autoharp is an accompanying instrument of exceptional beauty. It is easily played and can be used in many styles. The one problem with the instrument is the time it takes for tuning. There are many more strings than on a ukulele or guitar. The newer instruments, however, are constructed to hold their pitch better and consequently do not need to be tuned so often. Classroom teachers who have never played a string instrument would enjoy starting on a baritone ukulele and later explore the sounds of an autoharp. Students of all ages seem to be fascinated with the sound of an autoharp acompaniment.

The Guitar. There are many opportunities available to learn folk guitar which would be most helpful in accompanying singing in the classroom. The best way to learn would be to go to the finest guitar teacher available and have this teacher assist in the choice of an instrument and a good instruction book. Many people have taught themselves with the help of a good textbook and have enjoyed self-learning.

Percussion Instruments. Instruments of definite pitch as well as those of indefinite pitch that are played by striking or shaking are classified as percussion instruments. Resonators, bells, xylophones, marimbas, glockenspiels, metallophones, orchestra bells, drums, triangles, all have definite pitch and are similar to the piano keyboard (see Fig. 10–1). They are played with mallets and may be used to play the melody or a harmony part of a composition, either a chord sequence, contrasting melody, or all three. The number of sets of bells and the experience of the group will determine their use. In one classroom a teacher placed a set of bells across the front of her desk. Students volunteered to find the starting pitch of their favorite songs, played the melody, created new melodies for original songs, and countermelodies or descants for songs they knew. While these experiences cannot be classified as the traditional accompaniment, they do create a kind of accompaniment that helps children sing and adds interest and color to their singing.

Percussion instruments of indefinite pitch may be used to emphasize an important characteristic of a song from the simple beat on a tom-tom for Indian songs to the exciting rhythms of Mexican songs played on maracas. Mallets of different weight may be used to discover different timbres. A finger cymbal or triangle may be used at the beginning of phrases to call attention to a phrase ending, or point up a special effect in a song. Drums, wood blocks, shakers, jingle clogs, and tambourines are often used effectively to help children keep a steady tempo, create a special mood, and bring out interesting rhythmic patterns.

Like all equipment it is the use of these instruments which determine their value. This is especially true of percussion instruments, as they may often be used to create mere noise rather than music unless the performer has a real feeling for the music and uses the instrument as an extension of this feeling.

FIGURE 10–1   Exploring instrument sounds.

The quality of the instrument should be carefully considered. Instruments of definite pitch should always be in tune and other percussion instruments should be constructed so they will produce a musical sound. This does not mean there is no place for a "kitchen band"—the jug ensemble and the washboard rhythm section for fun and special occasions—but it does mean that, in general, the instruments used should be of such a quality that the experience will add to the child's musical growth.

Students may enjoy making some of their own instruments. (See pp. 107–108.) This can be a fascinating project but again the two questions which should be asked continually are, "How does it sound?" and "How can I play it to make the music more interesting?" There should be an opportunity for exploration and discovery in this area.

For example, contrast beans, corn, rice, and small stones in

FIGURE 10–2 *Tablespoons and other kitchen utensils can be used as melodic percussion instruments in composing music.*

paper cups, in the cardboard centers from toilet tissue, or in paper towel rolls to discover the best sound for a particular song. Or choose one sound best suited to the verse of a song, another for the chorus.

Examples of Styles of Accompaniment
(By performer)

Recordings
Baez, Joan, *Joan Baez Sings Folksongs,* Vanguard.

Belafonte, Harry, and Belafonte Singers, *My Lord, What a Morin'* (black spirituals), R.C.A. Victor.

English, Logan, *American Folk Ballads,* Monitor.

Ives, Burl, *Songs of the Colonies; Songs of the Revolution; Songs of the North and South; Songs of the Sea; Songs of the Frontier,* Columbia Records.

Lomax, John A., Jr., *Sings American Folk Songs,* Folkway Records.

Mills, Alan, *Oh Canada: A History of Canada in Folk Song,* Folkway Records.

Listen to the accompaniments on the basic song series recordings (see list, pp. 279–282).

Sounds in the Classroom

The children can explore and discover sounds in their classroom that may be used for musical purposes. Such resources are limited only by the imagination of the teacher and the children. Some sounds which may be used to accompany a song are: (1) chalk tapped on a chalkboard gives a delicate sound most adaptable to a song about rain; (2) a large group tapping pencils one against another will give a similar sound; (3) the sound of the back of the fist against a cupped hand imitates a tom-tom sound; (4) horses galloping may be illustrated rhythmically by shaking hands with yourself and slapping the palms together; (5) brushing the palms of the hands together as the arms go forward and backward creates a fine accompaniment for a train song; (6) finger snapping or clapping, slapping the thighs, and sounds made with the mouth may be used to create interesting and appropriate accompaniments for special songs.

Again, it is important to state that much attention must be given to the musical quality of the experience involving the use of percussive sounds as the experience can result in a nonmusical one. Children must understand the object of the exploratory activities is to find a variety of ways of adding to the musicability of a song. There is no limit to their discoveries if they accept this challenge.

The Piano. The piano may be used in many ways to create a musical experience for children's songs. It may be used to reinforce the melody, to add an interesting harmony part, to provide an exciting rhythm, or for any combination of these activities. The piano is used by some teachers who have a limited

FIGURE 10–3 Exploring human sounds.

technique to give support to the melodic line by playing the melody with the right hand. Other teachers may choose to use a chord accompaniment similar to that of a ukulele or guitar.

Students and teachers may enjoy improvising rhythmic patterns to initiate sounds around them or to add a special effect to a dramatization. For example a circus unit in a lower grade may call for an accompaniment for trained bears and elephants (the low register), trapeze artists swinging high above the crowd (high register), or following the imaginary steps of a high wire performer. A clown trying to climb a ladder may be reinforced in a comic way by ascending and occasionally descending the scale as he falls back only to start over again and eventually reach the top.

Often the rhythm of a well-known tune may be adapted to accompany a child's movements. Chant words or phrases to fit the motions and follow the pattern with the melodic line or improvisation.

The piano, as well as all instruments used in the classroom, should be kept in as perfect tune as possible. It should also be placed so teachers or anyone accompanying can see the class members easily. We, as teachers, wouldn't think of turning our backs to a class to read them a story. The basic principle of "teaching-eye" contact is a wise one in playing the piano as well as reading. Some teachers prefer to stand, looking over the top of the piano, to communicate with their students. The small electronic pianos available today are enjoyed by some not only because of their unusual tone but because of their lower height compared to many of the standard pianos. It would be wise to investigate all types of instruments, securing the best advice possible before purchasing a piano. Each year new advances are made, especially in the electronics field, making it impossible to suggest one make over another. Good tone quality and minimum upkeep are important points to be considered. The availability of service is of primary importance especially if the electronic pianos are being considered. A piano tuner could be most helpful in giving advice for the selection of the standard piano.

Percussion and Melody Instruments
(Include catalogs in your library)

Children's Music Center, 5373 West Pico Blvd., Los Angeles, Calif. 90019
Rhythm instruments, resonator bells, song bells, autoharp, Latin American instruments, flutophones, tonettes, song flutes, recorders, Carl Orff instruments.

Conn Corporation, 1101 East Beardsley St., Elkhart, Indiana. Song flutes, rhythm instruments.

T. C. Dragon, Inc., 1770 W. Berteau Ave., Chicago, Illinois 60613 Mallet percussion instruments.

Educational Music Bureau, Inc., 434 Wabash Ave., Chicago, Illinois 60605
American representatives of Orff instruments.

Gamble Hinged Music Co., 312 South Wabash Ave., Chicago, Illinois 60604
Rhythm band instruments, tonettes, song flutes, flutophones, recorders, tone bells, song bells, autoharps, pitchpipes.

Goya Music, Division of Avnet, Inc., 53 W. 23rd St., New York, New York 10010
Distributors of guitars, instruments, supplies.

Hargail Music Press, 157 West 57th Street, New York, N.Y. 10019 Imported recorders and recorder music.

Harmolin, Inc., P.O. Box 244, La Jolla, California 92037
Harmolin, resonator bells, psalteries.

Harmony Company, 4600 W. Diversay Ave., Chicago, Illinois 60639
Manufacturers of guitars, electric guitars, banjos, mandolins, ukuleles, amplifiers.

M. Hohner, Inc., Andrews Road, Hicksville, N.Y. 11802
Manufacturers of recorders, melodicas, rhythm band instruments, drums, guitars, accordians.
Ludwig Industries, 1728 N. Damin Ave., Chicago, Illinois 60647
Lyons Band Instrument Company, Industrial Drive, Elmhurst, Illinois 60126
Instruments for the classroom.
Magna-Music Baton, Inc., 6394 Delmar Blvd., St. Louis, Missouri 63130
Percussion instruments including Orff instruments.
Melody Flute Company, Laurel, Maryland 20810
Melody flutes and recorders.
Music Education Group, P.O. Box 1501, Union, N.Y. 07083
The attaché autoharp, as well as other musical instruments for the classroom sold by dealers.
Oscar Schmidt-International, Inc., 87-101 Ferry Street, Jersey City, N.J. 07307
Autoharps and guitaros.
Pacific Music Supply Co., 1143 Santee St., Los Angeles, Calif. 90015
Distributors of Jenco and Deegen percussion instruments, Oscar Schmidt autoharps.
Peripole Products, Inc., 51-17 Rockaway Beach Blvd., Far Rockaway, N.Y. 11691
Manufacturers and distributors of elementary classroom musical instruments, including bells, autoharps, and ukuleles.
Rhythm Band, Inc., Box 126, Fort Worth, Texas 76101
Distributors of rhythm equipment and supplies including resonator bells, autoharps, and ukuleles.
Targ-Dinner, Inc., 2451 N. Sacramento St., Chicago, Ill. 60647
American Prep Tone bells and teaching aids.
Trophy Products Company, 1278 West 9th Street, Cleveland, O. 44113
Flutophones.
Viking Company, 113 South Edgemount Street, Los Angeles, Calif. 90004
Resonator bells, music charts.
Walberg and Auge, 31 Mercantile Street, Worcester, Mass. 01608
Song bells, marimba bells, resonator bells, autoharps, rhythm instruments, Latin American instruments, song flutes, tonettes, flutophones, recorders.
Yamaha International Corporation, Box 54540, Los Angeles, Calif. 90054
Importers and distributors of musical merchandise. Franchiser, Yamaha Music School in the United States.
Zim-Gar Musical Instrument Corp., 762 Park Place, Brooklyn, N.Y. 11216
Rhythm band instruments, Latin American instruments,

autoharps, zithers, psalteries, flutophones, tonettes, song flutes, resonator bells, melody bells, orchestra bells, xylophones, step bells, recorders, pitchpipes.

Records

Starting a record library (especially on a minimum budget) is easier than it was a few years ago because of the fine educational albums available. Each recording may not be of top quality if you compare it to single stereo albums at the highest prices, but the quality in most cases is good, the accompanying guide books containing descriptions of the music are helpful teaching suggestions, and the price most reasonable by comparison to high quality records. There are recordings for listening, singing, and dancing that can be used in many different ways and for many different reasons, depending on the particular needs of the students. Although many of the albums contain selections for particular grade levels the teacher would do well to become acquainted with the *series,* as the records are frequently interchangeable depending on the sophistication of the children as well as the basic purposes for using the recording. For example, a selection such as Saint-Saëns' *The Swan* (Grade 3, Album II of the Adventure Series, R.C.A. Victor) might be used in nursery school, kindergarten, or primary grades for its quiet mood. In another grade the same record could be used to introduce the cello; in still another grade to analyze the melodic line or phrase structure; and in all grades because it makes for beautiful listening. It is also possible music included in albums selected for rhythmic activities (such as those included in the R.C.A. Basic Library) would serve as an excellent introduction to the listening program because of their rhythmic appeal, while those in the listening albums offer many opportunities for dramatization or movement as well as creative listening.

Selecting recordings for and with children can be a great adventure. Until children have had many experiences using music in the classroom, it might be helpful to choose music with strong or interesting rhythms, beautiful melodies, or unusual instrumental effects. The rhythm of Copland's "The Circus" from *The Red Poppy* or Kabalensky's *Comedian's Galop* tend to be irresistible. The lovely melodies in Victor Herbert's "March of the Toys," and "The Lullaby" from Stravinsky's *Firebird Suite* have a special appeal. The use of the piccolo, trombone, and percussion instruments in Sousa's *Stars and Stripes Forever,* or the new sounds of contemporary music may be of special interest to children.

Story records using music for background to create appropriate moods or special effects are sometimes a child's first introduction to recorded music in the classroom. Because of this it is important to choose those of good musical quality and to call attention to the music as well as the story. Asking questions such as: Did the music tell us anything about the story? Why do you think they used music with this story? Did the music help us understand the story better? How? All could help children become more aware of the music and would help them to begin to develop more satisfying listening habits.

Activity records are popular in early grades. Some require exact interpretation while others simply provide a music background for free interpretation. Both should guide the student toward good listening habits. The purpose of the lesson will determine the ones to be used. The records suggesting motions may be helpful in teaching a child to take directions and help build a vocabulary of motions that he may use to express himself. Some children, perhaps those who feel insecure, may respond most readily to these recordings, while others may enjoy the freedom of creating their own interpretation.

Recordings that accompany folk dancing are most valuable. Many of these have the directions on the record while others have excellent guides included in the albums. Older students may enjoy having the opportunity to work these dances out themselves. One class learned the traditional minuet and then created a modern version of the dance. As a result of this they taught their friends both dances so the experience went far beyond the classroom walls.

Song Book Series
(Books and Records)

Allyn and Bacon, Inc., *This Is Music*, 470 Atlantic Ave., Boston, Massachusetts 02210.

American Book Co., *New Dimensions in Music*, 55 Fifth Avenue, New York, N.Y. 10003.

Follett Publishing Co., *Discovering Music Together*, 1010 West Washington Blvd., Chicago, Illinois 60607.

Ginn and Company, *The Magic of Music*, 191 Spring Street, Lexington, Massachusetts 02173.

Holt, Rinehart, and Winston Inc., *Exploring Music*, 383 Madison Avenue, New York, N.Y. 10017.

FIGURE 10–4   *This child said, "I am listening, and I am thinking."*

Prentice-Hall Inc., *Growing with Music,* Englewood Cliffs, New Jersey 07632.

Silver-Burdett Company, *Making Music Your Own,* Park Ave. and Columbia Road, Morristown, New Jersey 07960.

Summy-Birchard, *Birchard Music Series,* 1834 Ridge Avenue, Evanston, Illinois 60204.

The song series are an excellent source of materials for teachers and students. They include books for the students, teachers editions with teaching suggestions, accompaniments, material for related listening experiences, and recordings of many songs in the texts.

Each book is adaptable in several grade levels.

Educational Albums and Records for Teaching
(Record Series for Listening)

Music (Series)

Bowmar Educational Records, *Bowmar Orchestral Library.* Three series, charts for classroom use included. 10510 Burbank Blvd., North Hollywood, California 91701

Canyon Press, Inc., Instructional recordings. P.O. Box 1255, Cincinnati, Ohio 45201.

C.M.S. Records, *UNICEF Series.* 14 Warren Street, New York, New York 10017.

Keyboard Publications, Inc. *American Indian, Argentina, Brazil and Mexico, and others.* Recordings, reading material, theme charts, visual material. 1346 Chapel St., New Haven, Conn. 06511.

Musical Sound Books. Records and accompanying texts: *The Crimson Book, The Green Book, The Blue Book.* (Texts written by Lillian Baldwin and published by Silver-Burdett.) Sound Book Press, Inc., 36 Garth Road, Scarsdale, New York 10583.

R.C.A. Victor *Library for Elementary Schools,* 155 E. 24th Street, New York, New York 10010. (*Listening Albums I–VI, Rhythmic Activity Albums I–VI.*)
Adventures in Music, a teacher's guide by Gladys Tipton and Eleanor Tipton. Notes for teachers prepared by Lilla Belle Pitts and Gladys Tipton.

Song series recordings are especially valuable.

Recordings of Instruments of the Band and Orchestra For Young Children

A Child's Introduction to the Orchestra. Music by Alec Wilder, lyrics by Marshall Barer, musical direction by Mitch Miller. Golden Records, Distributed by Affiliated Publishers, Inc.. Rockefeller Center, New York, N.Y. 10020.

Instruments of the Orchestra. Milton Cross, Narrator. Written by Ernest La Prade. Learn for Pleasure Cultural Activities, Ottenheimer: Publisher.

Instruments of the Symphony Orchestra. Produced by the Jam Handy Organization, manufactured by R.C.A. Victor Records. Record—1, 2, 3, 4.

Meet the Instruments. Stanley Bowman Company.

Independent Study and Upper Elementary Grades

First Chair, Philadelphia Orchestra. Eugene Ormandy Conducting. Columbia.

First Chair Encores. Philadelphia Orchestra. Eugene Ormandy Conducting. Columbia.

Instruments of the Orchestra. National Symphony Orchestra. R.C.A. Victor.

The Complete Orchestra. Wheeler Beckett Orchestra of New York. Wheeler Beckett, Conductor. Author Narrator, Music Education Record Corp.

The Orchestra. Leopold Stokowski conducting his Symphony Orchestra. Capitol Records (presented by sections).

Music of the World

Authentic records of music of the countries of the world are now available. Children must be well prepared to hear this music. Just as there are differences in the clothes worn around the world, the food eaten in different countries, the speech used by different groups, so is the music different. The *voice* quality of the oriental, the American, and the Western European illustrate three extremes in pitch and tone, while the African drums, the gamilons of Bali, and the English chamber music groups illustrate three extremes in the choice of instruments. The age old story of the traveling American who commented on the Englishman driving down the *wrong* side of the street, and who was corrected by his guest who said, "Shall we say just a *different* side" is appropriate here. Listening to discover the differences and similarities, studying the text, the different scales, and creating "your" own songs or rhythms using the important music characteristics of a different country can be an exciting experience to an individual as well as to a class.

One interesting project worked out by a student involved a trip around the world in a plane that had a very poor engine. Because of so much mechanical trouble the plane was forced down frequently. Somehow it always happened at night and the only way the student knew where he was, was to listen to the music of the country where he landed. Some selections were very easy to identify while others were more difficult, but the "trip" proved highly entertaining and the children really listened. These are some of the selections used.

Country	Composition	Composer
France	"Can-Can"	Offenbach
England	"Pomp and Circumstance"	Elgar
Italy	"Celeste Aïda"	Verdi
Mexico	"Mexican Hat Dance"	Folk song
America	"Rhapsody in Blue"	Gershwin
Bali	"Ketjak" (The Monkey Dance)	Folk music
Japan	Threshing Song	Folk song
	"Mugit-Suki-Uta"	
Puerto Rico	"San Severino"	Folk song

This idea can be expanded by listening to more music from each country. The objective of such a project should be one of exploration and expansion of repertoire. Children may be interested to discover composers are sometimes influenced in their writing by the music characteristics of other countries. For example, Bizet, a Frenchman, wrote an opera which includes Spanish rhythms. Charles Griffes, an American composer, wrote a composition, *The White Peacock*, which is described by some music crtics as French impressionist music. Letting children explore the idea of selecting music for such an imaginary "trip" can lead to many analytical listening experiences.

Recordings of Music of the World
(Check record company addresses, p. 303.)

AFRICA

Ethnic Folkways Records
    Africa South of the Sahara
    Negro Folk Music of Africa and America
Folkways Records
    Music of Equatorial Africa

AMERICA

Capitol Records
  Folk Songs of the Frontier
  Ode to Billie Joe
  Songs of Stephen Foster
  Virtuoso
Columbia Records
  Dangerous Sounds!—Pete Seeger
  The Freewheelin' Bob Dylan
  Old American Songs, Sets I & II
  We Shall Overcome—Pete Seeger
Desto Records
  Songs by American Composers
Ethnic Folkways Records
  Music of the Sioux and the Navajo
Folkways Records
  American Favorite Ballads
  Anthology of American Folk Music, vols. 1, 2 and 3
  Broadsides
  Folk Music
  Indian Music of the Southwest
  Negro Folk Music of Africa and America
  Poor Boy—Woody Guthrie
  Songs of the Civil War
RCA Victor Records
  Sea Chanties
  Stephen Foster Song Book
Reprise Records
  Arlo—Arlo Guthrie
SPA Records
  American Life
Stinson Records
  Leadbelly Sings and Plays
Unart Records
  Burl Ives Favorites
Vanguard Records
  America (An Epic Rhapsody)
  David's Album—Joan Baez
  Folk Festival at Newport, vol. 3
  Joan—Joan Baez
Vox Records
  Stephen Foster—His Story and His Music
Warner Brothers Records
  In the Wind—Peter, Paul and Mary
  Peter, Paul and Mary
  Peter, Paul and Mommy

CANADA

Ethnic Folkways Records
Indian Music of the Canadian Plains

CZECHOSLOVAKIA

Apon Records
Czech Polkas and Waltzes, vol. 2
Monitor Records
Czech, Slovak, and Moravian Folk Songs

ENGLAND

Capitol Records
Folk Songs of the Old World
Folkways Records
Broadside Ballads (London: 1600–1700)
Vox Records
The English Country Dancing Master

GERMANY

Vanguard Records
Best Loved German Songs

GREECE

Ethnic Folkways Records
Folk Music of Greece

HUNGARY

Folkways Records
Folk Music of Hungary

IRELAND

Capitol Records
Folk Songs of the Old World

ISRAEL

Artia Records
Jewish Religious Songs
Folkways Records
Holiday Songs of Israel

ITALY

Angel Records
Italian Song Book
London Records
Program of Spanish and Italian Songs
Riverside Records
Songs Children Sing: Italy

JAPAN
Folkways Records
    Music of Asia: Japan/China/Okinawa

MEXICO
Mercury Records
    La Fiesta Mexicana

NORWAY
Ethnic Folkways Records
    Folk Music of Norway

POLAND
Folkways Records
    Polish Folk Songs and Dances

RUSSIA
LSC Records
    Eight Russian Folk Songs
Mercury Records
    Memories of My Childhood—Life in a Russian Village

SCOTLAND
Capitol Records
    Folk Songs of the Old World

SOUTH AMERICA
Ethnic Folkways Records
    Music of Peru

SPAIN
Angel Records
    Songs from Spanish Songbook
London Records
    A Program of Spanish and Italian Songs
Westminster Records
    Songs and Dances of Spain, vols.: 1–5

TRINIDAD
Ethnic Folkways Records
    Cult Music of Trinidad

YUGOSLAVIA
Ethnic Folkways Records
    Folk Music of Yugoslavia

WALES
Capitol Records
Folk Songs of the Old World

GENERAL FOLK MUSIC
Capitol Records
Folk Songs of Western Europe
Ethnic Folkways Records
Demonstration Collection

Adventures in Music Series
(By countries)

ARGENTINA

Ginastera, Alberto, WHEAT DANCE from the Ballet Suite "Estancia." Grade 4, vol. 1, side 2, band 5.

ARMENIA

Khachaturian, Aram, WALTZ from "Masquerade Suite." Grade 4, vol. II, side 1, band 1.

AUSTRALIA

Grainger, Percy (Arr.), LONDONDERRY AIR (Irish Tune from "Country Derry"). Grade 4, vol. II, side 1, band 2.

AUSTRIA

Mozart, Wolfgang Amadeus, MENUETTO from "Divertimento no. 17, "K. 334." Grade 5, vol. II, side 2, band 2. ROMANZE from "Eine kleine Nachtmusik" (Serenade in G, K. 525). Grade 4, vol. 1, side 2, band 1.
Schubert, Franz, FIRST MOVEMENT (Allegro from "Symphony No. 5, in B-Flat"). Grade 5, vol. I, side 1, band 3.
Webern, Anton, SEHR LANGSOM (from five movements for String Orchestra). Grade 2, vol. II.

BELGIUM

Gretry, Andre Modeste, GIGUE from "Cephale et Procris." Grade 1, side 2, band 6. TAMBOURIN, Ballet Music from "Cephale et Procris."

BOHEMIA (Czechoslovakia)

Dvorak, Antonin, SLAVONIC DANCE IN C MINOR, Op. 46, No. 7. Grade 4, vol. II, side 2, band 5.

BRAZIL

Guarnieri, Camargo, BRAZILIAN DANCE from "Three Dances for Orchestra." Grade 6, vol. II, side 2, band 1.
Villa-Lobos, Heitor, THE LITTLE TRAIN OF THE CAIPIRA from "Bachianas Brasileiras No. 2." Grade 3, vol. 1, side 1, band 4.

CUBA

Lecunona, Ernesto, ANDALUCIA from the Spanish Suite "Andalucia." Grade 4, vol. 1, side 1, band 3.

CZECHOSLOVAKIA

Smetana, Bedrich, DANCE OF THE COMEDIANS from "The Bartered Bride." Grade 6, vol. II, side 2, band 4.

ENGLAND

Arnold, Malcolm, ALLEGRO NONTROPPO from "English Dances." Grade 2, vol. II.
Arnold, Malcolm, GRAYIOSO from "English Dances." Grade 1, vol. II.
Coates, Eric, KNIGHTSBRIDGE MARCH from "London Suite." Grade 5, vol. II, side 2, band 4.
Elgar, Edward, FAIRIES AND GIANTS from "Wand of Youth Suite No. 1." Grade 3, vol. I, side 2, band 1.
Elgar, Edward, SUN DANCE from "Wand of Youth Suite No. 1." Grade 2, vol. II.
Hoist, Gustav, THE SPIRITS OF THE EARTH, from "The Perfect Fool"—Ballet Suite. Grade 6, vol. II, side 2, band 5.
Rossini-Britten, MARCH from "Soirées Musicales." Grade 1, side 2, band 4.
Vaughan Williams, Ralph, "FANTASIA ON GREEN-SLEEVES." Grade 6, vol. II, side 1, band 1. MARCH PAST OF THE KITCHEN UTENSILS (3rd M.) from "The Wasps." Grade 3, vol. I, side 2, band 5.
Walton, William, VALSE from "Façade"—Suite. Grade 6, vol. II, side 1, band 3.

FINLAND

Sibelius, John, ALLA MARCIA from "Karelia Suite," Op. 11. Grade 5, vol. I, side 2, band 3.

FRANCE

Berlioz, Hector, BALLET OF THE SYLPHS from "The Damnation of Faust." Grade 1, side 1, band 8.
Bizet, Georges, THE BALL from "The Children's Games." Grade 1, side 2, band 7. THE CHANGING OF THE GUARD from "Carmen Suite No. 2." Grade 3, vol. II, side 1, band 2.

CRADLE SONG from "Children's Games." Grade 1, side 1, band 6. FARANDOLE from "L'Arlesienne Suite No. 2." Grade 6, vol. I, side 2, band 4. LEAP FROG from "Children's Games." Grade 1, side 2, band 8. MINUETTO from "L'Arlesienne Suite No. 1." Grade 4, vol. II, side 2, band 2. THE DRAGONS OF ALCALA from "Carmen Suite." Grade 2, vol. II.

Chabrier, Emmanuel, ESPANA, Rhapsody for Orchestra. Grade 5, vol. I, side 1, band 1. MARCHE JOYEUSE. Grade 4, vol. I, side 2, band 4.

Charpentier, Gustav, ON MULEBACK from "Impressions of Italy." Grade 5, vol. I, side 1, band 4.

Debussy, Claude, PLAY OF THE WAVES from "La Mer" (The Sea), Three Symphonic Sketches. Grade 6, vol. II, side 2, band 2. THE SNOW IS DANCING from "The Children's Corner Suite." Grade 3, vol. I, side 2, band 6.

Delibes, Leo, LESQUENCANDE from "The King is Amused." Grade 1, vol. II. SWANHILDE'S WALTZ from "Coppelia." Grade 2, vol. II. WALTZ OF THE DOLL from "Coppelia." Grade 1, side 1, band 9.

Faure, Gabriel, BERCEUSE from "Dolly" Op. 56, No. 1. Grade 2, side 1, band 5.

Gounod, Charles, WALTZ (DANCE OF THE NUBIANS) from Ballet Music from "Faust." Grade 3, vol. I, side 2, band 4.

Ibert, Jacques, THE LITTLE WHITE DONKEY from "Histories No. 2." Grade 2, side 1, band 2. PARADE from "Divertissment." Grade 1, side 2, band 3.

Kabalevsky, Dmitri, WALTZ from "The Comedians." Grade 1, vol. II.

Liadov, Anatol C., BERCEUSE from "Eight Russian Folk Songs." Grade 1, vol. II.

Lully, Jean Baptiste, MARCHE from "Ballet Suite." Grade 3, vol. II, side 2, band 6.

Massenet, Jules, ARGONAISE from "Le Cid." Grade 1, side 1, band 2.

Milhaud, Darius, COPACABANA from "Saudades de Brazil." Grade 4, vol. II, side 2, band 1. LARANJEIRAS from "Saudades de Brazil." Grade 4, vol. II, side 1, band 3. THE CONVERSATIONS OF BEAUTY AND THE BEAST from "Mother Goose Suite." Grade 5, vol. I, side 2, band 2.

Mozart, Wolfgang Amadeus, No. 8 from "The Little Nothings." Grade 1, vol. II.

Pierne, Gabriel, ENTRANCE OF THE LITTLE FAUNS from "Cyclalise" Suite No. 1. Grade 2, vol. II.

Saint Saëns, Camille, THE SWAN from "Carnival of the Animals." Grade 3, vol. II, side 1, band 5.

GERMANY

Bach, Johann Sebastian, BADINERIE from "Suite No. 2 in B Minor." Grade 3, vol. I, side 2, band 7. GIGUE from "Suite No. 3 in D Major." Grade 1, side 2, band 5. JESU, JOY OF MAN'S DESIRING from "Cantata No. 174." Grade 5, vol. I, side 2, band 5. LITTLE FUGUE IN G MINOR. Grade 6, vol. I, side 1, band 3. RONDEAU from "Suite No. 2" in B Minor. Grade 2, vol. II.

Van Beethoven, Ludwig, SECOND MOVEMENT from "Symphony No. 8 in F, Op. 93." Grade 6, vol. I, side 1, band 4.

Brahms, Johannes, HUNGARIAN DANCE No. 1 in G Minor. Grade 5, vol. II, side 1, band 1.

Gluck, Christoph, AIR GAI from "Iphigenie in Aulis." Grade 1, side 1, band 1. MUSETTE from "Armide" Ballet Suite. Grade 2, vol. II.

Handel, George Frederick, BOURREE AND MENUET II from "Royal Fireworks Music." Grade 3, vol. II, side 1, band 6. HORNPIPE from "Water Music." Grade 2, side 1, band 7.

Humperdinck, Engelbert, "Hansel and Gretel: PRELUDE." Grade 5, vol. II, side 1, band 5.

Meyerbeer, Giacomo, WALTZ from "Les Patineurs." Grade 2, side 2, band 7.

Offenbach, Jacques, BARCAROLLE from "The Tales of Hoffmann." Grade 3, vol. I, side 1, band 5.

Schumann, Robert, TRAUMEREI from "Scenes from Childhood," Op. 15. Grade 4, vol. 2, side 1, band 5.

Strauss, Richard, ROSENKAVALIER SUITE from "Der Rosenkavalier." Grade 6, vol. I, side 1, band 1.

Wagner, Richard, PRELUDE TO ACT III, from "Lohengrin." Grade 6, vol. I, side 2, band 5.

HUNGARY

Bartok, Bela, BEAR DANCE from "Hungarian Sketches." Grade 3, vol. 2, side 1, band 1. AN EVENING IN THE VILLAGE from "Hungarian Sketches." Grade 5, vol. II, side 1, band 3. JACK-IN-THE-BOX (Scherzando) from "Mikrokosmos Suite No. 2." Grade 2, side 2, band 6.

Kodály, Zoltan, ENTRANCE OF THE EMPEROR AND HIS COURT from "Hary Janos Suite." Grade 4, vol. II, side 2, band 3. VIENNESE MUSICAL CLOCK, from "Hary Janos Suite." Grade 2, side 2, band 1.

ITALY

Cimarosa, Domenico, NONTROPPO MOSSO from "Cimarosiana." Grade 2, vol. II.

Corelli, Arcangelo, SARABANDE from "Suite for Strings." Grade 6, vol. II, side 2, band 3.

Menotti, Gian-Carlo, SHEPHERD'S DANCE from "Amahl and the Night Visitors." Grade 5, vol. II, side 2, band 6.

Respighi, Ottorino, DANZA from "Brazilian Impressions." Grade 5, vol. II, side 2, band 2. PRELUDE TO "THE BIRDS." Grade 2, vol. II. THE PINES OF THE VILLA BORGHESE from "The Pines of Rome." Grade 4, vol. 1.

Rossini-Britten, MARCH from "Soirees Musicalés." Grade 1, side 2, band 4.

Rossini, Gioacchino, CAN-CAN from "The Fantastic Toyshop." Grade 2, side 1, band 6. FINALE from "William Tell Overture." Grade 3, vol. I, side 1, band 2.

Rossini-Resphigi, TARENTELLA from "The Fantastic Toyshop." Grade 3, vol. II, side 2, band 3.

Scarlatti, Comenico, NON PRESTO from "The Good-Humored Ladies." Grade 4, vol. II, side 2, band 4.

NORWAY

Grieg, Edward, IN THE HALL OF THE MOUNTAIN KING from "Peer Gynt Suite I." Grade 3, vol. II, side 1, band 3. NORWEGIAN RUSTIC MARCH from "Lyric Suite." Grade 4, vol. I, side 2, band 3.

RUSSIA

Borodin, Alexander, IN THE STEPPES OF CENTRAL ASIA. Grade 6, vol. I, side 1, band 2.

Gliere, Reinhold, RUSSIAN SAILOR'S DANCE from "The Red Poppy." Grade 6, vol. II, side 1, band 2.

Kabalevsky, Dmitri, MARCH AND COMEDIANS GALLOP from "The Comedians." Grade 3, vol. I, side 1, band 6. PANTOMIME from "The Comedians." Grade 1, side 1, band 4.

Khachaturian, Aran, DANCE OF THE ROSE MAIDENS from "Gayne Ballet Suite." Grade 1, vol. II.

Moussorgsky, Modeste, BALLET OF THE UNHATCHED CHICKS from "Pictures at an Exhibition." Grade 1, side 1, band 3. BYDLO from "Pictures at an Exhibition." Grade 2, side 1, band 4.

Prokofiev, Sergei, DEPARTURE from "Winter Holiday" Op. 122. Grade 2, side 2, band 3. MARCH from "Summer Day Suite." Grade 1, side 1, band 5. TROIKA from "Lieutenant Kije Suite." Grade 2, vol. II. WALTZ ON THE ICE from "Winter Holiday" Op. 122. Grade 3, vol. II, side 2, band 4.

Rimsky-Korsakoff, Nicholai, BRIDAL PROCESSION from "Le Coq d'or Suite." Grade 4, vol. I, side 1, band 5. DANCE OF THE BUFFOONS from the "Snow Maiden." Grade 2, vol. II.

Shostakovich, Dmitri, PETITE BALLERINA from "Ballet Suite No. 1." Grade 2, side 1, band 3. PIZZICATO POLKA from "Ballet Suite No. 1." Grade 1, side 2, band 9.

Stravinsky, Igor, BERCEUSE from "The Firebird Suite." Grade 1, side 1, band 7. INFERNAL DANCE OF KING KASTCHE I from "The Firebird Suite." Grade 5, vol. II, side 2, band 5. RUSSIAN DANCE from "Petrouchka." Grade 1, vol. II.

Tchaikovsky, Peter Ilich, DANCE OF THE LITTLE SWANS from "Swan Lake." Grade 1, side 2, band 2. DANCE OF THE SUGAR PLUM FAIRY from "Nutcracker Suite." Grade 1, vol. II. FOURTH MOVEMENT from "Symphony No. 4 in F Minor." Grade 6, vol. II, side 1, band 4. PUSS-IN-BOOTS AND THE WHITE CAT from "The Sleeping Beauty." Grade 3, vol. I, side 1, band 2. WALTZ from "The Sleeping Beauty Ballet." Grade 4, vol. I, side 1, band 2.

SPAIN

DeFalla, Manuel, SPANISH DANCE NO. 1 from "La Vida Breve." Grade 6, vol. I, side 2, band 2.

UNITED STATES

Anderson, Leroy, THE GIRL I LEFT BEHIND ME from "Irish Suite." Grade 5, vol. II, side 1, band 4.

Carpenter, John Alden, THE HURDY GURDY from "Adventures in a Perambulator." Grade 5, vol. II, side 2, band 3.

Copland, Aaron, CIRCUS MUSIC from "Red Pony Suite." Grade 3, vol. I, side 2, band 3. DREAM MARCH from "Red Pony Suite." Grade 2, vol. II. HOE-DOWN from "Rodeo—Ballet Suite." Grade 5, vol. II, side 1, band 3. STREET IN A FRONTIER TOWN from the Ballet Suite "Billy the Kid." Grade 6, vol. I, side 2, band 1.

Gottschalk, Louis Moreau, and Hershy Kay, GRAND WALK-AROUND from "Cakewalk." Grade 5, vol. I, side 2, band 1.

Gould, Morton, AMERICAN SALUTE. Grade 5, vol. I, side 2, band 4.

Griffes, Charles T., THE WHITE PEACOCK, Op. 7, No. 1. Grade 6, vol. I, side 2, band 3.

Grofé, Ferde, DESERT WATER HOLE from "Death Valley Suite." Grade 4, vol. I, side 2, band 3.

Hansen, Howard, BELLS "For the First Time." Grade 1, vol. II. CHILDREN'S DANCE from "Merry Mount Suite." Grade 3, vol. I, side 1, band 1.

Herbert, Victor, DAGGER DANCE from "Natoma." Grade 3, vol. I, side 1, band 3.

Howe, Mary, SAND. Grade 2, vol. II.

MacDowell, Edward, IN WAR TIME from "Suite No. 2, Op. 48 (Indian)." Grade 5, vol. I, side 1, band 2.

MacDowell, Karl, CHILDREN'S SYMPHONY: First Movement. Grade 3, vol. II, side 2, band 2. CHILDREN'S SYMPHONY: Third Movement. Grade 2, side 1, band 1.

McBride, Robert, PONY EXPRESS from "Punch and Judy." Grade 1, vol. II. PUMPKIN EATER'S LITTLE FUGUE. Grade 2, vol. II.

Menotti, Gian-Carlo, MARCH OF THE KINGS from "Amahl and the Night Visitors." Grade 1, vol. II.

Moore, Douglas, HARVEST SONG from "Farm Journal." Grade 1, vol. II.

Schuller, Gunthro, THE TWITTERING MACHINE from "Seven Studies on Themes of Paul Klee." Grade 2, vol. II.

Sousa, John Phillip, THE STARS AND STRIPES FOREVER. Grade 4, vol. I, side 1, band 4. SEMPER FIDELIS. Grade 3, vol. II, side 2, band 5.

Taylor, Deems, THE GARDEN OF LIVE FLOWERS from "Through the Looking Glass," Op. 12, A Suite for Orchestra. Grade 3, vol. II, side 2, band 1.

Thomson, Virgil, THE ALLIGATOR AND THE COON from "Arcardian Songs and Dances." Grade 3, vol. 2, side 2, band 1. WALKING SONG from "Arcadian Songs and Dances." Grade 1, side 2, band 1.

FRANCE–UNITED STATES

Calliet, Lucien, VARIATIONS ON THE THEME—"Pop Goes the Weasel." Grade 4, vol. I, side 1, band 1.

IRELAND–AMERICA

Herbert, Victor, MARCH OF THE TOYS from "Babes in Toyland." Grade 2, side 2, band 2.

ITALY–ENGLAND

Rossini-Britten, BOLERO from "Soirees Museolem." Grade 2, vol. II.

Story Records

Educational Audio Visual Aids, Inc., 29 Marble Ave., Pleasantville, New York 10510
Filmstrips and Records:
  Afternoon of a Fawn—Debussy
  Billy the Kid—Copland
  Rodeo—Copland
  West Side Story—Bernstein

Golden Records, Affiliated Publishers, Inc., Rockefeller Center, New York, N.Y. 10020
  I Love a Marching Band.
  Song-Stories from the Bible.
  Great Classic Treasury of Fairy Tales.

Society for Visual Education, 1345 Denersey Parkway, Chicago, Illinois
Filmstrips and Recordings:
   Nutcracker Suite—Tchaikowsky
   Sorcerer's Apprentice—Dukan

Young People's Records, Greystone Corp., 100 Sixth Ave., New York, N.Y.
   All Aboard
   Circus at the Opera
   Creepy, the Crawly Caterpillar
   Grandfather's Farm
   Hot Cross Buns
   Hunter at the Sea
   The Kings Trumpet
   Little Brass Band
   Little Rodeo
   The Lonesome House
   The Merry Toy Shop
   Pedro in Brazil

Recordings for Dramatizations and Rhythm Activity
(Activity Records)

Bowmar Orchestral Library, 10510 Burbank Blvd., North Hollywood, Calif. 91610
   Marches—Album #54.
Capitol Records Distributing Corporation, 1750 North Vine Street, Hollywood, Calif. 90028
   Listen, Move and Dance. Vols. I & II.
Children's Record Guild, The Greystone Corp., 100 Sixth Ave., New York, N.Y.
   Do This, Do That
   Einsie Weensie Spider
   The Circus Comes to Town
   My Playful Scarf
   A Walk in the Forest
   Sing-along Series
   The Monkey and the Donkey
   Sunday in the Park
   Visit to My Little Friend
   Big Rock Candy Mountain
R.C.A. Adventure Series
   Grade I   Massenet—*Argonaise* (from "El Cid")
   Vol. I   Tchaikovsky—*Dance of the Little Swan* (from "Swan Lake")
         Rossini—*Britten March* (from "Soirées Musicales")

Kabalevsky—*Pantomime* (from the "Comedians")

Shostakovich—*Pizzicato Polka* (from "Ballet Suite #1")

Delibes—*Waltz of the Doll* (from "Coppelia")

Grade II
Vol. I
Moussorgsky—*Bydlo* (from "Pictures of an Exhibition")

Herbert—*March of the Toys*

Shostakovich—*Petite Ballerina* (from "Ballet Suite #1")

Grade III
Vol. I
Offenbach—*Barcarolle* (from "Tales of Hoffman")

Copland—*Circus Music* (from "The Red Pony")

Debussy—*Snow Is Dancing* (from "Children's Corner Suite")

Grade III
Vol. II
Bartok—*Bear Dance* (from "Hungarian Sketches")

Grieg—*In the Hall of the Mountain King* (from "Peer Gynt Suite")

Saint-Saëns—*The Swan* (from "Carnival of Animals")

Prokofiev—*Waltz on Ice* (from "Winter Holiday")

Grade IV
Vol. I
Tchaikovsky—*Waltz* (from "Sleeping Beauty")

Grade VI
Vol. II
Walton—*Valse* (from "Façade Suite")

These selections have definite moods, strong rhythmic patterns, and appealing melodies which are excellent for interpretation.

Students and teachers wishing to extend their repertoire may enjoy listening to some of the following recordings. These are only a few of those available today. A wide variety is included, recognizing the varied tastes of both students and teachers.

Individual Recordings for Classroom Listening
(Listed by composer)

Alling, John. *Afro Fuga Percussion*. Golden Crest Records, Inc.
Anderson, Leroy. *The Typewriter Song*. Archives.
————. *Sleighride*. Archives.
————. *Syncopated Clock*. Archives.
Anthiel, George. *Ballet Mecanique* (airplane propellers, automobile horns, player pianos, annils, bells, percussion instruments). Columbia.

FIGURE 10–5   Dramatizing records provides another type of music experience.

Bach, J. S. *Air for the G String.* Strings by Starlight. Capitol.

————. *Concerto in G Major.* Harpsichord. Mercury.

————. *Little Fugue in G Minor* (from Album: "Family Fun with Familiar Music"). R.C.A. Victor.

————. *Toccata in D Minor.* E. Power Biggs, Organist. Columbia Records.

Bartok, Bela. *Concerto for Viola and Orchestra.* Bartok Records.

————. *Music for Strings, Percussion and Celesta.* Epic Records.

————. *Rhapsody #1 for Violin and Orchestra.* Vanguard Records.

Beethoven, Ludwig van. *Folk Dance.* (Album: Heifetz Encores.) R.C.A. Victor.

————. *Famous Overtures,* London Records.

Benson, Warren. *Variations on a Handmade Theme* (scored for Hand Clappers). Golden Crest Records, Inc.

Bernstein, Leonard. *What Is Jazz?* Columbia Records.

Borodin, Alexander. *Polovetsian Dances* from "Prince Igor." Columbia Records.

Brahms, Johannes. *Rubinstein Plays Brahms.* R.C.A. Victor.

————. *The Four Symphonies of Johannes Brahms.* Angel.

Britten, Benjamin. *A Young Person's Guide to the Orchestra.* London.

————. *Let's Make an Opera*. London.

————. *A Ceremony of Carols*. London.

Broadway Musicals. Sung by Mario Lanza. R.C.A. Victor.

Charminade, Cecili. *Spanish Dance*. (Album: "Violin Virtuosity.") Westminster Records.

Chopin, Frederic. *Chopin Nocturnes*. R.C.A. Victor.

Classical Music for People Who Hate Classical Music. R.C.A. Victor.

Copland, Aaron. *Appalachian Spring*. R.C.A. Victor.

————. *Billy the Kid*. R.C.A. Victor.

————. *The Children's Suite* from "The Red Pony." Decca Records.

————. *Concerto for Clarinet and String Orchestra*. Columbia Records.

————. *Fanfare for the Common Man*. Columbia Records.

————. *Lincoln Portrait*. Columbia Records.

————. *Organ Symphony*. Columbia Records.

Cowell, Henry. *Ostinato Pianissimo* (percussion and rice bowls). Folkways.

Curtain Up! *Favorite Overtures*. Mercury Records.

Debussy, Claude. *Afternoon of a Faun*. Columbia Records.

————. *En Bateau from "Petite Suite."*

————. *Clair de Lune—Westminster*.

————. *La Cathedral Engloutic*.

Debussy, Claude and Ravel, Maurice. *The Popular Music of Ravel and Debussy* (Arabesque #1. Sunken Cathedral, Fireworks, and others). Columbia Records.

————. *Debussy's Piano Music*. (Children's Corner Suite and others.) Columbia Records.

————. *Clair de Lune*. Columbia Records.

————. *Petite Suite from Piano Album—four hands*. Columbia Records.

————. *Reverie*. Capitol Records.

Dvorak, Antonin. *Slavonic Dance in C Minor, Op. 46, No. 7*. Adventures in Music Series, vol. 11. R.C.A. Victor.

Einene, Gottfried Von. *Capriccio for Orchestra, Op. 2* (Album: New Directions in Music and Sound). Decca Records.

Enseco, Georges. *Rumanian Rhapsody #1*. Westminster Records.

Ginastera, Alberta. *Estancia—Ballet Suite*. R.C.A. Victor.

————. *Wheat Dance* from the Ballet Suite "Estancia." Adventures in Music Series, vol. 1. R.C.A. Victor.

Grainger, Percy (Arr.) *Londonderry Air*. ("Irish Tune from Country Derry.") Adventures in Music Series, vol. 1. R.C.A. Victor.

Gretry, Andre Modeste. *Gigue* from "Cephale et Procris." *Tambourin* Ballet Music from "Cephale et Procris." Adventures in Music Series, grade 1. R.C.A. Victor.

Griffes, Charles. *Poem for Flute and Orchestra*. Mercury Records.

————. *The Pleasure Dome of Kubla Khan*. Mercury Records.

—————. *Clouds, Op. 7, #4.* Mercury.
—————. *The White Peacock, Op. 7, #1.* Mercury.
Grofé, Ferde. *Death Valley Suite, Grand Canyon Suite, Hudson River Suite, Mississippi Suite.* Capital Records.
Handel, George Frederic. *The Messiah.* R.C.A. Victor.
—————. *Water Music.* R.C.A. Victor.
Holst, Gustav. *The Planets, Op. 32.* Capitol Records.
Honegger, Arthur. *Pacific 231.* Westminster Records.
Humperdinck, Engelbert. *Children's Prayer from Hansel and Gretel.*
Ives, Charles. *Variations on Holidays Symphony.* Columbia.
Ivey, Jean Eichelberger. *Pinball.* Folk.
Japan, Its Music and Its People (and music of other countries). Desto Records.
Khachaturian, Aram. "Waltz" from *Masquerade Suite.* Adventures in Music Series, vol. 11. R.C.A. Victor.
Lecunona, Ernesto. "Andalucia" from the Spanish Suite *Andalucia.* Adventures in Music Series, vol. 1. R.C.A. Victor.
Liszt, Franz. *Rubenstein Plays Liszt.* R.C.A. Victor.
Mendelssohn, Felix. *Violin Concerto in E Minor.* London.
—————. *Hebrides* (Fingal's Cove Overture). Mercury.
Moussorgsky, Modiste. *Pictures at an Exhibition.* R.C.A. Victor.
Mozart, Wolfgang Amadeus. *Menuetto* from "Divertimento No. 17. K. 344." Adventures in Music Series, vol. 11.
—————. *Romanze* from "Eine kleine Nachtmusik." Adventures in Music Series, vol. 1. R.C.A. Victor.
Oliveros, Pauline. *Sound Patterns* (Improvised vocal sounds). Odyssey.
Phillips, Burrill. *John Alden and Priscilla.* Mercury.
—————. *Selections from McGuffey's Reader.* Mercury.
—————. *The Midnight Ride of Paul Revere.* Mercury.
—————. *The One Horse Shay.* Mercury.
Rimsky-Korsakoff, Nikolai. *Scheherzade Suite.* Columbia.
Saint-Saëns, Camille. *Carnival of the Animals.* Columbia Records.
—————. *Dance Macabre* (Album: "Invitation to the Dance"). Columbia Records.
Schubert, Franz. First Movement (Allegro from Symphony No. 5 in B-Flat). Adventures in Music Series, vol. 1. R.C.A. Victor.
Schuman, William. *New England Triptych.* Archives.
Schumann, Robert. *Concerto in A Minor, Op. 129.* Columbia Records.
Shostakovich, Dmitri. *Age of Gold.* Capitol Records.
—————. *Polka* from "The Age of Gold." R.C.A. Victor.
Smetana, Bedrick. *The Moldan.* Mercury Records.
Strauss, Johann. *The Blue Danube.* London.
—————. *Tales of the Vienna Woods.* London.
Tchaikovsky, Peter Ilich. *1812 Overture.* Mercury.
—————. *Nutcracker Suite.* Columbia.

Villa-Lobos, Heitor. *The Little Train of the Caipira* from "Bachianas Brasileiras No. 2." Adventures in Music Series, vol. 1, R.C.A. Victor.

Wagner, Richard. *Der Meistersinger*. London.

————. *Overture to Tannhauser*. R.C.A. Victor.

————. *Parsifal*. London.

————. *Prelude to Act III, Lohengrin*. Columbia.

Choral Groups—Mormon Tabernacle Choir. *Hymns and Songs of Brotherhood*. The Roger Wagner Chorale. *Folk Songs of the British Isles, Folk Songs of the Old World*.

Musicals—Bock, Jerry; Hornick, Sheldon. *Fiddler on the Roof*.

Rodgers, Richard; Hammerstein, Oscar. *Carousel*. Decca.

Oklahoma. Columbia.

South Pacific. Columbia.

Sound of Music. Columbia.

BOOKS

Children, like adults, tend to be influenced by their environment; therefore it is important that books about music be included in the room. Our emphasis on activity during the late years has sometimes deemphasized the importance of research in music in the elementary school and reading for pleasure in this area. The most effective activity programs include the search for information about music but often the emphasis on singing and playing leaves little time for other activities. Today's books are fascinating, well-written, and informative. Rotating the books available to children in your room may encourage reading and in this way stimulate greater interest in the subject. A child who reads one of the excellent biographies of Beethoven may be motivated to listen to his compositions.

This is a project which can be developed most effectively through the cooperation of the music teachers and the classroom teachers.

Stories about Music and Musicians
(With grade level indicated)

Aebersold, Maria. *The Enchanted Drum*. Parents' Magazine Press. 1969. K–3.

Alden, Raymond. *Why The Chimes Rang*. Bobbs. 1954. 4–6.

Alexander, Anne. *I Want a Whistle*. Hale. 1966. K–3.

d'Aulaire, Edgar, and d'Aulaire, Ingri. *Foxie: The Singing Dog*. Doubleday. 1969. K–3.

Bakeless, Catherine. *Story Lives of American Composers*. Lippincott. 1962.

Baldwin, Lillian. *Music for Young Listeners: Green Book, Crimson Book, and Blue Book*. Silver Burdett. 1951. 4–6.

Balet, Jan. *What Makes an Orchestra*. Oxford University Press. 1951.

Berkowitz, F. P. *On Lutes, Recorders and Harpsichords*. Atheneum. 1967. 4–6.

Bernstein, Leonard. *The Joy of Music*. Simon and Schuster. 1959.

Biemiller, Ruth. *Dance: The Story of Katherine Dunham*. Doubleday. 1969. 4–6.

Bonne, Rose, and Mills, Alan. *I Know an Old Lady*. Rand McNally. 1961.

Bothwell, Jean. *Little Flute Player*. Hale. 1966. K–3.

Brandenberg, Aliki, adapt. *Hush Little Baby*. Prentice-Hall. 1968. Pres–3.

Browne, C. A. *The Story of Our National Ballads*. Crowell. 1960. 4–6.

Buchanan, F. R., and Luckenbill, C. L. *How Man Made Music*. Follett. 1959. 4–6.

Bulla, C. R. *The Ring and The Fire*. Crowell. 1962. 4–6.

———. *Stories of Favorite Operas*. Crowell. 1959. 4–6.

———. *More Stories of Favorite Operas*. Crowell. 1965. 4–6.

Carmer, Carl. *America Sings*. Knopf. 1950. K–6.

Chapin, Victor. *Giants of the Keyboard*. Lippincott. 1967. Grade 6 and up.

Chappel, Warren. *The Nutcracker*. Knopf. 1958. 4–6.

Clare, Helen. *The Cat and the Fiddle and Other Stories*. Prentice-Hall. 1968. Pres–3.

Close, E. T. *The Magic Ring: Children's Tales from Richard Wagner*. Carleton. 1964. 4–6.

Collier, J. L. *Which Musical Instrument Shall I Play?* W. W. Norton & Co. 1969. P–6.

Commins, Dorothy Berliner. *All About the Symphony Orchestra and What It Plays*. E. M. Hale & Co. 1961. 4–6.

Cooke, D. E. *The Sorcerer's Apprentice*. Winston. 1947. 4–6.

Craig, Hean. *The Heart of the Orchestra, The Story of the Violin and Other String Instruments*. Lerner Publications. 1962.

———. *The Story of Musical Notes*. Lerner Publications. 1962.

Crozier, Eric. *The Master-Singers of Nuremburg*. Walck. 1964. 4–6.

De Mille, Agnes. *The Book of the Dance*. Golden Press. 1961.

———. *Dance to the Piper*. Little. 1952.

Deucher, Sybil. *Edward Grieg, a Boy of the Northland*. Dutton. 1946.

Distler, Bette. *Timothy Tuneful*. Crowell-Collier. 1968. K–3.

Dobrin, Arnold. *Aaron Copland: His Life and Times*. Crowell. 1967.

Eaton, Jeannette. *Trumpeter's Tale: The Story of Young Louis Armstrong.* Morrow. 1955. 4–6.

Emberley, Barbara, adapt. *London Bridge Is Falling Down.* Little. 1967.

————. *One Wide River to Cross.* Prentice-Hall. 1966. K–3.

————. *Simon's Song.* Prentice-Hall. 1969. Pres–3.

Erlich, Lillian. *What Jazz Is All About.* Julian Messner. 1962.

Ewen, David. *Panorama of American Popular Music.* Prentice-Hall. 1957.

————. *Popular American Composers.* Wilson. 1962. 4–6.

————. *With a Song in His Heart.* Holt. 1963. (Tells the story of Richard Rogers.)

Fletcher, Helen J. *The First Book of Bells.* Franklin Watts. 1959.

Fox, Lilla M. *Instruments of Popular Music.* Roy Publishers. 1966.

Fraser, Beatrice. *Arturo and Mr. Bang.* Bobbs. 1963. K–3.

Gilbert, W. S., and Sullivan, Arthur. *The Pirates of Penzance.* Watts. 1963. 4–6.

Gilmore, Lee. *Folk Instruments.* Lerner Publications, Co. 1962.

Givson, Enid. *The Golden Cockerel.* Walck. 1963. 4–6.

Grote, William. *Fiddle, Flute and the River.* Meredith. 1967. 4–6.

Hanley, Eve. *A New Song.* Weybright & Talley. 1968. 4–6.

Headington, C. *The Orchestra and Its Instruments.* 1965.

Higgins, Don. *Papa's Going to Buy Me a Mockingbird.* Seabury. 1968. Pres–3.

Hodges, Margaret. *One Little Drum.* Follett. 1958. K–3.

Hoffman, E. T. A. *Coppelia, the Girl with Enamel Eyes.* Knopf. 1965. 4–6.

Huges, L. *The First Book of Jazz.* Franklin Watts. 1955. 4–6.

Hume, Ruth, and Hume, Paul. *Lion of Poland.* Hawthorne. 1962. 4–6.

Huntington, H. E. *Tune Up, the Instruments of the Orchestra and Their Players.* Doubleday. 1942. 4–6.

Kaufmann, H. L. *The Story of 100 Great Composers.* Grosset. 1969. 4–6.

Keats, Ezra Jack. *The Little Drummer Boy.* Macmillan. 1968. K–3.

Kettelkamp, L. *Drums, Rattles & Bells.* Morrow. 1960. K–3.

————. *Flutes, Whistles & Reeds. Morrow.* 1962. 4–6.

————. *Horns.* Morrow. 1964. 4–6.

————. *Singing Strings.* Morrow. 1958. 4–6.

Key, F. S. *The Star Spangled Banner.* Doubleday. 1942. K–6.

Krisher, R. H. *Playback: The Story of Recording Devices.* Lerner Publishing. 1962. 4–6.

Kruss, James. *The Proud Wooden Drummer.* Doubleday. 1969. K–3.

Leodhas, S. N. *Always Room for Once More.* Holt. 1965. K–3.

Lerner, Sharon. *Places of Musical Fame.* Lerner Publishing. 1962. 4–6.

Lewiton, Mina. *John Philip Sousa, the Marching King*. Didier. 1944. 4–6.

Lobel, Anita. *The Troll Music*. Harper. 1966. K–3.

Lyons, J. H. *Stories of Our American Patriotic Songs*. Vanguard Press. 1942. 4–6.

Mandell, Muriel, and Wood, Robert E. *Make Your Own Musical Instruments*. Sterling Publishing. 1959. K–6.

Menotti, Gian-Carlo. *Amahl and the Night Visitors*. McGraw. 1952. 4–6.

Miller, N. *The Story of the Star Spangled Banner*. Children's Press. 1965. K–6.

Mirsky, R. P. *Johann Sebastian Bach*. Follett. 1965. 4–6.

————. *Joseph Haydn*. Follett. 1963. 4–6.

————. *Mozart*. Follett. 1960. 4–6.

Montgomery, E. R. *The Story Behind Popular Songs*. Dodd, Mead & Co. 1958. 4–6.

————. *William C. Handy: Father of the Blues*. Garrard. 1968. 4–6.

Moore, J. T. *Story of Silent Night*. Concordia. 1965. K-6.

Niles & Smith. *Folk Ballads for Young Actors*. Holt, Rinehart and Winston. 1962. 4–6.

————. *Folk Carols for Young Actors*. Holt, Rhinehart and Winston. 1962. 4–6.

Nussbaumer, Mares, and Nussbaumer, Paul. *Away in a Manger*. Harcourt. 1965. K–6.

Papas, William. *Tasso*. Coward-McCann. 1966. 4–6.

Posell, Elsa Z. *This Is an Orchestra*. Houghton Mifflin. 1950. 4–6.

Prokofiev, Serge. *Pete and the Wolf*. Watts. 1961. K–6.

Reidy, J. P., and Richards, Norman. *Leonard Bernstein*. Childrens Press. 4–6.

Richardson, A. L. *Tooters, Tweeters, Strings and Beaters*. Grosset and Dunlap Publishers. 1964. K–6.

Rublowsky, John. *Music in America*. Crowell. 1967. 4–6.

Samachson, Dorothy, and Samachson, Joseph. *The Fabulous World of Opera*. Rand McNally. 1962. 4–6.

Schackburg, Richard. *Yankee Doodle*. Prentice-Hall. 1965. K–6.

Shaw, Arnold. *The Rock Revolution*. Crowell-Collier. 1969. 4–6.

Shippen, K. B., and Seidlova, Anca. *The Heritage of Music*. Viking Press. 1963. 4–6.

Skolsky, Sidney. *Music Box Book*. Dutton. 1946. K–6.

Staddard, H. *From These Comes Music*. Thomas Y. Crowell. 1952. 4–6.

Stearns, Monroe. *Richard Wagner, Titan of Music*. Watts. 1969. 4–6.

————. *Wolfgang Amadeus Mozart, Master of Pure Music*. Watts. 1968. 4–6.

Stevenson, Augusta. *Francis Scott Key: Boy with a Song*. Bobbs. 1960. 4–6.

Suggs, William. *Meet the Orchestra.* Macmillan. 1966. 4–6.

Walden, Daniel. *The Nutcracker.* Lippincott. 1959. 4–6.

Warren, Dr. F., and Warren, Lee. *The Music of Africa.* Prentice-Hall. 1970. 4–6.

Weil, Ann. *John Philip Sousa, Marching Boy.* Bobbs. 1959. 4–6.

Wenning, Elizabeth. *Christmas Mouse.* Holt. 1959. K–3.

Wheeler, Opal. *Adventures of Richard Wagner.* Dutton, 1939. 4–6.

————. *Franz Schubert and His Merry Little Friends.* Dutton. 1939. 4–6.

————. *Frederic Chopin, Son of Poland, Early Years.* Dutton. 1949. 4–6.

————. *Frederic Chopin, Son of Poland, Later Years.* Dutton, 1949. 4–6.

————. *Handel at the Court of Kings.* Dutton. 4–6.

————. *H.M.S. Pinafore.* Dutton. 1946. 4–6.

————. *Joseph Haydn, the Merry Little Peasant.* Dutton. 1937. 4–6.

————. *Ludwig Beethoven and the Chiming Tower Bells.* Dutton. 1944. 4–6.

————. *Paganini, Master of Strings.* Dutton. 1950. 4–6.

————. *Peter Tchaikovsky and the Nutcracker Ballet.* Dutton. 1946. 4–6.

————. *Sing for Christmas, A Round of Christmas Carols, Stories of the Carols.* Dutton. 1946. 4–6.

————. *Stephen Foster and His Little Dog, Tray.* Dutton. 1941. 4–6.

————. *Story of Tchaikovsky.* Dutton. 1964. 4–6.

Yates, Elizabeth. *With Pipe, Paddle, and Song: A Story of the French-Canadian Voyageurs circa 1750.* Dutton. 1968. 4–6.

Yulya. *Bears Are Sleeping.* Scribner's. 1967. K–6.

Catalogues

Catalogues from these companies would be helpful in keeping up with new materials. Check with your local dealer for the latest releases and changes in catalogue listing.

A & M Records
1416 No. LaBrea
Los Angeles, California 90029

Archives
Check-Everest Records
10920 Wilshire Blvd.
West Los Angeles, California

Angel Records
1750 North Vine Street
New York City, New York 90028

Audio-Visual Enterprises
P.O. Box 8686
Los Angeles, California 90008

Austin Custom Records, Inc.
P.O. Box 9190
Austin, Texas 91601

Bell Records, Inc. (Distributors)
Affiliated Publishers
New York, New York

Bowmar Record Co.
10510 Burbank Blvd.
North Hollywood, California
  91601

Caedmon Records, Inc.
505 Eighth Avenue
New York, New York 10018

Camden Records
c/o RCA Records
155 East 24th Street
New York, New York 10010

Capitol Records
1750 N. Vine Street
Hollywood, California 90028

Chesterfield Music Shops, Inc.
12 Warren Street
New York, New York 10007

Children's Music Center, Inc.
5373 West Pico Blvd.
Los Angeles, California 90019

C.M.S. Records
12 Warren Street
New York, New York 10010
(Distributors for UNICEF
  Records)

Columbia Records
51 West 52nd Street
New York, New York 10019

Coral Records
445 Park Avenue
New York, New York 10007

Coronet Recording Co.
379 East Broad Street
Columbus, Ohio 43215

Crest Records
220 Broadway
Huntington Station, New York
  11746

Crown Records
5810 So. Normandie Avenue
Los Angeles, California

Decca Records
445 Park Avenue
New York, New York 10007

Desto Records
12 East 44th Street
New York, New York

Disneyland Records
Educational Division
156 Fifth Avenue
New York, New York 10010

Educational Record Sales
157 Chambers Street
New York, New York 10007

Enrichment Teaching Materials
246 Fifth Avenue
New York, New York 10001

Eye-Gote House Inc.,
146–01 Archer Avenue
Jamaica, New York 11435

Folkways Records
117 West 46th Street
New York, New York

Folkways/Scholastic
906 Sylvan Avenue
Englewood Cliffs, New Jersey
  07632

The Golden Record Library
A Musical Heritage for Young
  America
250 W. 57th Street
New York, New York 10019

Imperial Productions, Inc.
Dept. K
Kankakee, Illinois 60901

Kimbo Educational Records
P.O. Box 55
Deal, New Jersey 07723

Keyboard Junior
1346 Chapel Street
New Haven, Conn. 06511

Learning Arts
P.O. Box 917
Wichita, Kansas 67201

Listening Library
1 Park Avenue
Old Greenwich, Conn. 06870

Mercury Records
35 East Wacker Drive
Chicago, Illinois 60601

Odyssey
c/o Columbia Records
51 West 42nd Street
New York, New York 10019

RCA Victor Records
155 East 24th Street
New York, New York 10010

Schwann Inc. (Distributors)
137 Newbury Street
Boston, Mass. 02116

SPA Records
2519 East Erie
Chicago, Ill. 60611

Summy-Birchard
Evanston, Illinois 60204

Systems for Education
612 N. Michigan Avenue
Chicago, Illinois 60611

Time Records, Inc.
2 West 45th Street
New York, New York

Twentieth-Century Fox Records
c/o ABC Records, Inc.
8235 Beverly Blvd.
Los Angeles, California 90049

United Artists Records
729 Seventh Avenue
New York, New York

Vanguard Records
71 West 23rd Street
New York, New York 10010

Vista Records
800 Sonora Avenue
Glendale, California 91201

Vox Records
211 East 43rd Street
New York, New York 10017

Warner Brothers Records
4000 Warner Blvd.
Burbank, California 91505

Westminster Records
c/o ABC Records, Inc.
8255 Beverly Blvd.
Los Angeles, California 90048

Young Peoples Records
Children's Record Guild
100 Sixth Avenue
New York, New York 10013
(Franson Corporation
  Distributors)

SONG BOOKS

Carefully prepared song books and accompanying records, which have been discussed above, are available for all grade levels. Like the recording, the songs in one grade level may be adapted to several grades depending on the sophistication of the song, the class members, and the reason for choosing the songs. For example, a second-grade teacher might make it easier for children to transfer from one teacher to another by starting the year with the discovery she and the children know some songs in common. She could borrow "their" books, gradually making the transition to "new" books. Since building repertoire is important, many songs become part of our experience. Often a song can be changed by adding harmony through singing parts or descants or using more complicated accompaniments but, however it is sung, it offers pleasure to many ages.

Timing is important. Some groups could be most anxious to use graded books. In this case the emphasis would be changed. Familiar songs may be found in several books and new songs in these books added to the child's repertoire more quickly than usual. The new organizations of schools may eliminate this problem, placing the emphasis on sequential musical experience but unattached to grade-level material.

The teaching suggestions in the teacher's books are often excellent. They have been carefully thought out and at least offer a starting point, especially for new teachers. Their inclusion is not to dictate procedures but simply to offer suggestions which may help the teacher feel more comfortable and secure in bringing out certain elements in the song, which may add to the students' musical pleasure.

The vocal range of most songs included in the several series is lower than in previous publications. To the amateur they may still seem too high. A little practice, including humming and singing with the recordings which accompany the series, may be helpful in increasing range which is really excellent for children. If it proves to be too difficult for the teacher, the song may be presented in the teacher's range and the pitch raised later for the children.

The accompaniments vary in difficulty, from simple chords to more complex rhythmic patterns. Frequently songs are taught without any accompaniment or the melodic line is played on bells or piano, usually to help the teacher keep on pitch and give a little added security without overshadowing the text. Children must know what the song is about if we are to hold their interest and motivate them to learn the song. Therefore, the text must predominate at all times. The accompaniment can be added when the song is learned to make it a richer musical experience for the children.

Teachers who have never played the piano but wish to learn might enjoy one of the beginning piano methods in these series which emphasize the chord approach. In this way the piano may be used in place of the autoharp, ukulele, or guitar by following the chords outlined for these instruments.

The variety of songs in the basic song series is rich. Songs of many nations with authentic information included on origin and history expand the child's knowledge to learning the characteristics of the music of the people of the world as well as some of their interesting cultural backgrounds. Often the origin of a song can be the starting point for many interesting discoveries about music and people. For example, a comparison of the work songs of several countries: Compare a work song with a sea chanty or a spinning song of the Scandinavian countries. There are songs for fun, quiet songs, sad songs, songs for action, song stories, singing games—in fact every type of song plus a description of several recorded concert selections.

The texts are so well prepared that any teacher who has the interest and is willing to work could develop a music program for the students.

In addition to the basic song series there are many fine song books available for special interest groups. Several of these are listed in the bibliography.

The bibliography which follows includes only a few of the available materials. New books and recordings are being released so fast it is best for teachers to be on the mailing lists of the publishers (included below). In this way it is possible to be informed of new trends and publications.

Books

Addresses of Music Textbook Publishers
Allyn and Bacon Inc., 470 Atlantic Ave., Boston, Mass. 02210
American Book Company, 300 Pike St., Cincinnati, Ohio 45202
Follett Publishing Company, 1010 West Washington Blvd., Chicago, Illinois 60607
Ginn and Company, 191 Spring St., Lexington, Mass. 02173
Holt, Rinehart and Winston, Inc., 383 Madison Ave., New York, N.Y. 10017

Prentice-Hall, Inc., Englewood Cliffs, New Jersey 07632
Silver Burdett Co., Park Avenue & Columbia Rd., Morristown, N.J. 07960
Summy-Birchard Publishing Co., 1834 Ridge Ave., Evanston, Ill. 60204

Song Books
(Not in Series.)

Bailey, Charity. *Sing a Song with Charity Bailey.* Plymouth Music Co., New York, N.Y.

Beckman, Frederick. *Partner Songs and More Partner Songs.* Ginn and Co., Lexington, Mass. 02173

Bomemark, Guilan. *The Play Game Song Book.* Allyn and Bacon, Boston, Mass. 02210

Boni, M. B. *The Fireside Book of Favorite American Songs.* Simon & Schuster, Inc., 1 W. 39th St., New York, N.Y. 10018
————. *Fireside Book of Folk Songs.* Simon & Schuster, 1 W. 39th St., New York, N.Y. 10018

Bonne, Rose, and Mills, Alan. *I Know an Old Lady.* Rand McNally & Co., Chicago, Ill. 60680

Brand, Oscar. *Singing Holiday, The Calendar in Folk Song.* Alfred A. Knopf, New York, N.Y. 10022

Brandenberg, Aliki, adapt. *Hush Little Baby.* Prentice-Hall, Inc., Englewood Cliffs, N.J. 07632

Burrows, Abe. *The Abe Burrows Songbook.* Doubleday & Co., Inc., 501 Franklin, Garden City, N. Y. 11531

Carmer, Carl. *America Sings.* Knopf, New York, N.Y. 10022

Cole, William. *Oh, What Nonsense!* Viking Press, 625 Madison Ave., New York, N.Y. 10022

Coleman, Satis N., and Thorn, Alice G. *Singing Time, Another Singing Time.* John Day Co., New York, N.Y. 10010

Dallin, Leon, and Dallin, Lynn. *Heritage Songster.* William C. Brown & Co., Dubuque, Iowa 52001

Dawley, McLaughlin. *American Indian Songs.* Highland Music Co., 1311 North Highland Ave., Hollywood, Calif. 90028

de Angeli, Margaret. *Book of Favorite Hymns.* Doubleday & Co., Inc., 501 Franklin St., Garden City, N.Y. 11531

DeCesare, Ruth. *Folksong Collection.* Mills Music, 1619 Broadway, New York, N.Y. 10019

Dietz, Betty Warner, and Park, Thomas Choonbai. *Folk Songs of China, Japan, Korea.* John Day Co., 200 Madison Ave., New York, N.Y. 10019

Ehret, Walter, and Evans, George. *The International Book of Christmas Carols.* Prentice-Hall, Inc., Englewood Cliffs, N.J. 07632

Fukuda, Hanako. *Favorite Songs of Japanese Children.* Highland

Music Co., 1311 North Highland Ave., Hollywood, Calif. 90028

Grissom, M. A. *The Negro Sings a New Heaven.* Dover Publications, Inc., 180 Varick St., New York, N.Y. 10014

Hanley, Eve. *A New Song.* Weybright & Talley, 750 Third Ave., New York, N.Y. 10017

Kodály, Zoltan. *Fifty Nursery Songs within the Range of Five Notes plus 333 Elementary Exercises.* Boosey & Hawkes, Oceanside, N.Y.

Landeck, Beatrice. *Songs to Grow On and More Songs to Grow On.* Marks Music Co., 136 W. 52 St., New York, N.Y. 10019

Lenski, Lois. *Songs of Mr. Small.* Oxford University Press, 200 Madison Ave., New York, N.Y. 10016

McLaughlin, Roberta. *Folk Songs of Africa.* Highland Music Co., 1311 North Highland Ave., Hollywood, Calif. 90028

————. *Latin American Folk Songs.* Highland Music Co., 1311 North Highland Ave., Hollywood, Calif. 90028

————. *Children's Songs of Mexico.* Highland Music Co., 1311 North Highland Ave., Hollywood, Calif. 90028

Nye, Robert, et al. *Singing with Children.* Wadsworth Publishing Co., Belmont, Calif. 94002

Nye, Vernice T., Nye, Robert E., and Nye, Virginia H. *Toward World Understanding with Song.* Wadsworth Publishing Co., 10 Davis Drive, Belmont, Calif. 94002

Scott, Thomas J. *Song of America.* Thomas Y. Crowell Co., 201 Park Ave. S., New York, N.Y. 10016

Seeger, Ruth Crawford. *American Folk Songs for Children; American Folk Songs for Christmas; Animal Folk Songs for Children.* Doubleday and Co., Inc., 501 Franklin, Garden City, N.Y. 11531

Simon, H. W. *Christmas Songs and Carols.* Houghton Mifflin Co., 2 Park St., Boston, Mass. 02107

Snyder, Alice M. *Sing and Strum.* Mills Music Co., 1610 Broadway, New York, N.Y. 10019

Songs Children Like. Association for Childhood Education, 3615 Wisconsin Ave., Washington, D.C. 20016

Van Loon, H. W. *The Songs We Sing.* Simon & Schuster, 1 West 39th St., New York, N.Y. 10018

Wessells, Katharine T., ed. *The Golden Song Book.* Golden Press, New York, N.Y.

AUDIOVISUAL MATERIALS

In addition to the materials already mentioned certain audiovisual materials can greatly enhance the music program. The classroom teacher and the music teacher must not overlook the value of these materials as a classroom resource, particularly films, filmstrips, electronic equipment, and television.

Audiovisual Materials
(These catalogs for audiovisual material should be helpful)

Bell Telephone Company. Write directly to the nearest office.

Stanley Bowmar Company, 622 Radier Drive, Glendale, Calif. 91201

Churchill Films, 662 N. Robertson Blvd., Los Angeles, Calif. 90069

Contemporary Films (Orff Methods), 267 West 35th St., New York, N.Y. 10020

Coronet Instructional Films, 65 E. South Water St., Chicago, Ill. 60601

EMC Corporation, St. Paul, Minn. 55101

Encyclopedia Britannica Films, Chicago, Ill. 60611

Folkways Records, 121 West 47th St., New York, N.Y. 10011

Jam Handy Organization, 2821 East Grand Blvd., Detroit, Mich. 48211

National Education Television, Audio-Visual Center, Indiana University, Bloomington, Ill. 47401

Society for Visual Education, Chicago, Ill. 60614

United World Films, Universal Education and Visual Arts, 221 Park Ave., South, New York, N.Y. 10003

Audiovisual References: Books

Brown, James W. *A.V. Instructions; Materials and Methods.* McGraw-Hill Book Company, 340 W. 42 St., New York, N.Y. 10036

Fry, E. *Teaching Machines and Programmed Education.* New York: McGraw-Hill Book Company, 340 W. 42 St., New York, N.Y. 10036

Le Bel, C. I. *How to Make Good Tape Recordings*, 3rd ed. Audio Devices, Inc., 444 Madison Ave., New York, N.Y. 10022

Marvel, Lorene. *Music Resources Guide for Primary Grades.* Hall and McCreary Co., 527 Park Ave., Minneapolis, Minn. 55415

National Education Association, Dept. of Audio-Visual Instruction. "Mediated Self-Instruction." *Audiovisual Instruction* (May 1969), pp. 121, 421, 542.

Wyman, Raymond. "Audio Media in Music Education." *Journal* (Feb.–Mar. 1966), pp. 105–108.

Swartz, Elwyn. "Sources of Audio-Visual Aids." *Music Education in Action*, Archie Jones, ed. Dubuque, Iowa: William C. Brown, pp. 473–493.

Films and Filmstrips

Did you ever try using your eyes to hear? Visuals can be used to guide children to hear more in the music if they are carefully chosen and well used in the classroom.

Both films and filmstrips are excellent for independent study.

The catalogues listed below will provide complete information, including a description of the material as well as the prices.

Student producers in the late elementary grades may enjoy using this media to illustrate their musical ideas.

Film Resources

(Recommended for use in the classroom. See addresses at end of list for film companies.)

CODE

P.—Primary grades
I.—Intermediate grades
G.—All grades, K–6
Col.—College level

African Musicians
    (Western Cinema Guild, 16 min., c), I.
Afternoon of a Fawn
    (B F A, 10 min., b & w), I.
Aretha Franklin, Soul Singer
    (M G H, 25 min., c), I., Col.
The Autoharp
    J H, b & w, 19 min.), Col.
Ballet Girl
    (B F, 23 min., c), I.
Beethoven and His Music
    (CORF, 10 min., c), I.
Boogie-Doodle
    NFBC, 4 min., c), I.
Brahms and His Music
    (CORF, 13½ min., c), I.
Building Children's Personalities with Creative Dancing
    (UCX, c), Col.
The Capricious Arts (3 in set)
    (KSP, 20 min., c), I., Col.
Dance Squared
    (IFB, 4 min., c), I.
Dance Your Own Way
    (S, 6 min., c), Col.
Design to Music
    (IFB, 6 min., c), G.

Discovering the Music of Africa
(BFA, 20 min., c), I.
Discovering String Instruments
(BFA, 14 min., c), K–3.
Discovering the Music of Japan
(BFA, 22 min., c), I.
Discovering the Music of the Middle Ages
(BFA, 20 min., c), I.
Discovering the Sound and Movement of Music
(BFA, 16 min., c), P.
The Elements of Composition
(IU, 27 min., c), I.
Exploring the Instruments
(MGIT, 12 min., b & w), I.
Fiddle Dee Dee
(S, 7 min., c), K–Col.
Handel and His Music
(CORF, 13½ min., c), I.
Harmony in Music
(CORF, 17½ min., c), I.
Instruments of the Band and Orchestra: Introduction
(CORF, 11 min., c), G.
Instruments of the Orchestra
(D, 20 min., c), I.
Introduction to Music Reading
(SUTHP, 11 min., c), G.
Keyboard Experiences in Classroom Music
(AMC, 23 min., b & w), Col.
Liszt and His Music
(CORF, 13 min., c), I.
Listen and Sing
(MGH, 10 min., b & w), G.
Looking at Sounds
(MGH, 10 min., b & w), G.
Melody in Music
(CORF, 13 min., c), I.
Mozart and His Music
(CORF, 10 min., c), I.
Music for Children
(CF, 13 min., b & w), Col.
Peter and the Wolf
(Disney, 14 min., c), G.
The Pitch Pipe
(JH, 13 min., b & w), Col.
Reading Music: Finding the Melody
(CORF, 11 min., c), G.
Reading Music: Learning About Notes
(CORF, 11 min., c), G.

Rhythm and Percussion
(EBF, 12 min., b & w), G., Col.
Rhythm Instruments and Movements
(EBF, 11 min., b & w), Col.
Rhythm in Music
(CORF, 17 min., c), I.
Rhythm Is Everywhere
(CM, 11 min., b & w), G.
Schubert and His Music
(CORF, 11 min., c), I.
Sounds of Music
(CORF, b & w, c), G.
Stravinsky
(MGH, 50 min., b & w), I.
Toot, Whistle, Plunk and Boom
(Disney, 10 min., c), G.
Two Part Singing
(JH, 19 min., b & w), G., Col.
W. C. Handy
(BFA, 14 min., c), I.

Film Publishers

AMC
American Music Conference
332 South Michigan Avenue
Chicago, Illinois

BF
Brandon Films
221 W. 57th Street
New York, N.Y. 10019

BFA
Bailey-Film Associates, Inc.
11559 Santa Monica Blvd.
Los Angeles, California 90025

CM
Carl Mahnke Productions
215 E. 3rd Street
Des Moines, Iowa 50300

CF
Contemporary Films
267 West 25th Street
New York, N.Y. 10001

CORF
Coronet Films
65 E. South Water Street
Coronet Building
Chicago, Illinois 60600

DISNEY
Walt Disney Productions
Educational Film Division
350 S. Buena Vista Avenue
Burbank, California 91503

EBF
Encyclopedia Britannica Films
1150 Willmette Avenue
Wilmette, Illinois 60091

IFB
International Film Bureau
332 S. Michigan Avenue
Chicago, Illinois 60604

IU
Indiana University
Bloomington, Indiana 47401

JH
Johnson Hunt Productions
6509 DeLongpre Avenue
Hollywood, California

KSP
King Screen Productions
Seattle, Washington 98100

MGH
McGraw Hill Text Films
330 West 42nd Street
New York, N.Y. 10018

NFBC
National Film Board of Canada
680 Fifth Avenue
New York, N.Y. 10019

SUTHP
John Sutherland Educational Films, Inc.
201 N. Occidental Blvd.
Los Angeles, California 90028

Syracuse University Learning Resource Center
Syracuse, N.Y. 13210

UCX
University of California
University Extension
Education Film Sales Dept.
Los Angeles, California

Filmstrip Resources
(Recommended for use in the classroom. See addresses at end of list for filmstrip companies.)

CODE
P.—Primary grades
I.—Intermediate grades
G.—General—all grades K–6
Col.—College level

Aida—Verdi
> (JH, c), I., Col.
————. *And Virtuosi* (Michael Rabin, Violinist and Harry Moskovitz, Flutist) 2 filmstrips, 2 records
> (WS, c), I.
Bartered Bride, The—Smetana
> (JH, c), I., Col.
Biographies of Great Composers (with recordings):
> Haydn, Mozart, Beethoven, Schubert, Verdi, Puccini
> (Bowmar, 75 fr. ea., color), I.
Black Songs of Modern Times
> (SVE, Sq fr., c), I.
Composers of Many Lands and Times
> (Series: Bach, Haydn, Mozart, Beethoven, Mendelssholn, Chopin, Foster, Tchaikovsky, Greig)
> (Eye Gate, c), I.
Edvard Grieg
> (Eye Gate, c), G.
Felix Mendelssohn
> (Eye Gate, c), G.
Folk Instruments
> (Bowmar, c), G.
Folk Songs
> (Bowmar, c), G.
Folk Songs and the American Flag
> Part I, Part II
> Sung by Burl Ives (Records)
> (WS, c), I.

Folk Songs in American History (6)
    6 records
        Early Colony Days
        Revolutionary War
        Workers of America
        In Search of Gold
        The South
        Civil War
    (WS, c), I.

Folk Songs in American History
    6 records
        Reconstruction and the West
        Immigration and Industrialization
        World War I
        1920's and the Depression
        World War II
        Post War
    (WS, c), I.

Folk Songs in the Civil War (Records)
    Part I, Part II
    (WS, c), I.

Folk Songs and the Declaration of Independence
    Part I, Part II—Sung by Burl Ives
    (WS, c), I.

Folk Songs and Whaling Cowboys
    (Warren Schloat, c), I.

Folk Songs in the Great Depression
    Part I, Part II—Records
    (WS, c), I.

Folk Songs in the War of 1812
    Part I, Part II—Records, Sung by Burl Ives
    (WS, c), I.

Franz Schubert
    (EBEC, c), I.

Frederic Chopin
    (Eye Gate, c), G.

Hansel and Gretel—Humperdinck
    (JH, c), I., Col.

Heart of the Orchestra (Violin and Strings)
    (SVG, 52 fr., c), I.

Instruments of the Orchestra
    Eye Gate, c), I.

Intervals and Phrases
    (VSG, 58 fr., c), G.

It's Fun to Read Music
    (8 filmstrips: Major Scales, Key of C; Major Scales, Key of F, Key of A flat; Major Scales, E flat, A flat; Key of D flat, G flat, C flat; Key of G, Key of D, Key of A; Key of E, Key of B, F Sharp, C Sharp; Minor Scales, Chromatic Scales.
    (Eye Gate, c), I.

Johann Sebastian Bach
    (Eye Gate, c), G.
Johannes Brahms
    (EBEC, c), I.
Joseph Haydn
    (Eye Gate, c), G.
Keyboard Instruments
    (SVG, 38 fr., c), I.
Key Signatures
    (SVE, 54 fr., c), G.
Let's Learn About Music
    (8 filmstrips—The Music Alphabet, Sharps, Flats, Rests, Key Signatures, Rhythm, Time Signatures, Sharps)
    (Eye Gate, c), G.
Lohengrin—Wagner
    (JH, c), I., Col.
Ludwig Van Beethoven
    (Eye Gate, c), G.
Magic Flute—Mozart
    (JH, c), I., Col.
Major and Minor Scales, Accidentals and Chromatics
    (SVG, 56 fr., c), G.
Mastersingers—Wagner
    (JH, c), I., Col.
Measures, Whole Notes and Eighth Notes
    (SVG, 45 fr., c), G.
Meet the Instruments
    (Bowmar, c), K–6.
Musical Instruments
    Introduction to the Violin (4)
    Introduction to the Flute (2)
    With Records
    (WS, c), I.
The Nutcracker—Tchaikovsky
    (JH, c), I., Col.
Peer Gynt—Grieg
    (JH, c), I., Col.
Peter and the Wolf
    (EBEC, c), G.
Piotr Ilich Tchaikovsky
    (Eye Gate, c), G.
Rhythm, the Quarter Note, and the Half Note
    (SVG, 47 fr.), G.
Scheherezade—Rimsky-Korsakov
    (JH, c), I., Col.
Science Explains Music Sounds
    (CUMC, 48 fr., c), I.
Shining Brass
    (SVE, 48 fr., c), I.

Sleeping Beauty—Tchaikovsky
   (SVE, c), I., Col.
Songs of Slavery
   (SVE, 58 fr., c), I.
Sorcerer's Apprentice—Dukas
   (JH, c), I., Col.
Staff and Its Notes
   (SVE, 54 fr., c), G.
Stephen Collin Foster
   (Eye Gate, c), G.
Story of Handel's Messiah
   (SVE, 58 fr., c), G.
Story of John Sebastian Bach and His Christmas Oratorio
   (SVG, 74 fr., c), I.
Story of our National Anthem
   (LA, 40 fr., c), G.
Swan Lake—Tchaikovsky
   (JH, c), I., Col.
William Tell—Rossini
   (JH, c), I., Col.
Wolfgang Mozart
   (EBEC, c), I.
Woodwinds, The
   (SVE, 43 fr., c), I.

Filmstrip Companies

BOWMAR
Stanley Bowmar Co., Inc.
4 Broadway
Valhalla, N.Y. 10595

CUMC
Curriculum Materials Corp.
1319 Vine Street
Philadelphia, Pa. 19100

EBEC
Encyclopedia Britannica Educational Corp.
425 N. Michigan Avenue
Chicago, Illinois 60611

EYE GATE
Eye Gate House, Inc.
146–01 Archer Avenue
Jamaica, N.Y. 11435

JH
Jam Handy Organization
2021 E. Grand Blvd.
Detroit, Michigan

LA
Learning Arts
P.O. Box 917
Wichita, Kansas 67201

SVE
Society for Visual Education Inc.
1345 Diversey Parkway
Chicago, Illinois 60614

WS
Warren Schloat Productions, Inc.
Pleasantville, N.Y. 10570

Synthesizers, Loops, You Name It

Electronic equipment, although considered too expensive and too complicated for school use a few years ago, is now entering the classroom. Ease of use, more reasonable prices combined with student and faculty interest have made it possible for many schools to include these new sounds in the curriculum.

Superior demonstrations have been offered at music conferences by children who not only used the equipment well but gave evidence of complete involvement.

The authors suggest it is best to visit a school in the area using new equipment and write for specific information from the companies listed in the bibliographies.

This is a new frontier in music which is exciting and challenging.

Electronic Music

C E S Computers, Inc.
    P.O. Box 234, Hicksville, N.Y. 11802
Electronic Music Laboratories, Inc.
    P.O. Box H, Vernon, Connecticut 06066
Folkways Scholastic
    906 Sylvan Avenue, Englewood Cliffs, N.J. 07632

Ionecamera
    128 James St., Dept. I, Morristown, N.Y. 07960
R. A. Moog, Inc.
    Trumansburg, N.Y. 14886
Wurlitzer Company
    Dekalb, Illinois 60115

These are a few sources of information for teachers interested in widening their sphere of interest.

Television

The miracle of television offers educators the opportunity of equalizing one area of the music curriculum for all children. The authors make no claim it can do what a teacher sitting with a child can do but it can bring the finest artists into the classroom and augment the classroom program. The use of television is regional at present and somewhat limited by the kind and amount of equipment available, but teachers should check with local stations and the N.E.T. network for information concerning available programs.

Hearing and seeing a symphony orchestra is no longer an experience reserved for a privileged few but is available for all. The use of television is not always easy because of scheduling and demands both preparation and follow-up planning, but it does open the doors of the classroom and offer students another enrichment experience.

The use of closed circuit television offers many opportunities for students to share their talents and gain additional experience in using music to express their ideas. One fifth grade told the story of the development of the United States through music, using narration, songs, and dances. Students throughout the school watched on closed circuit television. The advantages over an assembly program with all the students in one large room were many. Every child could see and hear without having children on the stage strain their voices, the viewers were comfortable in their own room so there was a more controlled situation, the teachers could discuss the material presented with their students after the program which created more of a learning situation, the children saw and heard the results of their efforts which reinforced the experience for them, and it was possible to repeat the program for future study.

The TV trainer is a superior instrument for creating a learning situation. Like the tape recorder it must be used over a period of time so each person can become used to seeing and hearing himself, but it is invaluable as a teaching device. It not only helps individuals learning to play or sing correctly (as it mirrors their efforts), but it can be used to help children discover the effectiveness of their musical creations. Since the tape can be rerecorded, a class, for example, might record a song story, discover changes they would like to make in a song or dance, make the change, rerecord, and evaluate each before presenting their program.

Using television can be an exciting and effective way for both children and adults to learn. There are new developments that make it possible for teachers to record in the classroom and play back the material immediately. The TV trainer is easy to use, the camera can be handled by older children, and the improvement in performance is easily observed. Students should rarely be forced to this exposure, however, as the experience could be a negative one for those who are not prepared emotionally to evaluate themselves.

College students at State University College at Oswego preparing to teach found the experience most helpful. Each student recorded the music she felt most capable of presenting to her children. Some recorded a song. Others used visuals for a guided listening lesson, and some gave a lesson which illustrated the use of music to enhance another area of study. The experience served as a culminating activity for a music course. Students could rerecord if they chose until each was satisfied with his presentation.

Equipment is changing rapidly so it may be helpful to check with audiovisual departments and professional magazines for new developments.

Other Resources

Children's Music Center
5373 West Pico Blvd.
Los Angeles, California 90019

Just what it implies—
a center for all music
activities and materials.
Send for information.

The Continental Press, Inc.
Elizabethtown, Pa. 17022

Music includes dupli-
cating masters.

Dalcroze School of Music
Dr. Hilda M. Schuster, Director
161 East 73rd Street
New York, N.Y. 10021

First hand information
on the Dalcroze system.

E M C Corporation
180 East Sixth Street
St. Paul, Minnesota

Excellent resource for cassettes, filmstrips, and records.

General Words and Music Co.
525 Busse Highway
Park Ridge, Illinois 60068

Music for the classroom.

Indian House, Dept. 1
Tony and Ida Isaacs
Box 472
Taos, New Mexico 87571

Recordings of American Indian music.

Keyboard Jr. Publications
1346 Chapel Street
New Haven, Connecticut 06511

Materials on piano keyboard. Man and His Music Recordings. Keyboard material for all ages.

Music Educators' National Conference
Music Educators' Journal: The Official Magazine of the Music Education National Conference
1201 Sixteenth Street, N.W.
Washington, D.C. 20036

An excellent magazine about the teaching of music.

Music Minus One
46 West 61
New York, N.Y. 10023

Excellent music for accompaniment.

Music in World Cultures
Music Educators' Journal
1201 Sixteenth Street, N.W.
Washington, D.C. 20036

An excellent resource for the international music picture.

Music Educators' National Conference
1201 Sixteenth Street, N.W.
Washington, D.C. 20036

Monographs on current research for the classroom teacher plus other educational bulletins.

R. C. A.
Educational Sales
P.O. Box R C A 100
Indianapolis, Indiana 46291

Excellent source of records.

SUMMARY

Although resources for teaching music in each school vary widely, a significant factor in planning a music program is that *some* material is available for *all* types of programs. The classroom teacher and the music teacher, individually or jointly, need to inventory the materials available and proceed from there to purchase more materials if possible or to supplement the available materials with free or available resources.

The following music materials can be used to create an interest in music and to develop musical skills in the classroom.

1. Songs and recordings used to help children feel comfortable while in school.
2. Accompanying string instruments available and in tune.
3. Bells placed conveniently for exploration and accompaniment when children sing.
4. Percussion instruments of musical quality easily accessible, both commercial and those made by children.
5. Piano conveniently placed with interesting song book.
6. Books and pictures about music in the room.
7. Pictures children have made exhibited conspicuously.
8. Records and record player in good condition and available to the teacher and the children. Earphones would add to the ease of using the machine.
9. Films, filmstrips, and other audiovisual aids.
10. A television set, if possible.

TO THE COLLEGE STUDENT AND THE TEACHING TEAM

Have you tried . . .

1. Letting children tap feathers with soft music to emphasize the concept of softness?
2. Letting children use flashlights to trace melodic patterns on the wall? Introducing form by using different colors over a flashlight to illustrate the different sections?
3. Helping children learn their telephone numbers and street addresses by chanting them rhythmically?
4. Letting small children choose a song or record of the week and making their own book with pictures of their songs or records? Including a bulletin board of pictures of the favorite songs or records of "your" children?
5. Studying your community through music in intermediate grades: the ethnic groups, community music groups, church groups?

6. Attending a rehearsal of school choirs, bands, and orchestras with the children? Attending a rehearsal or concert of a professional music group?

7. Writing a song for "your" room, either using original music or writing new words to a favorite tune?

8. Listing all the different sounds the children can find in the room and then creating interesting combinations of these sounds?

9. Letting children create an accompaniment to movement with percussion instruments or create patterns on percussion instruments to be interpreted through movement?

10. Suggesting children report on the softest, loudest, highest, lowest, prettiest, worst sound they hear in a day.

11. Letting children create a "musical" map in the room, expanding from the United States to other countries, finding a folk dance, folk song, characteristic instruments, composer, and concert composition for each?

12. Turning a favorite story into a "junior" musical, setting words to familiar tunes or creating original songs with narration and action?

13. Encouraging students to create songs or dances in the style of a country or period in history: Calypso, Indian, Contemporary? Learning heritage songs of the students in the room?

14. Just enjoying, listening with the children? Singing too!

SELECTED BIBLIOGRAPHY

(Books of help to the classroom teacher.)

Andrews, J. Austin, and Jeanne Foster Wardian. *Introduction to Music Fundamentals: A Programmed Textbook for the Elementary Classroom Teacher.* New York: Appleton-Century-Crofts, 1963.

Austin, Virginia. *Learning Fundamental Concepts of Music: An Activities Approach.* Dubuque, Iowa: William C. Brown, 1970.

Baines, Anthony (Ed.) *Musical Instruments through the Ages.* New York: Walker (Penguin Books), 1961.

Barlow, Howard, and Sam Morgenstern. *A Dictionary of Musical Themes, the Music of More than 10,000 Themes.* New York: Crown, 1948.

Barnes, Robert A. *Fundamentals of Music: A Program of Self-Instruction.* New York: McGraw-Hill, 1964.

Benson, Warren. *Creative Projects in Musicianship.* Washington, D.C.: Music Educators' National Conference, 1967.

Blom, Eric. *Everyman's Dictionary of Music,* 4th ed. rev. New York: E. P. Dutton, 1962.

Boulez, Pierre. *Thoughts on Music.* Cambridge, Mass.: Harvard University Press, 1970.

Bureau of Elementary Curriculum Development. *Words, Sounds, and Pictures About Music.* Albany, N.Y.: The University of the State of New York (The State Education Department).

Carabo-Cone, Madeline. *The Play Around as Music Teacher,* vols. 1, 2. New York: Harper, 1959.

Cheyette, Irving, and J. Curtis Shake. *Basic Piano for the Classroom Teacher.* Bryn Mawr, Pa.: Theodore Presser, 1954.

Collins, T. C. (Ed.) *Music Education Materials: A Selected Annotated Bibliography.* Washington, D.C.: Music Educators' National Conference, 1967.

Colwell, Richard. *The Evaluation of Music Teaching and Learning.* Englewood Cliffs, N.J.: Prentice-Hall, 1970.

Crews, Katherine. "Music Every Day. You Should, You Can. Here's How!" *The Instructor* LXXX (December 1970), p. 37.

DeLong, P. D., et al. *Art and Music in the Humanities.* Englewood Cliffs, N.J.: Prentice-Hall, 1966.

Ewen, David. *The World of Modern Composers.* Englewood Cliffs, N.J.: Prentice-Hall, 1962.

————. *The New Book of Modern Composers,* 3rd ed. New York: Alfred A. Knopf, 1961.

————. *An Encyclopedia of Concert Music.* New York: Hill and Wang, 1959.

————. *The Complete Book of American Musical Theater.* New York: Holt, Rinehart, and Winston, 1958.

Garretson, Robert L. *Music in Childhood Education.* New York: Appleton-Century-Crofts, 1966.

Gilglend, David R., and Winifred E. Stiles. *Music Activities for Retarded Children.* New York: Abingdon Press, 1965.

Gordon, Edwin. *Psychology of Music Teaching.* Englewood Cliffs, N.J.: Prentice-Hall, 1971.

Hartshorn, W. C. *Listening to Music in the Elementary School.* Englewood Cliffs, N.J.: Prentice-Hall, 1966.

Kaplan, Max, and F. J. Steiner. *Musicianship for the Classroom Teacher.* New York: Rand, 1966.

Knuth, A. S., and William E. Knuth. *Basic Resources for Learning Music.* Belmont, Calif.: Wadsworth, 1966.

Lambert, Hazel M. *Early Childhood Education.* Boston: Allyn and Bacon, 1960.

Landis, Beth, and Polly Carder. *The Eclectic Curriculum in American Music Education.* (Contributions of Dalcroze, Kodály, and Orff.) Washington, D.C.: Music Educators' National Conference, 1969.

Leach, John R. *Fundamental Piano for the Teacher.* Englewood Cliffs, N.J.: Prentice-Hall, 1968.

Leonhard, Charles. *Recreation through Music.* New York: Ronald, 1952.

Murphy, Judith, and George Sullivan. *Music in American Society.* Washington, D.C.: Music Educators' National Conference, 1968.

Music Educators' National Conference. *Music in the Curriculum.* Washington, D.C.: M.E.N.C., 1967.

Nye, Robert E., and Bjornar Bergethon. *Basic Music for Classroom Teachers,* 2nd ed. Englewood Cliffs, N.J.: Prentice-Hall, 1962.

Pace, Robert. *Piano for Classroom Music.* Englewood Cliffs, N.J.: Prentice-Hall, 1970.

Pierce, Anne E. *Musicianship for the Classroom Teacher.* New York: McGraw-Hill, 1967.

Rosewall, Richard B. *Handbook of Singing.* Evanston, Ill.: Summy-Birchard, 1961.

Russcol, Herbert. *Guide to Low-Priced Classical Records.* New York: Hart, 1969.

Salzman, Eric. *Twentieth-Century Music: An Introduction.* Englewood Cliffs, N.J.: Prentice-Hall, 1967.

Schwadron, Abraham. *Aesthetic Dimensions for Music Education.* Washington, D.C.: Music Educators' National Conference, 1967.

Serposs, Emile H., and Ira Singleton. *Music in Our Heritage.* Morristown, N.J.: Silver Burdett, 1969.

Swanson, Bessie. *Music in the Education of Children,* 3rd ed. Belmont, Calif.: Wadsworth, 1969.

Szabo, Helga. *The Kodály Concept of Music Education.* New York: Boosey and Hawkes, 1968.

Weyland, Rudolph H. *Learning to Read Music.* Dubuque, Iowa: William C. Brown, 1961.

Winslow, Robert W., and Leon Dallin. *Music Skills for Classroom Teachers,* 3rd ed. Dubuque, Iowa: William C. Brown, 1970.

Winternitz, Emanuel. *Music Instruments and the Symbolism in Western Art.* New York: W. W. Norton, 1967.

INDEX

Ability, musical, 51, 224
Accompaniment:
  by children, 106
  creativity in, 175
  by instruments, 270–275
  primary level, 106, 177, 270
  selecting for stories, 177
  in song books, 306
  styles of, 273–274
Accompaniment instruments, 270–273
Activity records, 279, 294–295
Adaption, 27
Adventures in Communication (Smith), 140–142
Analytical listening, 140
"and" (&) sign, 128
Andrews, Gladys, 163
Andrews, Michael, 49
Appreciation, music, 51
  in the curriculum, 44–50
  forming early attitudes, 45–46
  using recordings to develop, 117
Appreciative listening, 140
Arranging, 138–139
Art, combining music and, 215–217, 245
Assembly programs, 151
Attentive listening, 140
Audio acuity, 260
Audiovisual aids, 77, 95–98, 309–310
Autosharp, 270–271

Barkan, Manuel, 3
Bellamy, Edward, 121

Body, expressing with, 93–95, 165, 167. *See also* Movement
Books:
  audiovisual, 310
  on music and musicians, 299–303
  with songs, 306–309
Brainstorming, 29–32, 251

Calypso music, 20
Carlyle, Thomas, 221
Catalogues, 303–305, 310
Ceremonial dances, 169
Chanting, 180, 181
Charades, 180, 185–186, 193
Choral speaking, 180, 230–231
Classroom teacher:
  in action, 78–86
  and the composer, 143–146
  music skills of, 90, 132
  and music teacher, 77, 117, 172, 257
  and the performer, 146–147
  self-inventory for, 155
Combining, 29
Competition, 45
Composers:
  books on, 299–303
  creating their works, 250–251
  learning about, 24, 136, 179, 283
  recordings of, 295–299
Composing, 15
  classroom teacher's role, 4–7, 17, 143–146
  encouraging, 4–7, 17, 144
  group songs, 145–146